COLLEGE OUTLINE SERIES

BARNES & NOBLE, INC., *Publishers*
105 FIFTH AVE., NEW YORK 3, N.Y.

[*Continued on next page*]

Jean Erin

EVERYDAY HANDBOOK SERIES

Barnes & Noble, Inc., Publishers
105 Fifth Ave., New York 3, N.Y.

About the Authors

Dorothy Mulgrave is Professor of Education at the School of Education, New York University, where she has taught for twenty-five years. Dr. Mulgrave also received her Ph.D. from New York University. She is the author of *Speech for the Classroom Teacher, Pocket Guides to Speech Practice,* and is co-author of *Conversations in Phonetic Transcription.* In addition, Dr. Mulgrave is a member of many professional organizations.

Wilbur Gilman has been Chairman of the Department of Speech at Queens College since 1945. Dr. Gilman received his Ph.D. from Cornell University. In the course of his academic career, he has taught at the University of Missouri, Cornell University, and the University of Michigan. He is a member of a number of speech, hearing, and language associations and has been an officer of many of them. Dr. Gilman is the author of *Milton's Rhetoric: Studies in His Defense of Liberty,* and he is co-author of *A Course Book in Public Speaking* and *The Fundamentals of Speaking.*

Wilbert Pronovost has been a director of the Speech and Hearing Center at Boston University since 1948. Dr. Pronovost received his Ph.D. from the University of Iowa and has taught at Purdue University and Queens College as well as having been employed by industrial organizations. He is currently vice-president of the New England Speech Association. Dr. Pronovost is the author of the *Elements of Speech Science.*

College Outline Series

SPEECH

A Handbook of Voice Training
Diction and Public Speaking

by
DOROTHY MULGRAVE
New York University

with chapters by
WILBUR GILMAN
Queens College

WILBERT PRONOVOST
Boston University

Barnes & Noble, Inc.
New York

PRINTED IN THE UNITED STATES OF AMERICA

Preface

This book has been written to serve (1) as a textbook and (2) as a general supplement for use with specialized textbooks.

It is suitable as a text because it surveys practically the entire field of speech. Because of its succinctness and highly organized format, the authors have been able to include a wider range of speech information than that found in the average college textbook. It is suitable as a supplementary volume because it provides detailed instructions and drill material on the sounds of English and on scientific voice training; it might, therefore, be used in conjunction with books specializing in public speaking, debating, and other speech arts.

This outline may also serve as a compact manual for students and general readers who wish to master the facts and principles of speech. It should be useful to the student who is studying any aspect of speech; it should be particularly helpful to those who are preparing to teach and who need a thorough orientation in the field of speech.

Because of the varied purposes of the book, the subject has been divided into two parts, which may be used together or independently depending upon the program of study which is desired. Readers interested mainly in the speech arts will find chapters on the use of words, public speaking, group discussions, argumentation and debate, and oral interpretation; these chapters (though fully cross-referenced) are so designed that they may be studied in any chosen order. Readers concerned especially with the speech sciences will find a concise but comprehensive treatment of the anatomy of speech and hearing, of voice training, and of English pronunciation.

In view of the scope of the subject matter, this volume may also be used (1) as a brief and practical textbook for adult study groups; whether they are concerned primarily with public speaking, with dramatics, or with speech correction and voice production, they will find a clear statement of principles and guidance for further study; (2) as a study guide for those who are seriously intent upon improving their own speaking personalities; (3) as an encyclopedic reference book for those who may have occasion to refer to the principles of parliamentary procedure or formal debating, to engage in group discussion, or to appear on radio or television; and (4) as a comprehensive review of the field of speech for those who need a general perspective.

Other values of this book are (1) its simplicity of style—even the chapters dealing with technical subjects are so written that they can be understood by the beginning student and the general reader; (2) its value for specialized study—the selected bibliographies provide guidance for readers who wish to make an intensive study of any aspect of the field of speech; and (3) its up-to-dateness—since the volume is one of the College Outline Series, both the content and the bibliographical information can be kept continuously up-to-date through frequent revisions.

Acknowledgments

To thank the numbers of students and friends who have helped in the completion of this book would be a manifest impossibility. I shall attempt here, therefore, to express gratitude formally to those who have worked most intimately with the material.

I wish to thank especially Dr. Wilbur E. Gilman, contributor of the three chapters on Public Speaking, Argumentation, and Debate, for his excellent suggestions, his detailed criticisms, and his invaluable help in preparing the entire manuscript; Dr. Wilbert L. Pronovost, contributor of the chapter on the Mechanisms of Speech and Hearing, for that chapter and for his co-operation in reading and criticizing the manuscript as a whole; Dr. David Guy Powers, to whom I am indebted for the idea of the book; Dr. Walter J. Derenberg for his advice on copyright law; Dr. Letitia E. Raubicheck, for her criticisms of the manuscript and for her kindness in reading and rereading it; Dr. Ruth Manser, for her many suggestions and her care in reading large sections of the manuscript; the following, for their help on various chapters: Mr. Charles F. Edgecomb, Dr. Leonard Finlan, Miss Evelyn Konigsberg, Miss Mary McGrath, and Mr. Nicholas Moss; Miss Mary Wallenius, for her illustrations for Chapter 11; Miss Hazel P. Brown for the transcription of the phonetic alphabet in Chapter 13; Miss Sylvia Fourdrinier for her invaluable assistance in proofreading; The Macmillan Company and the authors, for permission to use pages 571–573 from *The Fundamentals of Speaking* by Wilbur E. Gilman, Bower Aly, and Loren D. Reid; Alfred A. Knopf, for permission to use lines from Arthur Machen's *Hill of Dreams*; Prentice-Hall, Inc., for permission to use material in Chapters III and IV from *Speech for the Classroom Teacher* by Dorothy Mulgrave; Garden City Books, for permission to use in Chapter 11 four diagrams from *Fundamentals of Physiology* by Elbert Tokay; the editorial department of Barnes & Noble for their untiring efforts to improve the manuscript; and, finally, my mother, for her constant encouragement and for her invaluable co-operation without which this book could not have been written.

D. M.

Table of Contents

TABULATED BIBLIOGRAPHY
OF STANDARD TEXTBOOKS

This *College Outline* is keyed to standard textbooks in two ways:

1. If you are studying one of the following textbooks, consult the cross references listed here to find which pages of the *Outline* summarize the appropriate chapter of your text. (Roman numerals refer to textbook chapters, Arabic figures to corresponding *Outline* pages.)

2. If you are using the *Outline* as a basis for study and need a fuller treatment of a topic, consult any of the standard textbooks in the Quick Reference Table on pp. xvi–xvii.

Avery, Elizabeth; Dorsey, Jane; and Sickles, Vera A. *First Principles of Speech Training.* New York: Appleton-Century-Crofts, 1928.
I (3–7); II (143–160); III (161–170); IV (171–176); V (209–237); VI (184–198); VII (199–208); VIII (36–48); IX (21–35); IX (100–114).

Baird, A. Craig and Knower, Franklin H. *General Speech.* New York: McGraw-Hill, 1949.
I (3–7); II (238–245); III–IX (21–35); X (9–20); XII (21–35); XIII (161–170); XIV (171–237); XV (21–35); XVII–XVIII (21–35); XIX (49–63); XXI (36–48); XXII (100–114); XXIII (130–140).

Borchers, Gladys L. and Wise, Claude M. *Modern Speech.* New York: Harcourt, Brace, 1947.
I (3–7); III (161–170); IV (143–160); V (171–177); VI (238–245); VII (9–20); VIII (21–35); X (9–20); XIII (21–35); XIV (36–48; 49–63; 64–82); XV (83–100); XVI (100–114); XVII (125–128); XVIII (130–140).

Eisenson, Jon. *Basic Speech.* New York: Macmillan, 1950.
I (3–7); II (143–160); III (161–170); V (171–177); VI (184–237); VII (161–170); VIII (9–20); XI (36–48; 49–63; 64–82); XII–XIV (21–35); XVI (100–114).

Gilman, Wilbur E.; Aly, Bower; and Reid, Loren D. *The Fundamentals of Speaking.* New York: Macmillan, 1951.
I (3–7); II (21–35); III (161–237); IV (21–35); VI (130–140); VII (36–99).

Gray, Giles Wilkeson and Wise, Claude M. *The Bases of Speech*. (Rev.
    ed.) New York: Harper, 1946.
    I (3–7; 161–170); II–III (143–160); IV (171–237); VI (21–35);
    IX (9–20).
McBurney, James H. and Wrage, Ernest J. *The Art of Good Speech*.
    New York: Prentice-Hall, 1953.
    I–II (3–7); III (21–35); V–XII (21–35); XIX (161–170); XX
    (171–237); XXI–XXIV (21–35); XXV (36–48); XXVI (83–99;
    21–35); XXVII (130–140).
Monroe, Alan H. *Principles and Types of Speech*. (3rd ed.) Chicago:
    Scott, Foresman, 1949.
    I–II (3–7); III–VI (161–170); III–XVII (21–35); XVIII (9–20);
    XIX–XXIII (21–35); XXIV–XXVIII (21–35); XXIX (130–140);
    XXX–XXXII (36–48); XXXIII (83–99).
Monroe, Alan H. *Principles of Speech* (Rev. Brief Ed.) Chicago:
    Scott Foresman, 1951.
    I (3–7); II (21–35); III (143–170); IV–VII (21–35); VIII (36–
    48); IX (21–35); X (130–140).
Mulgrave, Dorothy. *Speech for the Classroom Teacher*. (Rev. ed.)
    New York: Prentice-Hall, 1946.
    I (3–7); II (143–160); III–IV (161–170); V (171–177); VI (178–
    183); VII (184–208); VIII (209–237); X–XII (238–245); XIV
    (100–114); XVI (115–129); XVII (21–35); XVIII (36–48); XIX
    (130–140).
Murray, Elwood; Barnard, Raymond, H.; and Garland, J. V. *Integrative
    Speech*. New York: Dryden, 1953.
    I–III (3–7); IV–VII (21–35); VIII–IX (9–20); X–XIV (21–35);
    XV–XVIII (36–48); XIX (83–99); XX–XXI (49–63; 64–82).
Oliver, Robert T. and Cortright, Rupert L. *New Training for Effective
    Speech*. (Rev. ed.) New York: Dryden, 1951.
    I–II (3–7); VI (36–48); VII (21–35); VIII–XII (21–35); XIII
    (161–170); XIV (171–237); XVI–XXI (21–35); XXII (83–99);
    XXIII (130–140).
O'Neill, James M. (Editor). *Foundations of Speech*. New York:
    Prentice-Hall, 1942.
    I (3–7); IV–V (171–237); VI–VIII (143–160); IX (161–170);
    X (36–48); XI–XII (100–114); XIII (36–48); XIV (21–35); XV
    (64–82); XVI (130–140); XVIII–XIX (238–245).
Powers, David G. *Fundamentals of Speech*. New York: McGraw-Hill,
    1951.
    I (3–7); II (9–20); III (161–170); IV (171–237); XV–XIX (21–
    35); XX (36–48); XXI (83–99); XXII (64–82); XXIII (100–114);
    XXIV (110–129); XXVI (130–140).

Sarett, Lew and Foster, William T. *Basic Principles of Speech*. Boston: Houghton Mifflin, 1946.

   I (3–7); II–VII (21–35); VIII–X (161–170); XII–XVII (21–35); XXIII (49–63); XXII (9–20); XXIII (130–140).

Thonssen, Lester and Gilkinson, Howard. *Basic Training in Speech*. (2nd ed.) Boston: D. C. Heath, 1953.

   I–V (3–7); VI–XI (171–237); XIII–XXI (21–35); XXII (100–114); XXIII (64–82); XXIV (36–48); XXV (49–63).

Weaver, Andrew T. *Speech Forms and Principles*. (2nd ed.) New York: Longmans, Green, 1951.

   I–II (3–7); V–VI (143–160); VII (171–177); XII (36–48; 64–82); XIII (21–35); XIV (100–114); XV (130–140).

References

Chapter in Speech	Topic	Avery, Dorsey, & Sickles	Baird & Knower	Borchers & Wise	Eisenson	Gilman, Aly, & Reid	Gray & Wise	McBurney & Wrage
1	Introduction	1–13	2–10	1–9		3–8 343–373 581–585	1–12	3–20
2	Semantics: Word Meanings		132–158	281–282	181–200	370	505–548	352–358
3	Public Speaking	195–213	298–402	326–350	258–291	11–154 237–339 377–435 484–515		60–61 79–133 135–154 225–243
4	Group Discussion	164–194	403–422	351–357	226–241	437–483		507–512 516–528
5	Argumentation	192–194	351–376	360–362	241–251	318–333		290–296
6	Debate	192–194	351–376	357–363	241–251	516–545		58 61–63 512–516
7	Parliamentary Procedure	190–192	403–422	364–373		546–578		520–528
8	Oral Interpretation of Literature	214–245	429–455	374–417	305–322	145–164		63–65
9	Dramatics			418–432				
10	Radio and Television			433–451		413–424		552–565
11	The Mechanisms of Speech and Hearing	14–47		39–66 67–91	14–40	165–194	70–138 139–216	393–422
12	Basic Speech and Voice Drills	252–365	223–236 246–258	92–127 128–189	149–179	172–194 202–236	15–42 197–198 205–206	393–422 430–434
13	The Sounds of English	72–83	238–258	39–66 92–127 128–190	66–91	195–236	217–302	426–434
14	Sounds in Connected Speech	136–163		115 152–153	88–91	227 230–232	476–481	434
15	English Vowels	105–127	245	108–120	73	200–205	195–197	426–427
16	English Diphthongs	127–135	245	111	70	206–207	486–488	427–428
17	English Consonants	84–104	245	44–66	71–72	207–226	38–39	428–429
18	Speech Pathology							

See pages xiii–xv for

TO STANDARD TEXTBOOKS

are to pages

Monroe	Monroe Brief ed. rev.	Mulgrave	Murray, Barnard, & Garland	Oliver & Cortright	O'Neill et al	Powers	Sarett & Foster	Thonssen & Gilkinson	Weaver
25-36	1-22	1-14	2-24	4-24		8-13	3-12	3-10	1-16
358-368		5-7	180-210 211-236	7		35-57			149-162
149-358 369-471 483-575	2-7 14-20 265-279	363-369	297-324 325-344	382-513	339 364-368	175-260	439-466	170-206 210-271 278-307	260-304
575-631	8-13 225-264	370-393	448-516	130-145	231-264	263-378	466-470	387-395	233-238 274-276
	111-194		541-544	412-419	348-350 381	302-316	439-477	256-277	238-248
436	195-223		549-566 567-589	531-535	370-399	302-316	439-466 471	363-386	238-248
631-644	225-262		517-533	516-535	235 394	279-301		395-400	248-259
		243-256	579-580		265-287 288-320	319-326		321-337	305-328
		330-352	286-296			327-342			
544-574	84-85 281-289	394-413	345-374	543-548 549-551	400-417	350-370	569-592	338-341	329-339
78-90	26-28 72-78	15-25		320-333	105 136 137-164 165-199				76-89 343-354
90-98 139-148	71-82 85-94	36-48 50-56		346-361	202-230	66-75 80-85 88-95	208-222	74-89	
		59-74		350-351	26-104			112-130	
	95-109	75-79			79-82				130
		80-99			41-62	129-148		115-116	355-360
		99-110			55-61	149-163		116	360
		111-143			162-178	103-128		112-114	360-362
		201-242			439-459			89-92	

complete list of titles

SPEECH

A Handbook of Voice Training
Diction and Public Speaking

1

Introduction

There are probably no more accurate gauges of a person's emotional, mental, and physical well-being than voice and speech. Speech is an integral part of the total personality, revealing the speaker's environment, social contacts, and education. Other aspects, such as dress or grooming, are external, but speech is inherent.

A person learns to speak at too early an age to remember the process. The child imitates the sounds he hears. If the models are good and he has a good ear for sound, he may speak well. However, if the models are poor and if they are imitated correctly, he will probably speak poorly. Conversely, if the models are good, but the ears are a poor recording instrument, the speech is likely to be faulty.

Unless there is a conscious effort to improve speech, the individual may betray more of his background than he intends, or he may fail to speak as well as his background indicates he should. Fortunately, the main requisite for improving speech is the desire to improve it. A second requisite is working in a systematic fashion to improve defective sounds, faulty intonation, and unpleasing voice quality.

THE DEFINITION OF SPEECH

According to the dictionary, speech is the faculty of uttering articulate sounds or words to express thoughts. By an extension of this definition, speech may be said to be a system of audible and visible signs utilizing many of the muscles and tissues of the body for the purpose of communicating ideas. It is, furthermore, a form of human behavior which utilizes physical, psychological, neurological, semantic, and linguistic factors so extensively that it may be considered man's most important instrument for social control.

Speech, then, is more than the articulation of sounds or of words. It is a means of communicating ideas organized and developed according to the needs of the listener. It is an instrument that reveals to an audience almost immediately whether or not the speaker understands both his subject and his listeners; whether or not he is poised and well-adjusted as he communicates his ideas; and whether or not he is alert and enthusiastic.

THE AIMS OF SPEECH

The primary aim of speech is to communicate. In order to convey thoughts effectively, the speaker must understand the meaning of what he wants to communicate; he must be able to evaluate the effect of his communication on his audience; and he must know the principles underlying all speech situations, whether public or private.

Speech should serve as a means to an end rather than as an end in itself. Indistinctness, inaudibility, or slovenly articulation will mar its effectiveness, while speech that is too conspicuously proper may attract attention to itself, thereby interfering with communication. Even in acting and singing, speech serves the useful purpose of communicating ideas and emotions.

People sometimes fear that they will sound affected if they change their mode of speech. This fear is really the expression of a defense mechanism. It is hard to admit that such an inherent part of one's personality as speech is deficient.

Obviously, it would be a superficial and affected change to cultivate an artificial quality of voice or to substitute markedly British stage diction for poor American speech. The object in improving a speech pattern is not to acquire unnatural mannerisms and a veneer, but rather, through analyzing the production of all English sounds and their use in connected speech, to learn how to use speech effectively and efficiently as an instrument for communicating one's own ideas and for interpreting the ideas of others.

Speech as a Social Tool. Many persons believe that only public speakers or actors or singers need to analyze their speech. They argue that the majority of people rarely speak formally from a platform. Actually, however, every normal individual who carries on conversations, speaks on the telephone, recites in class, participates in club activities, or takes part in civic discussions uses speech as a means of social control. The speaking activities of most persons may be classified as "private" rather than "public," but whether the individual talks to an audience of one or of a thousand, he is, consciously or unconsciously, using speech as a means of adjusting to his surroundings.

Speech as a Business or Professional Tool. In business and professional life, as in social life, an audible, pleasant voice and good speech techniques are desirable. The applicant for a position, for example, is judged on the basis of his entire personality. No matter how excellent the letters of recommendation, no matter how superior the previous record, the applicant is appraised generally on his ability to present ideas concisely, clearly, and effectively. In some branches of industry and in many professions, good speech is an absolute necessity for entrance; in others, it is essential for advancement.

SPEECH EDUCATION

The basic concepts underlying speech education may be grouped in three categories: (1) those concerned with the nature of speech; (2) those that set forth the intellectual processes required to develop the ability to speak well; and (3) those that enable one to attain the skills of speaking.

In order to understand the nature of speech, it is necessary to think of it as a type of human behavior having social, economic, and cultural implications in the life of each individual, and to realize that speech is a complex activity in which the relationships between the speaker and the audience may be profoundly affected by the speaker's ideas and emotional tone as well as by his manner of expression. It is also necessary to envision speech as a universal means of communication, having world-wide as well as community implications.

An analysis of the intellectual processes required to develop ability in speaking shows the necessity of organizing material for oral presentation; of analyzing an audience, adapting ideas and arrangement to the listeners; of using clear, effective expression for communication with that particular group; and of learning to listen carefully and appreciatively.

Since the field of speech is customarily divided into two general areas: (1) functional or applied speech (the speech arts) and (2) fundamental speech knowledge (the speech sciences), this volume is so arranged. Those who need knowledge of and guidance in public reading or speaking will find instructions and suggestions in the chapters in Part One, The Speech Arts.

Part Two, The Speech Sciences, contains chapters concerning the production of voice and speech sounds. Just as in music a knowledge of the technique of playing an instrument may deepen one's appreciation, so, too, in speech a knowledge of the scientific background of the production of sound is essential not only for the improvement of one's own speech but also for a better analysis of the attributes of the successful speaker and for a greater enjoyment of the spoken word.

PART ONE

Speech Arts

2

Semantics: The Understanding of Word Meanings

According to dictionary definition, a *word* is an articulated sound or series of sounds which stands for and communicates an idea. It is, furthermore, the smallest unit of speech that has meaning.

WORDS AS SYMBOLS

To say that words are symbols means that they stand for an idea or object, not that they are identical with the idea or object. The approximation between the speaker's use of a word and his listener's understanding of that word will be closest when speaker and listener have had similar experiences. When their experiences are totally dissimilar, or when the speaker uses words foreign to the vocabulary of his listener, communication cannot take place.

Referent, Denotation, and Connotation. In analyzing word meanings, one must bear in mind the concept that words are merely symbols that are used to express ideas. Words do not have inherent meanings; they acquire meanings through association. To know the meaning in a given text, it is necessary to know which associations, of the many possible ones, the word brings to mind. Once the *referent* of the word, that is, all the characteristics of and associations with it, has been defined, limitations are placed on its meaning.

A word with which the speaker or listener has not had experience will mean nothing to him in isolation and might possibly mean nothing even in context. Nor will an unknown foreign language evoke a response in a reader or listener. He is able to respond to a word only when he knows its meaning in the partic-

9

ular context of a specific sentence. The meaning does not reside in the words themselves, but in the reactions they cause in the listener or reader.

Dictionaries provide word definitions which merely denote accepted meanings. The *denotation* of *home,* for example, may be a place where one has lived with his family for many years. The word *home,* however, may have various personal and emotional associations for the speaker or listener or reader. Such personal and emotional associations constitute the *connotations* of the word. These emotional implications distinguish the denotations of words from their connotations.

A word in isolation may have quite a different connotation from the same word in context. The same word in context may differ from one sentence to another. *Pull,* for example, in one sentence may mean to exert physical force, but in the next sentence it may signify a person's social influence. *Long* may refer to the extent of an object from end to end, but it may mean "to yearn for" in the next context. A person may be described as *base* in his motives, but he may also be said to *base* his motives on the wrong principles. Examples of this kind abound in the language.

The Science of Semantics. The study of word meanings is known as the science of *semantics.* Since words are the most fascinating and useful tool of the speaker, he should always be aware of the need for precision in their use. Perhaps care in the selection of words is even more important for the speaker than for the writer, for speech is ephemeral, whereas writing is permanent. The reader may reread at will, look up words that are unfamiliar to him, consult authorities, or close the book without trying to interpret the words on the printed page.

The listener, however, is more or less at the mercy of the speaker. He may not always be permitted to interrupt the speaker to find out his exact meaning; he may not remember unfamiliar words or know how to spell them if he wishes to check them in a dictionary; and he may not be able to adjust easily to changes in the rate of speech or the volume of voice.

Precise oral and written communication is difficult because words remain static while the objects to which they refer change. The speaker or writer, therefore, is obliged to be as explicit as occasion demands. The words *Abraham Lincoln,* for example, may suggest to some persons a young rail splitter; to others, a struggling lawyer; to still others, a bearded president. In like manner, *war* conveys different meanings to different persons. To some, it suggests valorous deeds; to others, carnage; to some, glory; to others, death.

Some writers advocate using a symbol or a date with a word to show, for example, that *war* $_{1812}$ is not the same as *war* $_{1914}$ and that neither is the same as *war* $_{1941}$. They would also indicate that *John Smith* $_{1950}$ is not the same as *John Smith* $_{1951}$. This procedure is unwieldy and impractical.

Fortunately, not all concepts have to be dated so rigorously. The speaker should know, however, when to be specific and when not to be unduly precise. There are occasions when being as specific as possible is of the greatest importance. In contracts, in business, in diplomacy, and in legal matters, much may depend upon even the slightest misinterpretation of a single word.

CHANGES IN THE MEANING OF WORDS. Two common processes involved in semantic change are *generalization* and *specialization,* or *semantic widening* and *narrowing.* As these terms imply, some words come into the language with a rather restricted meaning, but eventually embrace much more than their origins would imply. Others are adopted into the language with a fairly broad interpretation and in time narrow their meanings.

Bribe (from the Old French *bribe,* "crumb," "piece," especially "a piece given to a beggar") has changed to mean "a price, reward, gift, or favor bestowed or promised with a view to pervert the judgment or corrupt the conduct of a person in a position of trust."

Candidate (from the Latin *candidatus,* "clothed in white," to express the purity of intention in seeking office) has become any aspirant for an office or honor. *Bible* (from the Greek *biblia,* plural of *biblion,* diminutive of *biblos,* "book," "papyrus") has narrowed to refer to the Holy Scriptures. *Critical* (from the Greek *kritikos,* "able to discuss," from *krinein,* "to judge") has narrowed until it now means "inclined to unfavorable criticism."

The English word *meadow* originally meant all grassland annually mowed for hay, but especially "that land by the side of a river or brook." In New England, the word now means "low, swampy land." The term *neck* was used along the Atlantic coast in the sense of "meadow," eventually contributing the name *little neck clam.* In modern American usage, *neck* means "an isthmus, cape, or narrow stretch of land." Colloquially, it is used to refer to a part of an isolated or distant section, as in the phrase *neck of the woods.*

CHANGES IN OBJECTS SYMBOLIZED. Other semantic processes are known as *degeneration* and *elevation.* Word meanings cannot remain static because they grow from the constantly changing configurations in men's minds. When a word has become less dignified or less respectable in its meaning, it is said to have "degenerated." Conversely, when the object symbolized has changed to something more reputable, or the meaning has become more favorable, the word is said to have been "elevated" or "ameliorated."

Examples of word degeneration include *villain* from Old French *vilain,* "worker on a villa, or farm." This change may have been brought about by the city dweller's contempt for the country worker. In time, the term was attributed to "anyone given to evil." *Doom* (from Anglo-Saxon *dom,* any "legal judgment," whether favorable or adverse) in modern usage represents "an unhappy or irrevocable fate."

Words that have become elevated include *nice* (from Latin *nescius,* "ignorant"), which went through a number of changes until in modern English it became "capable of discriminating or judging delicately." A person capable of nice distinctions was a nice person; hence the word was extended to mean "any pleasing or agreeable thing."

CHANGES DUE TO NEED FOR NEW WORDS. Although American English began as seventeenth-century British English, it naturally diverged from the parent tongue because of features of American life that were nonexistent in England and because language is an outgrowth of life as it is being lived rather than as it has been lived. New uses of words and new combinations of words emerged from life in the new country. There was no English word to describe the colonial backwoods and backwoodsman, no word to describe backlog or log house. The term *log cabin* came much later. In many cases, the early settlers formed a new word out of English elements. Sometimes they used an old word but gave it a slightly different meaning from its English one. The American red-breasted thrush became a *robin; blackbird,* which denoted a wild thrush, was used in America for a variety of birds having black plumage.

Some words changed and others fell into disuse because of the physical conditions of the land. The colonists used many English words such as *branch, bluff, pond, hollow,* and *swamp.* Other words, such as *spinney, combe, fen, wold, copse,* and *heath,* while still widely used in British English, have become quite obsolete in American English.

Moreover, just as "foreign" words changed their meanings as they came into English, so, too, have English words been changed in American usage. A waistcoat has become a *vest;* a lift, an *elevator;* a pavement, except regionally in a few areas, a *sidewalk;* and a flat, an *apartment.*

PROBLEMS OF VERBAL COMMUNICATION

Thoughts or ideas cannot be exchanged or conveyed without a common understanding of words. The speaker, therefore, must keep his vocabulary within the intellectual range of his listeners. He can accomplish this more easily by using a denotational rather than a connotational approach.

Problems Arising from Connotation. Recognition must be made of the emotional reactions to words and the subsequent interpretations and consequent misunderstandings of what was said. The speaker must be sure that the audience not only understands his vocabulary but also interprets his words and phrases as he intended.

The devices of using subscripts and of dating terms have already been mentioned as methods used to clarify statements. Some speakers use examples, anecdotes, parallel or analogous situations, or definitions to make sure the audience does not "miss the point." Still another technique is the use of modifying words to limit generalized statements. Expressions such as *from my point of view* or *it seems to me* remove some of the inclusiveness from a statement like *This candidate is dishonest.* Use of modifying words tends to create an atmosphere of sincerity and to show the desire for accuracy. Undue repetition of these words will weaken the speech and make the speaker sound insecure and overly careful.

Problems Arising from Changes in Word Meanings and in Objects. Many words have been in the language so long and have been taken for granted so generally that they seem to have inherent meanings. Actually, they are no more than sequences of sounds or letters which because of general agreement have come to stand for certain objects or experiences. Many other words change from decade to decade and certainly from century to century. The phrase *entangling alliances* meant one thing to an eighteenth-century president and means quite another to twentieth-century isolationists. *Frontier,* which still in British English designates a boundary between two countries, assumed fairly early the American sense "the border of settled regions within a country."

The speaker must bear in mind the changes that have taken place in usual meanings assigned to words, and he must also know any regional or special connotations. The word *Tammany,* for example, no longer refers to the Delaware chief who lived in the latter part of the seventeenth century, but to the powerful Democratic organization in New York City. References to *Tammany* as the name of the club, which was founded in 1789, occur from 1790 onwards.

Problems Arising from the Use of Abstractions. Since no word or symbol can represent all the aspects of any object, general or abstract terms, in which associations are made between the symbol and the object, are used for the purpose of immediate identification. A symbol, however, is meaningless unless the reader can associate it with an object. Music notes, editing or proofreading marks, and traffic and road signals are unintelligible unless the viewer is able to make the correct association. In the process of abstraction, some characteristics are selected as representative of an object, while others are rejected. The rejected ones may be just as important as those selected.

Abstractions are clarified or limited by the use of descriptive words or phrases. For example, the phrase *long sharp yellow pencil* will bring to mind a more concrete image than the word *pencil.* The term *writing implement* represents an even higher abstraction, for it may refer to a pen, pencil, crayon, quill, or piece of chalk.

Constant use of high-order abstractions may eventually lead to the replacement of some symbols by *stereotypes.* Slogans or labels may become so associated with general or abstract terms that they are used for every member of the general classification regardless of individual differences. Moreover, there is little attempt to investigate the manner in which such labels became attached in the first place. The *absent-minded professor* or *miserly Scotsman* are examples of stereotypes that have little real basis in truth.

LEGITIMATE USES OF ABSTRACTIONS. Abstractions are a great convenience, for without them every single object in the world would have to be identified individually. Assume that three boys are each holding a round, red object in their hands. Since the objects have many similarities, the use of the general term *apple*, rather than an expression of ownership by means of a different word in each case, is a decided convenience. The term *apple*, then, is an abstraction since each apple is different from the other two and possesses different characteristics. *Fruit* would represent a higher abstraction, for even less would be known about the object.

Stereotypes may also be useful among specialized groups. Publishers think of their "typical" readers, merchants of their "typical" customers, public speakers and actors of their "typical" listeners. That there are extensive ranges of differentiation within the ranks of these "typical" groups is understood at the outset.

DANGERS AND PITFALLS OF ABSTRACTIONS. Abstractions and overused stereotypes tend to make language meaningless. Slogans, labels, hackneyed phrases, and epithets are used indiscriminately by those who have no firsthand knowledge of the issues or persons involved.

The O. Henry story *Man about Town* is an excellent example of the frequent absurdity of high-order abstractions. The teller of this story was run over by an automobile while in quest of the "typical man about town." After recovering consciousness, he had his nurse read him the newspaper item concerning his accident. To his amazement, the report concluded with the sentence: "He appeared to be a typical 'man about town.'"

To say that a person is a "typical man about town," or "typical New Yorker," or "typical politician" is usually to attempt to categorize too emphatically. Every person in a group is different from every other person in that same group. The popular acceptance of stereotypes or similar verbal mannerisms, because of their emotional impact rather than their accuracy, may block thought rather than stimulate it.

SPEECH TECHNIQUES AS AIDS
IN CONVEYING MEANING

Word meanings may be conveyed not only by the context but also by the tone or inflection of the speaker's voice. The intellectual and logical presentation of a subject may differ little from one speaker to another, but the emotional interpretation will be influenced by his feelings about the subject and will eventually determine whether or not he reaches his audience. In view of the fact that psychologists have fairly well established that there is no such thing as a "pure idea" without some emotional coloration or connotation, the importance of the voice for conveying the logical or emotional elements of meaning cannot be over-emphasized.

Appropriate Voice Quality. The voice characteristic that is most important in affecting attitudes and emotions is quality or timbre. The quality of voice must match the essential mood of the material.

A gay poem such as Hunt's *Jenny Kissed Me* should not be read in the muted tones of Shelley's *A Dirge*. A harsh command should not be given as a mere piece of conversational small talk, nor should an original speech on a serious subject be read in the light tones of a humorous anecdote. The use of an inappropriate vocal quality will set up an insurmountable barrier between the speaker and the audience because the sound and the sense of the words will fail to coalesce.

Appropriate Volume. Volume should also be appropriate for the type of material under consideration. An oration, for example, requires more volume because of its content than a narrative poem. This is an intrinsic requirement apart from such extrinsic factors as the size of the room or the number of persons in the audience. Too loud a tone may jar on the ear of the listeners, distracting their attention; too low a tone may cause them to lose much of the content. The speaker must learn to gauge the amount of volume he needs for his material as well as for a specific room.

Appropriate Intensity. Intensity of force may be applied to any sentence to change its meaning. Variations in intensity express logical meanings in much the same way that variations in quality express changes in mood. The sentence "Why are you doing that?" may have five or more interpretations, depending upon which word or combination of words is stressed. The accompanying tone of voice permits even more interpretations.

Appropriate Pitch. Changes in pitch are of great importance in conveying ideas as well as emotions. Moods such as anger or gaiety require wide variations in pitch. An emotion such as grief or depression, on the other hand, requires but slight variation.

Appropriate Timing. In order to indicate both the logical and the emotional elements in meaning, timing is of great importance. A rapid rate will set up a different mood in an audience than a slow deliberate tempo. To a large extent, the nature of the material will dictate the tempo. For example, the seething turbulence of Southey's *The Cataract of Lodore* must be read in a faster tempo than James Stevens' measured lines in *Chill of Eve*. The spontaneity of O'Shaughnessy's *Ode* ("We are the music-makers") provides an interesting contrast to the staid and stately lines of Amy Lowell's *Patterns*.

THE USE AND ABUSE OF WORD SYMBOLS IN SWAYING AUDIENCES

Because of the general or specific associations they bring to mind, some words may be said to be emotionally charged. Such words may be properly used when a speaker attempts to arouse his listeners to give a fair consideration to a problem. When he uses them, however, to appeal to the fears, hatreds, or prejudices of his listeners in order to distract them from a fair analysis of facts and evidence, he is using them improperly or perhaps even dishonestly.

The study of semantics should encourage in both speakers and listeners a more thoughtful approach to words in all contexts. The former need to know how to employ emotionally charged words in order to secure attention; the latter need to be wary of them—particularly of the "devices" that are commonly used by unscrupulous speakers.

Emotionally Charged Words. A crowd may be lulled into feelings of false security by symbols evoking emotional reactions. Words such as *home, mother, hearth, democracy,* and *honor,* for example, may set up a chain of associations that will impede objective thought. In like manner, words such as *traitor, socialist, anarchist,* and *spy,* when applied without evidence, but merely as name calling, may move a mob to lynching or riot without any analysis of the facts or of the symbols being used to evoke emotional responses.

The Devices of Propaganda. Propaganda is conspicuous in modern life. Some propaganda, such as requests for plasma for blood banks and solicitations of money for heart funds or cancer research, is useful and contributes to the welfare of humanity. On the other hand, another type of propaganda, such as demagogic political speeches or false advertising, is pernicious, not only because its source, methods, and procedures are questionable, but also because it is concerned not with the ultimate welfare of humanity, but with its exploitation.

Whether propaganda is a source of good or bad, it should be analyzed carefully. The more high-order abstractions it contains, the more it should be subjected to minute evaluations to determine whether the propagandist is using words to blind rather than to enlighten. The common propaganda devices are: (1) the "name calling" device; (2) the "glittering generalities" device; (3) the "transfer" device; (4) the "testimonial" device; (5) the "plain folks" device; (6) the "card stacking" device; and (7) the "band wagon" device.[1]

NAME CALLING. This is a device to make the listener form a judgment without examining the evidence on which it should be based. The propagandist appeals to dislikes, hatreds, and fears by giving "bad names" to those individuals, groups, nations, races, policies, practices, beliefs, and ideals he would have his audience condemn and reject.

GLITTERING GENERALITIES. Here the propagandist identifies his program with respectability by using "virtue words." He appeals to the emotions of love, generosity, and brotherhood by using such words as *truth, freedom, honor, democracy, the American way,* and *upholding the Constitution.* Since practically every citizen believes in these ideals, the propagandist has only to identify the aims of his particular group with these idealistic words in order to have the audience support his cause. Glittering generalities may be contrasted with name calling in that

[1] Institute for Propaganda Analysis, "How to Detect Propaganda," *Propaganda Analysis,* I (November, 1937), 1–4.

it is a device to make the audience *accept and approve,* while the purpose of the latter is to have the listeners *reject and condemn.*

TRANSFER. Transfer is a device by which the propagandist carries over the authority, sanction, and prestige of something respected and revered to something he would have his audience accept. For example, most people respect and revere their church and nation. If the propagandist succeeds in getting representatives of the church or government to approve a campaign in behalf of some program, he thereby transfers their authority, sanction, and prestige to his program.

TESTIMONIAL. This device is frequently used in advertising. A widely-known person is quoted as saying he uses a special brand of cigarettes, or a motion-picture star is induced to give advice on a particular brand of cosmetics. The hope of the propagandist is that the audience will be led to follow the expressed or implied advice of the widely-known individual. Counter testimonials may be used by rivals, especially in connection with social, economic, and political issues.

PLAIN FOLKS. Politicians, labor leaders, and others use this device to win the confidence of the audience. During election years especially, the devotion of political candidates to small children, picnics, fishing, family ties, and church responsibilities is usually indicative that they are trying to show the audiences (the voters) that they are just like everyone else—just plain folks.

CARD STACKING. Here the propagandist seeks to befuddle and divert those in quest of facts he does not want to reveal, no matter how pertinent they may be. He "stacks the cards" against the truth by using overemphasis and underemphasis to dodge issues or to evade facts. He resorts to lies, censorship, and distortion. He omits facts. He offers false testimony. He creates a smoke screen of clamor by raising a new issue when he wants an embarrassing matter forgotten. This device is also called the "red-herring" device in reference to the early hunting custom of distracting the hounds by drawing a red herring across the trail.

THE BAND WAGON. "Follow the crowd" is the theme used here. By playing on the desire of the individual to conform, the propagandist who uses as his theme "Everybody's doing it" may readily win the audience to his cause.

The Responsibilities of Speakers and of Listeners. The speaker has an ethical responsibility to clarify his motives, to state his thesis in a straightforward manner, and to express himself clearly and concisely. The audience should assume he is honest until something in his technique warns them otherwise.

The audience must be especially wary of blatant political promises that have no possibility of fulfillment, and of convincing voices that make excessive and seemingly sincere promises for a wide variety of unrelated products and services. It is only through the careful study of the inner meanings of words and through penetrating analysis of high-order abstractions that an audience can be armed to understand and, hence, to resist the constant pressure and techniques of unethical individuals and groups.

Exercises

1. Make a list of nonverbal symbols that you use commonly in daily life.

2. What is your first reaction to the word *liberal?* Ask five friends or acquaintances to write their reactions to this word. Compare the results of this experiment with your own reaction.

3. The following words according to Webster's *New International Dictionary* have been used or are being used in a great many senses: *blank, blind, call, cast, clear, jump, stand,* and *well.* Write sentences to show how many uses you can make for each word. Check with the dictionary to see how many more uses you might have shown.

4. Analyze the propaganda techniques used in a magazine or newspaper advertisement.

5. Analyze the propaganda techniques used in a recent local or national political speech.

3

Public Speaking

Public speaking applies principles of direct and purposeful oral communication on a wide range of subjects for a wide variety of audiences and occasions. In contemporary society it is a most effective means of influencing thought and action.

THE PURPOSES OF PUBLIC SPEAKING

The fundamental purpose of a speech, whether it be simple, personal, daily speaking, or an eloquent address to a large audience on an important occasion, is to gain acceptance in the form of interest, understanding, approval, belief, or action. In many circumstances the speaker will seek only *to inform* his listeners by explaining a subject to them. In some instances he will wish *to entertain* his hearers by pleasing and amusing them. On ceremonial occasions he will endeavor *to impress* his listeners by paying tribute to the attainments or merit of an individual or a group. Concerning controversial matters, he will seek *to convince* his audience by striving to establish or to change beliefs. When action is to be taken, he will speak *to persuade* by trying to induce his listeners to do what he thinks is desirable.

When the speaker attempts to convince or to persuade, he should seek agreement from his hearers that his idea or his proposal is worthy of attention and acceptance, is more desirable than other plans, or is the most suitable of all possible solutions to a problem. In seeking this agreement, he relies on facts and evidence to support his proposition or assertion, and uses details for clarification.

But the public speaker should want his listeners to do more than understand the facts, evidence, and details. He should want them to accept his interpretation of those facts, to agree with the judgment or decision he has reached, to be willing to adopt the belief, to vote for the policy, or to follow the course of action established by the facts as necessary or desirable. Step by step he should endeavor to lead his hearers to a sound conclusion about what to think or about what to do, about what is expedient, or just, or significant: to a conclusion that will accomplish the result which he was considering when he was planning his speech.

THE OCCASIONS FOR PUBLIC SPEAKING

The occasions for public speaking may be divided into four general categories: (1) policy-forming, (2) professional, (3) social, and (4) ceremonial. Each type makes special demands upon the speaker.

Policy-Forming Occasions. The policy-forming, or deliberative, occasion is especially important in a democracy. The essence of democracy is the opportunity to deliberate and to hear conflicting points of view on what should be done. Whether the issue concerns such vital matters as condemning property or requiring military service, or such trivial activities as arranging an annual celebration or redecorating a meeting hall, and whether the speaker be a member of a group or an elected official, he is expected to offer his best judgment on the wisest or most expedient course of action to be taken.

Among specific kinds of policy-forming addresses are the keynote address of a convention, the speech of nomination, the campaign talk, the inaugural address, and the legislative speech. In each instance the speaker is supporting a policy, whether it be suggesting a platform, urging the fitness of a candidate, seeking votes in an election, announcing and defending a course of action upon assuming office, or advocating the passage of a statute in a legislative assembly.

Professional Occasions. Professional occasions for speaking vary widely, from the ritualistic occasions of the ministry to the commercial efforts of the salesman. Whether the speaker be a lawyer, an engineer, a journalist, a teacher, a physician, or a diplomat, he must be able to speak (1) in his professional capacity to his associates, and (2) in a semiprofessional capacity to great variety of nonprofessional groups.

A lawyer may speak as the attorney for the defense, as a judge on the bench, or as a member of his bar association, but he may also speak as a technically informed citizen to a service club in favor of abolition of the jury system. In the first three instances he is speaking to discharge his professional duties; in the last he is speaking to interpret an aspect of his profession to the lay public.

Social Occasions. On some social occasions the speaker seeks only to interest and to amuse his listeners; on others he may wish to entertain and at the same time to accomplish a serious purpose. In either case, he will do well to consider the expectations of the audience.

Usually his listeners will anticipate a treatment of the topic that will be easy to follow. In a popular lecture they will want a great deal of illustration, spiced with humorous personal experiences. In an after-dinner speech they will expect a light or satirical touch, enlivened with pertinent anecdotes and a vivid style. The speaker should be especially careful to avoid the trite, the bitter, and the offensive in seeking to be colorful.

The speaker should not use social occasions for a serious speech unless he knows that the audience will be receptive, or unless he thinks the problem so urgent that it cannot wait for a more appropriate time, or unless he feels that he should take advantage of a unique opportunity. In general, the social occasion calls for a speech which will enable the audience to relax and to enjoy the speaker's experiences.

Ceremonial Occasions. A ceremonial occasion calls for a speech to impress. Whether the speaker is making an introduction, presenting a gift, dedicating a building, celebrating an anniversary, eulogizing a founder, or participating in a commencement, his essential technique is that of dwelling upon an idea until its full significance is impressed upon the listeners. He may focus attention upon the character of an individual or upon the steadily increasing importance of an institution and may amplify those aspects most worthy of praise. Appropriate thought, feeling, style, and delivery will all contribute to the desired effect. The speaker may need to check a tendency, common in ceremonial speaking, toward the artificial and the stilted. If he is sincere, he should be able to manage his facts, language, organization, and presentation to create a response of genuine appreciation.

THE QUALIFICATIONS OF A SPEAKER

To achieve both the general and the specific purposes on a given occasion, a speaker must be able to construct a speech that will satisfy both the intellectual and the emotional needs of his listeners. He must be able to present it with directness, sincerity, and force in order to gain the desired response. He must recognize his limitations, and he must understand the moral requirements he should meet and the principles he should master.

At all times he should distinguish between mere exhibition of skill as an end in itself and genuine communication of thought and feeling for the accomplishment of a practical purpose. If any aspect of the art of speaking calls attention to itself, then display of skill has replaced the relationship that should exist between speaker and audience for the sincere communication of meaning.

Recognition of Limitations. When the speaker draws his material from what has happened in the past, he interprets it as accurately as his knowledge and ability permit. When he deals with the present, his nearness to events makes objectivity difficult, but in informing his listeners he does the best reporting he can, and in persuading he acts as an advocate to make the best case he can from an honest interpretation of the facts as he understands them.

When he is concerned with what is best for the future, he must exercise well-considered judgment in drawing inferences from what has happened in the past and from what current conditions indicate as desirable. Unlike the scientist, the speaker cannot hope to establish a high degree of certainty: he must establish probability.

Moral Responsibility. Every speaker should constantly bear in mind that speechmaking is a powerful instrument for either good or evil as he chooses to employ it. He has a solemn obligation to find the available facts and to interpret them as honestly and as intelligently as he can. Before he undertakes to induce others to agree with him, he should be sure, after full investigation and analysis, that his decision on the problem is what he sincerely believes to be desirable for the group he is addressing. Since he is acting as a leader, he should be fully aware of his responsibility to be guided by the highest ethical standards and to use his knowledge and skill for worthy ends.

Mastery of Principles. In order to accomplish his purpose with his listeners, the speaker must understand and follow principles of effective speaking observed, systematized, and applied in many forms for more than twenty-five centuries. The statement that orators are born, not made, reflects a failure to appreciate how the best speakers have acquired their ability. The testimony of accomplished speechmakers throughout history emphasizes that the art of public speaking, like other arts, requires full understanding of its fundamental principles. It also requires continuing experience in intelligently applying these principles to practical uses in order to develop skill and confidence.

THE METHODS OF DELIVERING SPEECHES

The purpose of the speech, the occasion, the audience, or the opportunity for preparation may prescribe the method of presentation, or the speaker himself may decide upon the best of the four possible methods. Whether the speaker talks (1) impromptu, (2) extemporaneously, (3) from manuscript, or (4) from memory, he has the problem of concentrating on what he is going to say, and of focusing his attention upon his ideas as he presents them.

Impromptu Delivery. An individual who is not scheduled to speak may be called upon with little or no warning and therefore may have time only to choose his central idea before he must begin to talk impromptu. He must draw upon his experience for the necessary development and adaptation as he proceeds. The simpler he makes his organization, the better. Anecdotes or incidents from his experience will usually be his best supporting material.

Extemporaneous Delivery. The speaker who wishes to utilize the advantages of maximum adaptability to the immediate occasion and audience may prepare as fully as the time and available material permit, but he should not depend upon a specific wording of his ideas. He should know his central idea and the exact sequence of his ideas, but he should choose his language as he speaks. Rehearsals should make this choice easier. In general, the fewer notes he uses the better because they hamper a fluent, forceful presentation and interfere with transitions. If they are used, the notes should be restricted mainly to statistics and quotations and should be on small cards easy to consult. Each card should be limited to a single item with clear headings indicating topic and source.

Delivery from Manuscript. Manuscript delivery is expected on very important occasions and is often used for broadcasts. The speaker must be able to grasp the significance of what he reads and to maintain close contact with his listeners. He should look at his audience as much as possible and at his manuscript as little as possible. He must be able to re-create the thought each time he presents it to an audience, with a genuine interest in the response of his listeners.

Delivery from Memory. Successful memorized speaking requires the speaker to have his speech so completely mastered that he has no problem in recalling the language and can devote his full attention to the direct communication of his thought and feeling. His memorization, however, should permit him the same spontaneity that he would have in extemporaneous presentation, to the point of interpolation if the circumstances require it.

THE PREPARATION OF A SPEECH

If a speaker is to proceed systematically, he must be aware of the sequence of steps in preparing a speech. Since the time of Aristotle, four major steps have been recognized: (1) investigation, (2) organization, (3) expression or choice of language, and (4) mastery of the content and language.

Investigation. In determining his topic, the speaker must consider the purpose of the speech, the nature of the occasion, and the characteristics of the prospective audience. After he has chosen his topic, he should proceed with an analysis of his subject in relation to his audience. He must then gather the data which this analysis indicates as necessary.

Choice of Topic. Frequently the speaker is invited to talk on a specific subject; if not, his first problem is to select one. He should begin his investigation by listing possible topics and selecting the one best suited to all aspects of the situation: his own interests and qualifications, the requirements of his specific purpose, the amount and the accessibility of information on the subject, the limitations, traditions, and significance of the occasion, and the expectations and characteristics of the audience.

The speaker may obtain suggestions for topics by considering the needs of the particular community. He may also obtain them by analyzing the political, sociological, economic, and educational questions, developments, attitudes, and trends of the day as revealed through newspapers, magazines, lectures, broadcasts, the movies, the theater, and literature, and by comparing the customs, standards, traditions, and manners of his own area with those of other cities, regions, or countries.

ANALYSIS OF THE AUDIENCE. The speaker should analyze his prospective audience in the light of the topic, the purpose of the speech, and the occasion. He must be concerned with such matters as the range of ages represented in the audience, the education and experience of the group, their knowledge and opinions on the topic, and their possible attitude toward him. He must adapt his speech as specifically as possible to the audience he is likely to face, keeping in mind that he may have to include interpolations, or to modify or to change the content to overcome hostility, boredom, or restlessness during his presentation.

The public speaker needs more than a superficial knowledge of the differences in the interests of men and women, children and adults, rich and poor, educated and uneducated, experienced and inexperienced. He should understand the beliefs, opinions, and prejudices of people of different political parties, religions, races, countries, professions, and economic and social levels. He should try to learn whether the audience has any previous knowledge and opinions of himself, his background, and his ideas so that he may be able to judge accurately that his reception is likely to be favorable, unfavorable, or indifferent.

The speaker should never fail to consider the emotional state of his audience so that he will be able to establish a common ground of feeling. Pride, anger, hatred, hope, fear, or grief may determine how the listeners will receive a speech. He must analyze and utilize their motives and interests if he is to relate what he has to say to their habits of thought and feeling. To choose the right appeals to re-enforce his evidence and reasoning, he must know as much as possible about the behavior and needs of the people he will address.

In some instances the nature of the assigned topic will give the speaker a hint as to the character of his prospective audience; in others, previous speeches made to the same group and subsequent criticisms and comments will help him to decide on specific adaptations in his own speech. He may obtain information about the prospective audience from the representative who arranged for the speech to be given. Psychological and sociological studies of group behavior will also prove valuable to the speaker in helping him to apply his speechmaking techniques to all kinds of groups.

COLLECTION OF MATERIAL. With his analysis of the audience in mind, the speaker should consider his own knowledge and experience concerning the topic and should then start his research and the collection of data. He should talk to both experts and laymen to get the facts and the opinions he needs for background. He should attend lectures and should consult newspapers, periodicals, and books. The library card catalogues, the *Readers' Guide to Periodical Literature,* and *The New York Times Index* are only a few of the many excellent guides to reference material. In his collection of material, the speaker should be sure to find concrete and specific examples to illustrate each of the units of his speech.

Organization. The second step in the speaker's preparations is determining the structure of the speech. He must decide both the logical requirements of the subject and the most appropriate way to adapt it to the prospective audience. Only after a speaker has selected his topic, has analyzed his particular audience, and has collected his material will he be properly equipped to plan the structure of his speech.

THE RELATION OF ANALYSIS TO STRUCTURE. At the end of his investigation, the speaker should formulate a statement of his central idea. He should word this sentence with extreme care to set forth exactly the point of view determined by the investigation. He should then select material to substantiate this statement. For example, if the speech is to inform, the supporting material should consist of specific details to clarify the statement; if the speech is to persuade, the supporting material should consist of reasoning and evidence to justify the proposition or resolution offered.

Not only will the systematic analysis completed in the first step of preparation indicate the logical structure of the subject, but it will also determine the requirements for adapting the subject to the audience. In other words, the needs of the specific audience in relation to the subject will indicate the best order and method of presentation of ideas: e.g., whether to begin the development with a statement of the central idea, with specific illustrations or examples, or with comparisons and contrasts. The systematic analysis should also suggest the best type of introduction and conclusion for the particular audience.

THE PARTS OF A SPEECH. The speaker should understand clearly the nature and functions of the three parts of a well-planned speech: the *introduction,* the *body,* and the *conclusion.* Although a more elaborate plan is possible for long speeches, a threefold division is adequate for all practical purposes.

The introduction may include such subdivisions as the *exordium* (or approach), the *narration* (or background), the *statement* (or proposition), the *partition* (or analysis), and such items as definitions, qualifications, and limitations when needed. The body may include the explanation or the argument and the contrast or the refutation, as well as digressions. The *peroration* (or conclusion) may include a recapitulation or summary and an exhortation or appeal.

The Introduction. The essential functions of the introduction are to gain attention, to give a favorable impression of the speaker, to create the right state of mind in the listeners, to lead into the subject, to state the central idea, and to indicate the divisions to be developed. A personal experience of the speaker may be the source of a good approach, particularly if it is amusing enough to break down any reserve that may exist.

The Body. The body of the speech should develop the central idea in accordance with the plan best suited to the immediate audience. Instead of a straightforward presentation of ideas from generalizations to specific instances or from effect to cause, usually followed in an outline or a brief, the speaker may decide to proceed from the specific to the general or from cause to effect. He may find it desirable to proceed from the familiar to the unfamiliar or from the known to the unknown, using comparison and contrast.

The speaker may want to use *reductio ad absurdum* (developing the arguments he is refuting to the point of absurdity); reversal of position (beginning with the statement of a popular position and following with the refutation of each of the generally accepted arguments); or proof, proposition, and more proof (creating suspense by offering some proof before stating the central idea and then following the central idea with additional proof).

The Conclusion. The conclusion should state or restate the central idea in such a way that the audience will clearly understand and remember it. By concisely summarizing his development, the speaker should leave no doubt about the concept or process he has been trying to explain, the belief he has sought to establish, or the action he wants the audience to take. The conclusion should also serve an emotional purpose as well as an intellectual one: it should establish the right attitude toward the speaker and the cause he supports.

Choice of Language and Style. The third step in building a speech is to express the thought and feeling in language that will communicate to the audience exactly what the speaker intends. Since the listener cannot interrupt the speaker, the speech must be instantly intelligible. The speaker's sentences should be easy to follow. His vocabulary must be suited to the understanding of the audience: it should be appropriate for the age and education of the group, and free from clichés, difficult and abstract words, and technical terms.

Furthermore, the style should possess the characteristics that sustain interest: vividness, variety, and force. The concrete and the specific, the personal relationship of speaker to audience through the use of *I* and *you* and direct address (my fellow-members), the unexpected turn of phrase, the sequence of action verbs rising to a climax of emphasis—these and many other devices of style enable the speaker to say what he means in a way that will hold the attention of his audience.

Mastery of Content and Language. The fourth step in preparing to address an audience is mastering the content and language of the speech with particular concentration upon the sequence of ideas. The speaker should fix firmly in mind the structure and plan of his speech, and he should know how he will progress from one idea into another. At the moment he speaks each idea, he must have a full realization of the exact meaning of what he is saying. He must also keep in mind the kind of response he expects from his listeners.

THE MEANS OF GAINING AUDIENCE ACCEPTANCE

The speaker has at his command three essential means of persuading the audience to accept his ideas. These resources, often called "kinds of proof," include (1) the establishment of his reliability, (2) the use of logical reasoning, and (3) the appeal to motives and feelings.

The Establishment of Reliability. If the speaker is known to his audience before his speech, his reputation may be either an asset or a liability. Through what he says and the way he says it, he may either confirm an impression or establish a new one.

Of greatest importance will be the respect the audience has for the speaker's judgment. The more willing his listeners are to follow the development of his ideas without mentally challenging his assertions, the easier his task becomes. Moreover, the more certain his listeners are that he is sincere, honest, trustworthy, and genuinely interested in their welfare, the more likely they are to have confidence in his facts and findings and to be willing to accept his proposal. If the audience suspects that the speaker has selfish motives and is guilty of exploitation, his reception will be cool indeed.

The Use of Logical Reasoning. The second of the three kinds of proof refers to the type of reasoning the speaker uses. Two methods of drawing inferences are available: "specific to general" and "general to specific."

With either type of reasoning, the speaker should make sure that his inferences are valid, that he does not generalize from too few or nontypical instances, and that he has left no loophole for an opponent to attack. He should familiarize himself with types of arguments, kinds of evidence, fallacies, and methods of refutation as well as with the requirements of adequate definition, logical classification, and systems of explanation.[1]

For the intelligent listener, logical and fully demonstrated proof is the main requisite of persuasion. When the speaker seeks only understanding, he may rely upon a systematic explanation with adequate reference to the facts the listeners already know. When he seeks action, he must associate with his arguments appeals to the specific interests and motives of his audience.

[1] See Chapters 5 and 6.

REASONING FROM SPECIFIC TO GENERAL. For the audience that is likely to be skeptical, the speaker will find the method of generalization from specific instances effective. If the particular examples are so familiar that the listeners immediately identify and confirm them, the speaker should be able to construct a chain of reasoning the audience cannot refuse to accept.

In urging slum clearance, for example, the speaker may begin by vividly describing three specific instances of well-known slums in different parts of the city. From these familiar instances he may gain acceptance for the idea that slum conditions are so bad for the inhabitant and so widespread in their effects on the city that immediate clearance for better housing is imperative. If he had begun with the general statement that slums must be replaced with new housing, his audience might well give first consideration to the cost to the taxpayer rather than to the plight of the slum-dweller and the possible spread of disease to all parts of the city.

REASONING FROM GENERAL TO SPECIFIC. Since the process of reasoning from "specific to general" usually requires more details and therefore more time, the speaker will want to use the method of "general to specific" when he knows that his hearers are prepared to cover ground rapidly. Usually a single representative instance is sufficient to give the audience the idea.

In attempting to induce voters to register for a coming election, the speaker would probably find readily acceptable the general idea that citizens should discharge their responsibility at the polls. The striking instance of a recent election of a corrupt politician whose administration cost the city large sums in taxpayers' money would probably suffice to make the audience understand the argument.

Appeal to Motives and Feelings. The last of the three kinds of proof is developed when the speaker appeals to the motives or arouses the feelings of his listeners in support of his proposition. Irresponsible speakers use emotional appeals apart from logical proof to exploit their listeners, but responsible speakers make legitimate use of the feelings of their hearers to re-enforce their reasoning.

Since we are not coldly logical in our behavior, the speaker will find it necessary to employ emotional as well as logical support for his proposition. He will consider such fundamental interests of his listeners as health, wealth, power, reputation, security, home, and family. By identifying his proposal with the attainment of their wishes, he can provide a strong incentive for them to adopt the course of action he advocates. By arousing such feelings as pride or shame, fear or confidence, love or hate, joy or grief, contempt or reverence, he can greatly strengthen the persuasive effect of his arguments.

THE PRESENTATION OF A SPEECH

The final test of the speaker's study and preparation is his presentation of his speech. Regardless of the method he uses to deliver his speech, the speaker must know exactly what he is saying at the very moment he says it in order to convey the full meaning with all the necessary shades of emphasis. Absent-mindedness or partial comprehension will quickly reveal to the audience that the speaker is either not very enthusiastic about his topic or not very well prepared.

The main responsibility of the speaker is to gain and to hold the attention of the listeners so completely that they will think along with him and will respond as he intended. To gain such intimacy and to elicit such a response, the speaker must look at his audience and must be quick to adapt his delivery to the reactions he senses: boredom, bewilderment, disagreement, hostility. He should know when his audience is interested, pleased, amused, enlightened, convinced, or persuaded.

The speaker should adjust his volume, rate, pausing, animation, and force to the kind of response he sees. His facial expressions, gestures, and movements should always contribute to the communication of his meaning and should never call attention to themselves.

SUGGESTED TOPICS FOR SPEECHES

The finding and testing of topics is always a specific problem related to the immediate circumstances. No list of topics can do more than suggest what other speakers have talked about. The topics on the following page are classified according to the purpose of the speaker.

To Inform:
How to Form a Club
How to Operate Radar
How to Make a Camp
How to Weave a Rug
The City-Manager Plan
Editing a College Paper
A Trip to Mexico
The Latest Type of Fighter Plane
The Federal Conciliation Service
UNESCO

To Entertain:
How to be Graduated without Studying
How Not to Win Friends
Freshmen Are Funny
The Joys of Living Alone
Oh! For the Good Old Days
Where Do We Go from Here?
I Couldn't Let Well Enough Alone
An Embarrassing Moment
The Ordeal of Being a Kid Sister
Politics Make Strange Bedfellows

To Impress:
The Greatest Teacher in My Life
America's Finest Painter
The Founders of Our Organization
The Immediate Challenge to the Graduates of Today
The Significance of Our Gift
Our Hopes for This New Building
A Tribute to American Inventiveness
A Welcome to Our Visitors
A Greeting to Our New Members
"Of Thee I Sing"

To Convince:
Has Democracy Failed?
The Futility of Censorship
Our Inherited Responsibilities
The Need for Leadership
The Functions of a Liberal Education
The Need for Higher Income Taxes
Why We Must Help Our Neighbors Abroad
Is Peace Possible in Our Time?
Can Our Standard of Living Continue To Rise?
The Importance of Vocational Guidance

To Persuade:
Vote for the Most Experienced Candidate
Support the Civil Rights Program
Give All You Can to the Red Cross
Make the Membership Drive a Complete Success
Join the Hospital Insurance Plan
Help in the Campaign for Better Roads
Heed the Warning: Safety First
Become a Regular Blood Donor
Enlist in the Branch of the Service You Prefer
Urge Board Members to Increase Salaries

Exercises

1. What are the purposes and occasions for public speaking?
2. Explain the methods of delivering a speech.
3. What are the major steps in preparing a speech?

4. Prepare an outline for a speech to inform. List the type of prospective audience and the sources for reference material.

5. Analyze a speech that has appeared in the newspapers. What kind of reasoning did the speaker use? Are there any loopholes in his arguments? Do you find any examples or anecdotes in the speech? Are the introduction and the conclusion adequate?

4

Group Discussion

Group discussion takes place when persons who are interested in a specific problem gather to discuss it *purposefully* in the hope of arriving at a solution or clarification. Although long-distance group discussion can obviously take place by letter, by contributors' columns in periodicals, and by other means, the present chapter will deal specifically with group discussions that are centered in one place—the classroom, the committee room, the broadcasting studio.

For effective discussion, the term *group* must mean more than a mere collection of individuals. A group is a dynamic whole with properties which are different from the properties of its parts.[1] For example, a group of six persons will produce ideas which no one of the six could have produced by himself. Individuals in a group are interdependent and must identify themselves with the whole group if they are to work co-operatively in related activity toward a common goal. A group, in other words, represents a plurality of individuals, but the end result of group endeavor is singular, not plural. So that the group may not lack direction, one member is designated as chairman or discussion leader.

Group discussion—which differs from public speaking where individuals explain their ideas to groups, and from debating where speakers defend the *pros* and *cons* but do not seek group thinking upon problems—is an excellent tool when the outcome of group thinking is really wanted. If an employer, for example, wants to know the reactions of his staff to a specific problem, and if he is willing to act on their collective thinking and experience, group discussion will be a satisfactory method. However,

[1] Kurt Lewin, "Field Theory and Experiment in Social Psychology," *American Journal of Sociology*, XLIV (May, 1939), 868–96.

if he has decided to put a plan into operation regardless of the attitude of his staff, discussion with them would be a waste of time. In other words, if the result of group thinking is going to determine policy or in some way affect the outcome, group discussion is invaluable. Otherwise, a lecture, some kind of demonstration, or perhaps a printed pamphlet may be a more desirable form of communication.

TYPES OF DISCUSSION GROUPS

There are many kinds of group discussion. Those that are explained here are the usual types, each valuable in its way, depending upon the purpose of the discussion, the number of participants, and the type of audience.

One of the most valuable features of group discussion is the *forum*, or question and answer period, which may follow any type of discussion or presentation. The open forum gives the audience an opportunity to secure further information, to introduce additional material, which might not otherwise have been included, and, most important of all, to ask questions and to participate actively in the discussion.

Classroom Groups. The lecture method in classrooms has been widely superseded by the use of discussion. There are many ways in which discussion may be used in the classroom. Sometimes a subject is assigned for discussion and a leader is appointed; sometimes a topic is introduced spontaneously in relation to the subject being studied, and the teacher or a student may lead the discussion; or else a subject allied to the one assigned for study leads to discussion. As in all forms of discussion, the leader must try to evoke responses from as many students as possible and must be aware of time limitations for each speaker.

The Conference. The term *conference* is used to indicate a variety of discussion groups. Generally, the conference is thought of as a small group, sometimes consisting of only two persons. More loosely, it is a name given to round-table meetings (in which a maximum of about twenty persons may participate), to public discussions, and even to conventions. Where the conference is sufficiently restricted in numbers, everyone has an opportunity to speak.

The chairman generally states the problem, sees that everybody has an opportunity to suggest a proposal, helps to work out the most likely solution, and then arranges for a committee to formulate the plan agreed upon. He then summarizes the work of the group and if necessary, arranges for a future meeting. This type of discussion is widely used in colleges, in industry, in professional organizations, and in political and legislative groups.

Informal Groups. R. D. Wagner and C. C. Arnold in their *Handbook of Group Discussion* [2] indicate three common types of informal discussions: (1) the study group; (2) the policy-forming group; and (3) the committee.

STUDY GROUPS. The study group might be an outgrowth of a desire to obtain information. In the classroom, for example, a study group might be assigned the problem of ascertaining the contributions of a specific dramatist.

POLICY-FORMING GROUPS. A policy-forming group of a college faculty might decide whether the works of the author in question were to be included in the curriculum and, if so, where they might be most advantageously placed.

COMMITTEES. The greatest part of the actual work of most organizations is done by committees. Because it is easier for small groups to work together than for large groups, a committee has advantages which enable it to work more efficiently than a parent organization. A committee can spend more time in investigation and discussion than a large organization; it can study troublesome or controversial subjects without the publicity that sometimes attends larger groups; and it can permit more informal procedure than is possible with large groups.

Committees may be elected by the organization or appointed by the presiding officer. They are usually classified as *special* or *standing*. The function of a special committee is to perform some specific task. Unless additional work is delegated to such a committee, it ceases to exist when its final report has been submitted. Organization projects which may be completed in a few days or weeks are usually the work of special committees. Long-range tasks, such as program planning or membership drives, are the responsibility of standing committees. Generally, standing committees serve from one election of officers to the next.

Since the chairman of the committee is in a most strategic po-

[2] R. D. Wagner and C. C. Arnold, *Handbook of Group Discussion* (New York: Houghton-Mifflin Co., 1950, pp. 159–65.

sition, it is essential to committee action that he be thoroughly acquainted with the nature and limitations of the committee assignment. His tasks are to apportion assignments of members; to amalgamate the findings of the committee; to know when and how to postpone decisions so that the committee will not be divided in action too soon; and to know when adjournment is advisable if members of the committee need additional time to investigate material or to discuss their differences informally.

The Panel. The panel is a discussion group in which the speakers are generally experts and the audience often participants. Seating arrangements not only should permit members of the panel to see and hear one another readily, but also should enable the audience to communicate easily with the speakers. Placing the speakers' chairs in a semicircle is one solution. Whether the panel should be seated on the same level with the audience or on a platform depends upon the size of the room and the size of the audience. If an informal tone is to be kept, and if the audience is not too large, it is advisable to have the audience and the members of the panel on the same level.

The number of speakers varies; probably six should be the maximum. Otherwise, it is difficult to carry on a discussion that is intelligible to an audience and that gives them any time for participation.

Members of the panel and the subject to be discussed should be introduced by the chairman. He should also inform the audience of the procedure to be followed, i.e., whether there are to be questions after each speech or at the end of the panel. After he has finished his introductory remarks, he should sit down and then open the discussion with a statement or query that will focus attention on an important facet of the problem. He must draw the members of the group into informal discussion. Through his expertness in summarizing, asking questions, and general elucidation, he can keep the audience informed of the trend of ideas, thereby helping them to formulate their questions.

The Symposium. The symposium consists of a number of individual speeches. Ordinarily, there are from three to six speakers, each of whom speaks about five to twenty minutes.

Since the speakers usually are experts in their respective fields, they should be chosen for their knowledge of group-discussion techniques. The speaker who is likely to be too dogmatic in his point of view and who discourages audience participation is not a good choice for a symposium.

The chairman should introduce the problem to be discussed, indicating its importance and preparing the audience for a breakdown of aspects of the subject to be developed by the speakers. He should also introduce each speaker, make the necessary transitions between the speakers, and summarize each speech briefly at its conclusion.

The symposium is usually followed by an informal panel discussion before audience participation is invited. This procedure lessens the formality of the symposium and prepares the way for group discussion.

Radio and Television Groups. Through presentation of group discussions on controversial and noncontroversial subjects, both radio and television have contributed to the democratic process. The main objective of these discussions is to offer an interesting and well-organized presentation of an important subject in such a way that more than one point of view will be available to listeners.

Some of the disadvantages of radio discussion are due to the fact that the speakers are not seen by the listeners, except for a comparatively few persons in the radio audience. For this reason, television programs in which the speakers sit around a table and discuss in an informal manner may prove a more effective device for group discussion. In neither form, however, is the audience usually able to participate in a very direct way, unless the program is held in a large hall or auditorium and roving microphones are used. Limitations of time and problems of production are other factors which prevent audience participation.

Nevertheless, the fact remains that many persons would prefer to listen to a discussion by a number of experts than to read the opinions of one author. One of the advantages of radio and television discussion is that they reach much larger audiences than those reached by any other discussion group. The discussions must have no perceptible lags, however, or the listeners will promptly turn the dial to something more interesting.

Because of the nature of radio and television discussion, the materials to be used must be gathered early and the procedures planned carefully with regard to the clarity and progression of ideas. The problem under discussion should be restated from time to time, and the chairman should make more summaries than are needed in other types of discussion for the sake of people who tune in after the program has begun or who have been distracted by activity in their homes. In general, the round-table or panel discussion seems to be best adapted to radio and television. The symposium-forum may be successful, but it is more difficult to conduct, and there are too few participants compared to the number of listeners.

Every participant in a broadcast discussion should learn the hand signals used during the broadcast to guide and direct the performers regarding their volume of voice, nearness to the microphone, or position on the set. The participant should also remember that the audience will consist of small family groups and should therefore use a conversational tone and style and speak as if he were talking to a few friends instead of to a million listeners. Sentences should be shorter, and personal pronouns may be used more than in other forms of discussion. Unlike the newspaper, magazine, or book reader, the broadcast listener cannot "turn back" to examine something he failed to understand. Consequently, all facts and figures must be carefully marshaled and arranged so that the listeners will have no difficulty understanding the material.

The tempo should be slower than that for nonbroadcast addresses, but not so slow that the material lags. Audiences cannot sustain interest if the effect is drawling or devitalizing. Subject matter and the experience of the speaker, as well as his natural tempo, will undoubtedly affect the speed of a broadcast speech, but a rate of a hundred and thirty-five to a hundred and fifty words a minute is considered adequate.

RADIO DISCUSSIONS. Although there are many similarities, the problems of broadcast discussions vary for radio and television. The radio speaker must know the distance to stand from the microphone; he must remember to turn his head when coughing; and he must avoid rattling papers or making unnecessary noise.

TELEVISION DISCUSSIONS. Television speakers must consider the visual as well as the auditory effects; they must be concerned with how they look as well as with what they say. For example, the task of the discussion leader is more difficult on television than on radio, for here it may be easily noted if he dominates the group instead of guiding it, or if he has mannerisms that intrude on his performance. He must also learn to check the time unobtrusively so that the audience will not be distracted by his looking at the clock.

ADVANTAGES OF GROUP DISCUSSION

One of the greatest advantages of group discussion is that it provides more resources for problem-solving than are available when one person makes decisions about problems affecting a group. It is also valuable when two opposing views have been set forth and an "either-or" outcome is in the offing. The introduction of new points of view may break the deadlock.

Through group thinking and planning, ideas can be tested more adequately and dispassionately than they can when the group is under the spell of a convincing though sometimes shortsighted or self-interested speaker.

Group discussion is essential to democratic government. From the earliest meetings of the colonists to the latest political convention, from the earliest "cracker-barrel" groups in the village store to the most recent discussion of scientific farming, people in America have been free to discuss, to differ, to use their democratic prerogative of free speech, to pool the results of their cooperative and reflective thinking. Herein lies hope for the future of the democratic way of life.

PROBLEMS FOR GROUP DISCUSSION

The problems selected for group discussion should be those which cannot or should not be decided without an exchange of ideas and opinions. Topics selected for discussion should also be within the intellectual scope of the members of the group.

Kinds of Problems. Problems that lend themselves to group discussion are many and varied. For convenience, they may be grouped under three general classifications: (1) problems involving group action; (2) problems involving determination of public policy; and (3) problems involving a mode of conduct.[3]

[3] Cf. William E. Utterback, "Group Thinking and Conference Leadership," *Techniques of Discussion* (New York: Rinehart & Co., Inc., 1950).

PROBLEMS INVOLVING GROUP ACTION. Problems involving group action are those which are imminent and so vital that they demand immediate consideration. Their solution may be placed in the hands of a committee which may be empowered to recommend a plan of procedure after investigation and discussion. The policy-forming committee, the grievance committee, the community council, and all kinds of local organizations engaged in the management of their own affairs deal primarily with problems involving group action.

PROBLEMS INVOLVING PUBLIC POLICY. Problems involving the determination of public policy include municipal, state, national, or international conditions about which the average citizen can clarify his point of view by listening to and participating in intelligent group discussions. Plans for a new library, road, or state park might have been formulated before the discussion. The object of the discussion is to help the citizen come to an individual decision.

Those who believe that the best questions involve a course of action recommend the inclusion of the word *should* in questions of policy: "Should there be a world language?" "Should the federal debt limit be raised?" "Should we have federal aid in education?" "Should tariff barriers be lowered?" "Should news be censored?"

PROBLEMS INVOLVING A MODE OF CONDUCT. Problems involving a mode of conduct generally pertain to group rather than to individual conduct. How can the teacher deal with tardiness or lateness in his classes? What should be the attitude of a small business man toward attempts to unionize his plant? What should be the attitude of young people toward the support of the aged or infirm? These and innumerable other topics are not so much personal problems as group problems and should be treated as such.

Phrasing of the Problem. Since the prime purpose of group discussion is problem-solving, the phrasing of the problem assumes great importance. If it is phrased in vague terms or embraces a whole field of human endeavor, it will not be a satisfactory topic for group discussion. Topics such as "The contributions of the Mayan civilization," "The necessity for decreasing absenteeism in industry," or "The role of socialized medicine in a democracy" are examples that are not sufficiently specific for discussion. Such topics tend to be overpowering rather than to stimulate constructive thinking.

Concrete wording, preferably in the form of a question, is desirable. Discussion questions concern fact, value, or policy. Those concerned with fact should involve research and interpretation; otherwise, they are not suitable for discussion. "Is the rainfall greater this year than last?" "Are there more tenants in housing project A than in B?" "Are there more high schools in the state than there were two years ago?"—these are all poor discussion topics because the information in each case is readily available. The facts are there; no discussion can grow out of the answers.

QUALIFICATIONS AND DUTIES OF GROUP MEMBERS

The qualities that make for successful group-discussion members are those that make for successful adjustment generally, for they represent the total personality of the speaker. Perhaps the prime requisite for a group member or leader is his willingness to participate in such a program and, having entered it, to try to improve his presentation of material as well as his listening and speaking habits. Open-mindedness; respect for others, including courtesy, tact, and willingness to listen; command of speech techniques, including those relating to audibility; and interest in people or in group co-operative planning are all required for the successful participant in group discussion.

The Role of the Discussion Leader. The discussion leader can frequently be the deciding factor in avoiding a dull, disorganized group discussion and obtaining an interesting, constructive one. His preparation for the discussion and the use of his intelligence, imagination, and ingenuity during the conference are important aspects of the role he must play.

PREPARATION. The discussion leader sets the tone of the meeting. He must gauge his subject, his speakers, and the possible interaction of the speakers on one another in order to determine the degree of formality or informality to try to attain. He must keep in mind the goals of the meeting and do everything in his power to bring about their fulfillment.

If the discussion leader is acquainted with a group, the problem of preparing the order of the conference is minimized. If he does not know the group, or if the subject matter is very complicated, he may have to hold preliminary meetings with one or more members in order to work out an adequate plan of action.

Before the meeting begins, the chairman should be sure that the speakers agree on their definitions of terms. Otherwise, groups are likely to be bored by quibbling that might have been avoided had the discussion leader planned carefully.

The chairman should also try to find out how much agreement exists among the speakers on the goals of the meeting and should endeavor to ascertain the possible solutions that are going to be offered. In this way, differences of opinion may be gauged, and procedures may be planned. He should then outline his material, indicating the time sequence that will be most effective and the order of solutions. This schedule should be kept in mind but should not interfere with the spontaneity of group thinking.

His voice, of course, must have good pitch, volume, and quality, for in no field of speech activity is it more important to have excellent voice control than in the field of discussion leadership. If defective, these voice characteristics may be improved through training and practice (see Chapter 12). The discussion leader must be heard at all costs. If the group is a small one in a small room, he will have to sound conversational. If the audience is a large one in a large room, he will have to maintain some informal quality even if he has to achieve volume. The problem is especially difficult if he has to deal with a small audience in a large room.

QUALIFICATIONS. Since the discussion leader is likely to be a layman, in contrast to the speakers who are experts, he must necessarily have an intelligent understanding of the subject and its problems. Without such understanding, he cannot hope to guide the discussion, ask intelligent questions, or help significantly in the solution of the problem.

He must exercise intelligence, imagination, courtesy, and tact. He must be able to use judgment in deciding whom to call on, which problems to set up, how to make transitions, and when to summarize.

The quality of his voice will help set the tone or mood of the meeting. His opening remarks are also important, for they tend to create interest in the subject, to condition the audience, and to start them thinking about the problem and the possible solutions. The enthusiasm of a chairman may awaken an enthusiastic response from the audience. In like manner, a dull, lifeless introduction may dampen the spirits of the group so that no cooperative thought can possibly ensue.

Another qualification of importance to the discussion leader is an accurate sense of timing. He must know when to interrupt the speakers; when to let them continue; when to inject a salient point or summary; when to interfere if questions are too involved or digressive; and when to summarize his material to bring the meeting to a close.

The discussion leader must be able to control the discussion as it develops. He must also try to keep loquacious speakers or those with badly organized presentations from monopolizing the time, and he must be sure that all material is relevant to the main purpose of the discussion. He must be ready to ask stimulating questions when the discussion lags or becomes tedious. A timely transition may serve to start the group thinking about the next topic instead of lingering on one too long, especially if there is little hope of agreement anyway.

If the group has wandered from the main problem, he will have to use his ingenuity in getting the members back to it. He must also judge when an amusing story will break the tension or when an aside will have the desired effect.

The closing of a discussion is as important as the opening. The summary should include all items agreed or disagreed upon, the general conclusions that have been reached, the matters for further study, and any particular contributions that have been made to the solution of a problem. The chairman must be objective and must be sure that he is not distorting the conclusions in the directions of his personal bias or convictions.

The Role of the Speakers. Each speaker has a responsibility to participate in the discussion. He cannot do this unless he understands and has an interest in the subject to be discussed. Audiences are quick to sense a lukewarm or indifferent attitude and are correspondingly unresponsive. The speaker must also familiarize himself with discussion methods and procedures in order to be able to make effective contributions.

PREPARATION. Members of discussion groups should be thoroughly versed in the subject under discussion. They should not only have in mind outstanding points that they want to make by way of individual contributions, but they should also have a reservoir of information which will make the forum period interesting and enlightening. They should have specific, challenging questions ready.

One of the principal requirements for the group-discussion member is audibility. Sometimes the listeners hear only the answers to questions which members of the discussion group have asked; or they may hear only the questions and not the answers. A member of the group discussion should know how to use his voice effectively and easily. If his voice is ineffective or his speech is markedly defective, he should seek remedial help before he engages in public discussion.

QUALIFICATIONS. A member of a discussion group should not be oratorical or dramatic, but he should be able to present his ideas forcefully and accurately and with vivid and enthusiastic language. He must also know how to listen intelligently and critically. Many speakers are so involved in what they themselves plan to say that they do not really hear what is being said by others.

Each member should listen carefully to the information contained in the speeches of other panel members, as well as to the emotional overtones and the progression of thought in such speeches. Sometimes it is helpful to take notes, in order to understand the relationship of each speaker to the total program. The speeches of others may help a member of the group to clarify his own thoughts.

The group-discussion speaker must also learn to gauge the reactions of the audience as well as those of other members. Some speakers quickly feel the antagonism or enthusiasm of audiences; others have to acquire this sensitivity through long experience with groups.

Although open-mindedness is one of the qualifications for a discussion-group member, the individual must also have the courage of his convictions. Unless he is proved to be wrong during the discussion, he should be able to retain his beliefs. He should not, however, try to force them on others, especially on an unwilling audience.

The Role of the Audience. The role of the audience will vary according to the type of discussion group. The audience may consist of silent listeners and of participants who contribute either to the entire discussion or to the forum period only.

Regardless of their role in the discussion, members of the audience should have a knowledge of the subject in question. Every member of the audience should feel his share of responsibility for the success of the whole discussion. He can do this in part by according respect and consideration to those speakers with whose opinions and ideas he differs. Moreover, every member must learn to listen carefully and to note overtones in each speaker's voice. Sometimes these overtones indicate far more than the actual words spoken.

Inexperienced participants sometimes feel that there is some personal criticism of them or of their thinking if their ideas are not accepted by the group. Techniques of group discussion call for a high degree of objectivity; no one tries to hurt the feelings of a speaker. But the fact remains that not all ideas are equally good, and many will be rejected.

Each idea or opinion, however, should be considered, and, if possible, reasons should be given for its rejection. Everyone should be treated fairly and justly in order to establish a friendly rapport. There can be no question of unequal social or intellectual status if the group is to work on a co-operative basis. Unless this spirit is present, reflective group action is practically impossible.

Exercises

1. Analyze the discussion carried on in some group to which you belong. To what extent did the group as a whole conduct itself with regard to participation? To what extent did the leader qualify?

2. Assume that you are to lead the discussion in one of the following situations; outline the question for discussion: (a) a discussion meeting of some social club to which you belong; (b) a discussion meeting of some professional or business organization to which you belong; (c) a meeting of the planning committee of your club; (d) an informal evening discussion at your home.

3. Study the uses made of public discussion in your community. Write an evaluation of as many discussion groups as you can observe in a week.

4. Make an analysis of the ways in which radio and television are being used in your community to modify group thinking.

5. Study the archives of a town or village. Evaluate the place of the town meeting in the annals of the town in any five-year period.

5

Argumentation

Argumentation is the technique of establishing the logical probability of a proposition by means of evidence, reasoning, and, when necessary, refutation of reasoning used against the proposition. The speaker needs this technique in speechmaking, in discussion, and in debate.

In order to be effective in argumentation, the speaker should know the nature and kinds of evidence and how to test its validity, the types of argument and the requirements for sound inferences, the various means of refutation and the opportunities for using them advantageously. Knowledge and skill in argumentation are needed: (1) to persuade an audience to accept arguments for or against a proposition; (2) to enable the speaker to anticipate and to prevent possible attacks upon his reasoning; and (3) to refute the arguments of opponents who have already expressed their views.

EVIDENCE

The basic resource in argumentation is the body of pertinent evidence from which inferences may be drawn. Directly observed or accurately reported facts, based upon events, analyses, experiments, or other kinds of experience, provide the foundations for establishing acceptable arguments.

The Nature of Evidence. Facts must be distinguished from opinions. As soon as a speaker proceeds from what he has observed to what he thinks his observations indicate, he is making a judgment and is therefore giving an opinion. A general's official report of military positions can be accepted as *evidence of fact;* his judgments on the need for re-enforcements must be classified as *evidence of opinion.* Opinions must be scrutinized with special attention to the qualifications of the individual to make a sound and honest judgment as well as to his ability to report accurately and completely what he has seen and has heard.

CATEGORIES OF EVIDENCE. In order to present his own arguments logically, to protect his reasoning from attack, and to refute the reasoning of his opponents, the speaker should be aware of the categories of evidence and the relative merits of each. He should be able to distinguish evidence according to form, source, and degree of relevancy.

Form of Evidence. In *form,* evidence may be real, testimonial, positive, or negative. An object, such as the shattered radiator of a damaged car, is "real evidence." An account of an accident given by the driver of one of the vehicles is "testimonial evidence." The serious damage to the center of the radiator is "positive evidence" that the collision was head-on. The absence of serious injuries to the occupants of the automobiles is "negative evidence" that the speed was moderate.

Source of Evidence. According to *source,* evidence may be original or hearsay, written or unwritten, and ordinary or expert. The statement of the officer who arrived on the scene just after the accident occurred is "original evidence," whereas the impressions given by a friend of one of the drivers who talked with several witnesses of the accident is "hearsay evidence." Original evidence is primary; hearsay, secondary.

A signed report of the accident submitted to the insurance company is "written evidence"; the garage mechanic's oral explanation of the repairs needed is "unwritten evidence." A bystander's story of the collision is "ordinary evidence"; the physician's report on the physical condition of the drivers is "expert evidence."

Degree of Relevancy of Evidence. According to the *degree of relevancy,* evidence may be direct or indirect. The description of the movements of the two cars by the driver of one of the cars is "direct evidence," whereas the positions of the two cars when the police arrived is "indirect evidence." Testimony of an eyewitness is direct, but evidence requiring the drawing of an inference is indirect or circumstantial.

TYPES OF EVIDENCE. Evidence may also be classified according to types. It may consist of instances, statistics, or opinions.

Instances. Instances may be general, specific, hypothetical, or analogous. "General instances" form the basis for the assertion that our national defense has been entrusted to very competent leaders in the Army, Navy, Air Force, and Marine Corps. "Specific instances" support the declaration that Generals X, Y, and Z are providing excellent leadership for the Army. "Hypothetical instances" are suggested in the observation that if these leaders retire, equally brilliant officers can be found to take their places; enumeration of specific possibilities would strengthen the case. "Analogous instances" may be literal or figurative. When the results of a particular type of military training in other countries are used as the basis for arguing that a similar plan would produce similar results in this country, the analogous instances are literal. When the training of soldiers is compared with the training of members of a football team, the analogous instances are figurative.

Statistics. Figures and percentages may show relationships. Comparison of the census reports of 1940 and 1950 will show the increase or decrease in population of the several states. Unless exact figures are definitely needed, round numbers will best serve the speaker's purpose.

Opinions. Opinions may be personal, lay, or expert. When a general makes a criticism of the President of the United States, he is giving a "personal" opinion. When he comments on the functioning of political parties, he is stating a "lay judgment." When he discusses the strategy of warfare for a section where he has been in command, he is offering the "judgment of an expert."

The Testing of Evidence. If a speaker is to select data wisely and to refute arguments presented by opponents, he must have criteria for testing not only the evidence he finds, but also what he hears from others. Evidence may be evaluated according to its *quality, source,* and *suitability.*

TESTS OF QUALITY. Criteria for the quality of evidence are *consistency, completeness, accuracy,* and *recency.* All four tests should be applied to each item of evidence to be used.

Consistency. Evidence should be consistent with itself, with established facts, with common experience, and with human behavior. A village resident who testified that he had devoted the last Sunday in November to Christmas shopping, after having admitted complete lack of funds and credit, demonstrated all four kinds of inconsistency. He could not shop without funds or credit on a day when stores are closed.

Completeness. Evidence should be complete: it should present all necessary details including negative instances. A character witness who cites a few examples of an individual's honesty, but who suppresses the many instances of his dishonesty, creates a totally false impression, since he is giving only the facts that support his testimony.

Accuracy. Evidence must be accurate. Instances or statistics offered must be unprejudiced, representative, adequate, and verified. Unless the examples or figures are objective, typical, sufficient, and dependable, they will distort and perhaps invalidate the reasoning based upon them. Statistics on our standard of living compiled by the National Association of Manufacturers and those compiled by the American Federation of Labor should both pass these four tests of accuracy.

Recency. Evidence should be recent. Statistics and examples may become worthless if they are out-of-date. The most recent figures and instances should be used in dealing with a problem that is subject to rapid change. Facts about the aviation industry today are very different from those compiled ten, five, or even two years ago.

TESTS OF SOURCES. Since the dependability of evidence rests upon the reliability of the source, the merits of each item of evidence must be determined individually after a thorough examination of the specific conditions of its use. In general, however, real evidence is more convincing than testimonial because the human factor is subject to many influences, both physical and psychological. Positive evidence is usually more valuable than negative because it is more definite. Original evidence is clearly more dependable than hearsay; written more dependable than unwritten; and expert more dependable than ordinary; but the importance of the evidence in each case must also be taken into account. The drivers' signed reports of an accident might be less important than the garage mechanic's oral explanation of the repairs needed, because the latter might contribute more essential information. Direct evidence is usually more valuable than indirect, but indirect evidence can be very powerful if all the circumstances point to a single conclusion. The special tests of sources are acceptability, competence, and certainty.

Acceptability. To be acceptable to speakers and listeners alike, a source should be disinterested in the outcome of the argument, favorably known in the field being discussed, and in a position to know the specific facts. The conductor of the New York Philharmonic Orchestra would be a highly acceptable source on orchestral music because of his necessarily outstanding reputation, his long experience, and his intimate acquaintance with orchestral scores, but he would be unacceptable on any dispute in which his orchestra was being contrasted with another symphony orchestra.

Competence. To be considered competent, a source or authority should be thoroughly trained in his field, abreast of developments, and mature enough to have good judgment. The conductor of a leading orchestra would meet all of these requirements. When the ideal witness or authority is not available, a person of lesser acceptability and competence should not be rejected, but the usefulness of such a source will necessarily be more limited.

Certainty. The degree of certainty of the source is especially important. A primary source should be cited whenever possible, and the specific source should be fully identified and checked for qualifications with reference to the particular item of evidence being used.

The extent to which an authority has the opportunity to observe or to know the facts, the kind of records he has kept, the reliability of his memory, the state of his health, the beliefs he holds—all these and other conditions determine the degree of certainty of evidence presented. For example, evidence by a labor leader of a local union against the president of the national union would be more valuable than that by a local manufacturer, unless other circumstances offset the criticism of the belief he would be expected to hold.

TESTS OF SUITABILITY. The suitability of evidence depends upon the direct relation to the support of the argument and to the needs of the listeners. Data may be complete, accurate, and recent, but if it is irrelevant or "over the heads" of the audience, it has little value. Instances and examples not quite to the point, or statistics so complicated that the listeners cannot follow or interpret them, will not serve the speaker's purpose because the audience must be able to perceive their applicability.

The Presentation of Evidence. The better the evidence, the better presentation it deserves. The speaker's language should interpret the evidence clearly and fairly with enough concrete and specific details to leave no doubt in the listeners' minds about the significance of the data. Charts and other visual aids, when possible, will help the audience to understand the full meaning of statistical evidence and will make the material more interesting.

Although evidence is always more persuasive if it is cited from more than one source, a speaker should never exaggerate by saying "authorities agree," when he means "three out of seven authorities agree." Keeping within the bounds of strict accuracy in reporting evidence and even seeming to be overcautious in presenting his facts will enhance the speaker's credibility. If his veracity is questioned, even on a small point, he will probably lose much of the ground he has gained, or expects to gain, with the rest of his evidence.

ANALYSIS OF THE PROBLEM

Before proceeding to reason from the available evidence, the speaker should check the clarity of his proposition and the terms associated with it. He should enumerate all of the main contentions *for* and *against* the proposition in order to determine the major issues. He should be able to present the major reasoning against his proposition as fully as he can present the main arguments for it.

The Proposition. The proposition should be worded so that it offers a single idea in simple, direct, unequivocal language. It should be an affirmative, unprejudiced assertion. Examples of acceptable statements for argumentation are: "The electoral college should be replaced with direct election of the president by a plurality of the votes cast," and "The United States should assist in the economic development of backward countries."

Terminology. All terms used in an argument should be fully, clearly, and precisely defined. Confusion about the meanings of words almost certainly leads to fallacies in reasoning by both speaker and listeners. Technical terms, though clear to the speaker because of his specialized knowledge, may be very troublesome to listeners unfamiliar with the special area concerned. Words like "sovereignty" and "federalism" in an argument about world government need exact definitions.

Main Contentions. After the speaker has exactly phrased his proposition and clearly defined his terms, he must set forth the main contentions that support the affirmative side of the proposition in opposition to those that support the negative side. He must make certain that he lists the major supporting ideas for both sides if he is to determine accurately all of the main issues.

The Issues. By contrasting these main contentions for and against the proposition, the speaker can determine the points at which clashes of opinion occur. The issues will then be those questions to which the two sides answer "Yes" and "No" respectively.

When speakers maintain various points of view, as, for example, in a group discussion, several sets of issues appear. If the proposition is "A plan of compulsory health insurance should be adopted in the United States," and five participants in a discussion offer five different plans of compulsory health insurance, a separate set of issues will be developed with reference to each plan. An issue common to all the plans might be, "Will the proposed plan eliminate inadequacies in the existing system of private medicine?"

TYPES OF ARGUMENT

After the speaker has obtained sufficient appropriate evidence to support his reasoning, and after he has determined the issues he must meet, he should then construct his arguments. Four major types of arguments are available: deduction (including *enthymematic reasoning* or *reasoning from sign*) and three types of induction: *causal relationship, example* or *generalization,* and *analogy.*

Deduction proceeds from general assumption to specific conclusion. Causal relationship proceeds from effect to cause, from cause to effect, or from effect to effect. Generalization proceeds from specific instances to general conclusion. Analogy proceeds from known resemblances to probable resemblance.

Deductive Argument. The speaker uses deductive reasoning when he proceeds from a general assertion to a specific conclusion. The general assertion must be acceptable to the audience if he is to gain approval for the specific conclusion. If it is not acceptable, the speaker must go back one or more steps in his reasoning until he does find a point at which he can begin a chain of deductions from a general assertion acceptable to the listeners.

If the assertion, "Eighteen-year-olds are mature enough to understand the issues in a political campaign," is not acceptable, the speaker may be able to start with "High-school students study current political problems." To be accurate the word "most" would have to be used in each case. The inference then is that most eighteen-year-olds would have had high-school training on political problems. They would constitute a specific group of those who have had such training.

THE CATEGORICAL SYLLOGISM. A deductive argument can be fully and logically expressed in the form of a syllogism, consisting of a *major premise*, a *minor premise*, and a *conclusion*. The major premise sets forth the general observation; the minor premise states the particular instance of the general principle; and the conclusion draws the inference from the two premises.

Syllogistic reasoning may be illustrated by this inference:

> All American citizens are in need of information about the activities of our government. (*major premise*)
> You are an American citizen. (*minor premise*)
> Therefore you are in need of information about the activities of our government. (*conclusion*)

A syllogism uses three and only three *terms*. The *major term*, "in need of information about the activities of our government," appears in the major premise and in the conclusion. The *minor term*, "you," is found in the minor premise and in the conclusion, while the *middle term*, "American citizens," is used in the major and minor premises. Each term must have the same meaning each time it appears in order to make a valid inference possible.

In at least one premise, the middle term must include *all* members of the class or group described. "American citizens" is so used in the major premise. A term may include all members of the class in the conclusion only if it has done so in the premise in which it appears. In the above example, the term, "in need of information about the activities of our government," in both the major premise and the conclusion, refers to *some* people, not to all people. Thus, "all people are in need of information about the activities of our government" could not be equivalent to "all American citizens." The latter is a part of the larger group.

If one premise is specific or particular, the conclusion must be also: *you* in both the minor premise and the conclusion is specific since it refers to the individual. If one premise contains a negative statement, a conclusion cannot be drawn, and, of course, the conclusion is valid only if both premises are valid.

The syllogism so far discussed is the *categorical* type. It presents a definite assertion in the major premise.

THE HYPOTHETICAL SYLLOGISM. When a speaker wishes to present the dependence of a desirable result upon a specific condition that must be fulfilled, the *hypothetical* syllogism meets his need in concise form. In this type of deduction, the major premise consists of a conditional clause called the *antecedent,* and a main clause called the *consequent.*

> If the nations are to form a stable world government (*antecedent*), they must sacrifice some of their sovereignty. (*consequent*)
> The nations will not sacrifice some of their sovereignty.
> Therefore they will not form a stable world government.

To be valid, the *minor premise must affirm the antecedent or deny the consequent.* If the minor premise denies the consequent, as it does in the above example, then the conclusion must deny the antecedent. If the minor premise affirms the antecedent, the conclusion must affirm the consequent. To say that the nations will form a stable world government but will not sacrifice any of their sovereignty would be a false inference because the minor premise would affirm the antecedent and the conclusion would deny the consequent.

THE DISJUNCTIVE SYLLOGISM. When the audience must choose one of a series of alternatives, the *disjunctive* syllogism provides the direct pattern of argument. In the disjunctive syllogism, the major premise offers two or more alternatives. The minor premise must accept one alternative or reject the others. If the minor premise accepts one alternative, the conclusion must reject the others and vice versa.

> American colleges and universities are static, declining, or expanding. (*major premise,* three alternatives)
> They are neither static nor declining. (*minor premise,* rejection of two alternatives)
> Therefore they are expanding. (*conclusion,* acceptance of remaining alternative)

The alternative possibilities offered in the major premise must be all-inclusive, and all of the possibilities offered in the major premise must be mutually exclusive.

THE CONJUNCTIVE SYLLOGISM. The disjunctive syllogism says in effect that *A is either b or c.* The complementary *conjunctive* syllogism states that *A cannot be both b and c.*

> You cannot be both married and single. (*major premise*)
> You are married. (*minor premise*)
> Therefore you are not single. (*conclusion*)

In the conjunctive syllogism, the minor premise must affirm one member of the conjunction. Moreover, the two members of the major premise must be explicitly contradictory.

THE DILEMMA. The *dilemma* refers to a situation in which only two solutions are available but neither is desirable; it is most useful in attacking an existing practice or plan. It consists of a major premise composed of two hypothetical propositions, a minor premise composed of two disjunctive propositions, and a conclusion showing two undesirable results. In arguing for the segregation of students with good grades, the speaker may contend that:

> If a teacher plans his class hours for the upper half of his class, the lower half is bewildered; and if he plans his class hours for the lower half of his class, the upper half is bored. (*major premise*)
> Either he plans for the upper half or for the lower half of his class. (*minor premise*)
> Therefore either one half of the class is bewildered or the other half of the class is bored. (*conclusion*)

To attack the dilemma, an opponent may offer other possibilities. In the foregoing illustration, he may demonstrate that some class activities may be adapted to each half of the class so that both parts will be interested. He may show that one of the alternatives will not necessarily produce the alleged consequence (for instance, he may demonstrate that adapting class activities to the lower half would not bore the upper half if the teacher used the kind of illustrative material that would hold the interest of everyone). He may also construct another dilemma, thereby reaching a conclusion directly opposite to the one in the dilemma that he is attacking.

THE ENTHYMEME OR "ARGUMENT FROM SIGN." The *enthymeme*, the traditional form of reasoning in public address, is based upon probable premises and leads to probable conclusions. The enthymeme is parallel with the logical syllogism in its method of reasoning, but it rarely sets forth both premises and conclusion. For example, the enthymeme, *Our instructor has examination booklets under his arm; therefore he will give our class a test*, might have been formally stated:

All instructors with examination booklets under their arms give their class a test. (*major premise*)
Our instructor has examination booklets under his arm. (*minor premise*)
Therefore he will give our class a test. (*conclusion*)

Arguments from sign proceed from the assumption that two or more variables are so related that the presence or absence of one indicates the presence or absence of the other. An instructor with examination booklets under his arm may be regarded as a sign that his class will take an examination. Four tests may be applied to the argument from sign: (1) Is the relationship accidental? (2) Is the relationship reciprocal? (3) Is the relationship dependent upon special circumstances? (4) Is the inference from one sign re-enforced by other signs?

The instructor might be carrying examination booklets to give to a colleague, while he himself might be giving an examination without using booklets; hence, giving an examination would not be dependent upon the instructor's having booklets. If he were carrying booklets during a vacation period, persons familiar with campus life would not interpret his action as the sign that he was about to give an examination. If, in addition to the examination booklets, he were carrying mimeographed question papers, and if, upon his arrival in the classroom, he asked his students to take alternate seats, then inferences from these two signs would re-enforce the inference drawn from the first sign.

Inductive Argument. The speaker uses inductive reasoning when he proceeds from specific evidence to a general conclusion. The major types of inductive reasoning are: (1) *argument from cause*, (2) *argument from example*, and (3) *argument from analogy*.

ARGUMENT FROM CAUSE. *Causal arguments* seek to set forth the reason why propositions are true; they answer the question

"Why?" Four tests may be applied to causal arguments: (1) Are all of the links evident in the chain of reasoning from cause to effect? (2) Is the inference free from interference of other causes? (3) Is the cause sufficient to produce the effect? (4) Does the cause produce only the indicated effect?

In the causal argument, "Students are failing in their history course because they are not giving enough time to the assigned readings," it may be said that there is an intervening link: inability to answer the instructor's questions. Other causes may be ill-health, too many other subjects, too much time devoted to outside interests. The failure could also be in part the result of inadequate background, inattention to the lectures and discussions in class, or inefficient habits of study. Other effects produced by the same cause, i.e., not giving enough time to assigned readings, could be confusion about the interpretation of events, and imagined inconsistencies observed in the readings completed.

ARGUMENT FROM EXAMPLE. *Argument by example or generalization* is the drawing of a conclusion from one or more instances. Four tests may be applied to argument by example: (1) Have fair instances or samples been used? (2) Do these examples represent a large enough part of the group to permit an inference involving the whole category? (3) Do the examples offered show the relationship being generalized? (4) Have negative instances been considered?

If, from the examples of four varsity debaters who are the highest-ranking students in their economics class, we conclude that debaters are the highest-ranking students in the college, our argument is open to criticism. Someone might point out that the four students are not typical of varsity debaters as a group. Someone else might note that the four debaters and the economics class do not constitute a fair "sampling," that is, they do not represent a sufficient number of students to permit a generalization about the *whole* student body. Another critic might comment that the four debaters are all majoring in economics and therefore do not show the relationship between training in debate and success in college studies. Someone else might observe that the negative instances of two debaters who are not high-ranking students were not considered.

ARGUMENT FROM ANALOGY. In *argument from analogy*, the resemblance between two instances or classes of instances in a certain number of respects leads to the inference that the resemblance applies to some other respect known to be pertinent to one instance but not known to be pertinent to the other. Three tests should be used: (1) Are the compared instances alike in all essential respects? (2) Are differences in the compared instances adequately explained? (3) Does the reasoning become stronger with an increase in the number of comparisons?

Let us say that two groups of college students are compared to determine their aptitudes for the curriculum they are pursuing. One group has successfully completed a year of work; the other is just beginning. Both groups are found to be similar in economic and social background, in high-school preparation, and in scholastic averages. The group that has completed a year of work has done well in the curriculum; by analogy the inference is drawn that the new group will do well. If the two groups compared are found to differ in any essential respect, for example, in having the opportunity to use a similar amount of time to study, then the analogy is invalid. If an apparently important difference between the two groups is shown to be unimportant—if, for example, an apparent difference in programs is shown to be negligible—the analogy will still have high probability. If the results of other comparisons strengthen the analogy—for example, similarity in age, in study habits, and in outside interests—then the degree of probability will be increased.

TECHNIQUES OF REFUTATION

Not only must the speaker construct sound arguments to support his own position, but he must also be able to expose the weaknesses, inconsistencies, inadequacies, false inferences, and irrelevant arguments presented in opposition. A complete understanding of the subject, a thorough knowledge of evidence and the types of argument, the ability to analyze and to evaluate, and a good command of the grammar and the structure of the English language are essential for effective refutation.

The speaker must determine how much of his time to devote to refutation and at which points to use it. Frequently it is necessary for a speaker to sacrifice some of his less important arguments in order to make an adequate counterattack. If an audience has been influenced to a great extent by an opponent, the speaker may need to begin with a strong refutation. In some instances he may be able to weave his refutation in with his constructive arguments.

To try to list all the common errors in thinking and in expression would be a tremendous undertaking. The speaker, however, must familiarize himself with the major types of errors so that he may be alert in detecting them both in his own reasoning and in that of others.

Attacking the Definitions. A fundamental requirement for straight thinking on any problem is clear, accurate, and adequate definitions. Just as the speaker should check his own definitions, so, too, should he demand specific definitions of others. Pointing out inaccurate, confused, or inadequate definitions constitutes a strong attack on an opponent's reasoning.

Attacking the Wording. Language difficulties are a major source of confusion. The substitution of the abstract for the concrete, of the general for the specific, and of the vague for the exact word, the lack of parallelism and subordination, and looseness in structure and syntax frequently result in a hopeless entanglement of ideas. To show an opponent's misuse of language is to undermine his inference and, more important, the reliance of his audience upon his trustworthiness.

Attacking the Analysis. Distorted analysis, especially through omission of important negative arguments, maximizing favorable aspects of the case, minimizing unfavorable aspects, and raising false issues, will make a sweeping attack necessary. A re-examination and re-evaluation of the issues will show the failure of the opponent to make an accurate, complete, and fair analysis.

Attacking the Use of Evidence. Careless or inadequate use or intentional misuse of evidence cause many of the mistakes in reasoning. Support for an argument must include accurate and consistent facts clearly stated, in sufficient numbers, and from established sources. Refutation should point out all these shortcomings in simple, direct, and factual development. The speaker may attack the quality, sources, and suitability of his opponent's evidence.

Attacking the Reasoning. Failure to comply with the laws of reasoning makes refutation easy. False assumptions, such as that an assertion which is true of the whole is necessarily true of each part, that because one occurrence succeeds another in time, the first is the cause of the second, or that because an authority is competent in one field, he is competent in another, clearly invalidate arguments. False inferences, such as drawing an affirmative conclusion from negative premises, generalizations from insufficient and unrepresentative instances, or analogies based on inadequate resemblances, can lead only to wrong or inadequately substantiated conclusions. Fallacies of deduction and induction in the opponent's reasoning should be systematically exposed. Reducing the opponent's reasoning to an absurdity (*reductio ad absurdum*) by carrying it to a ridiculous conclusion is one strong method of attack.

Attacking the Appeal to Emotion. Ignoring the proposition by using irrelevant arguments and appeals will not fool the discriminating listeners but may win the less discerning members of an audience. Appeals to such emotions as fear and pride and to such interests as health and wealth are justifiable only when they re-enforce the logical reasoning supported by evidence, and therefore can be readily attacked when they bear no relation to the reasoning. Language that is prejudiced or emotional may be completely misleading. (See Chapter 2.) "Name calling," ridicule and denunciation, and identification of one's opponent with unpopular causes may be answered in kind, but they can be more effectively refuted with strong arguments based upon undisputed facts.

Exercises

1. Distinguish between deductive and inductive reasoning. Give examples.

2. Read Edmund Burke's *Speech on Conciliation*. (a) Are there appeals to the emotions of his listeners? (b) List two examples of deductive and inductive reasoning. (c) Analyze the refutation. Give examples of the techniques he uses.

3. Analyze an argumentative speech as it appears in your local newspaper. (a) List and explain any fallacies in the reasoning. (b) List the possible sources the speaker used for his evidence. (c) Classify the evidence according to form and type.

4. Prepare an outline for an argumentative speech. What are the issues? Enumerate your sources of evidence, the possible arguments of your opponents, and your steps in refutation.

5. What is a syllogism? Prepare in syllogistic form the arguments you used in Question 4.

6

Debate

After the members of a group have used discussion in reaching the best available solution to a problem, they use the principles of debate to influence others outside the group to adopt the proposal selected. Neither technique can be substituted for the other. *Discussion* is illustrated in the deliberations of a committee assigned the task of recommending a policy for an entire group or parent organization. *Debate* is illustrated in the *pro* and *con* speeches in the larger organization before voting on the adoption of the proposed policy.

THE USES OF DEBATE

Wherever and whenever a proposal is offered and opposition to the proposal is presented, a debate is in progress. In our democratic society debate plays an important part in legislation, in politics, in business, in law, and in education.

Legislation. When a bill or statute is introduced in a legislative body, the proponent speaks in favor of the measure, and opponents speak against it. Amendments may be introduced, and debate on the desirability of the amendments will precede action upon them. If amendments are adopted, then the bill as amended becomes the proposition for debate.

If the debate on both sides brings out a full analysis of the merits and shortcomings of the bill, the legislators ought to be prepared to vote on it with a good understanding of its advantages and disadvantages to the interests they serve. Although party or group loyalty may determine many votes, nevertheless advocates and opponents of the bill argue for their cause in the hope that there are undecided members who are willing to evaluate the proposal on its merits and whose votes would carry the decision.

Politics. During political campaigns, joint debates enable voters to hear opposing candidates from the same rostrum defend and attack party platforms and past records in office. The Lincoln-Douglas joint debates in the senatorial campaign of 1858 in Illinois are probably the best-known examples.

Business. Boards of directors and executive committees use debate as well as discussion in reaching decisions on policies. After they have discussed and rejected all possible solutions but the one favored by the majority, a debate may ensue between the majority and the minority whether the adoption of this solution is better than no action at all.

Law. In courts of law a man's life frequently depends upon the debate before a jury by the prosecution and the defense. Property rights, civil rights, claims for damages, and many other problems of citizens and noncitizens require adjudication. Lawyers for the plaintiff and for the defense present the issues, the evidence, and the reasoning in legal debates.

Education. On some college and university campuses, debate has become an important means of acquainting the community with the issues on leading public questions. Such debate is especially useful when it is followed by analytical comment by a panel of three or four experts and an open forum for questions.

TYPES OF DEBATING

Several classifications of debate according to form, purpose, and method may be made, as, for example, the following classification into three types or categories: (1) assembly or parliamentary debating, (2) cross-examination debating, and (3) formal, conventional, or educational debating. All three types are used in schools and colleges, but parliamentary debating is characteristic of legislative bodies; cross-examination is a technique developed in the law courts; and formal debating is based on the conventions of the joint political debate.

Assembly Debating. The purpose of assembly debating is to gain support for a specific measure, and all members who wish to express their views speak for or against the proposal from the floor of the assembly. Time limits on individual speeches or on the length of the debate may be set by parliamentary action of the assembly. Student assemblies of representatives of schools or colleges extend over two or three days and debate a limited number of previously chosen public questions. Committee sessions for hearing testimony of experts and for discussing various solutions to problems precede the introduction of the committee-drafted bills on the floor of the assembly.

Cross-Examination Debating. The purpose of cross-examination debating is to ask a series of skillfully related questions that will induce the individuals questioned to support the position the questioner hopes to establish. In law courts attorneys cross-examine witnesses; in intercollegiate debates speakers cross-examine each other. On the debate platform one speaker on each side gives a constructive case; the negative cross-examines the affirmative; the affirmative cross-examines the negative. Then one speaker on each side summarizes the whole case as established by the constructive speech and the answers to questions, and offers rebuttal to the position taken by the other side.

Questions must be concisely worded, and answers must be brief, preferably "Yes" or "No." Time limits for each speaker are previously agreed upon, ranging usually from eight to fifteen minutes per speaker. The number of speakers on each side may range from one to three, depending upon how many of the three functions—constructive argument, questioning, and summary and rebuttal—one speaker fulfills.

Formal Debating. The purpose of formal debating is to provide an opportunity for two teams of speakers to present to an audience the arguments for and against a proposition. Each side is allotted an equal amount of time for the constructive and the rebuttal speeches.

If there are two speakers on each team, usually the first affirmative speaker will give the background of the debate, including the origin and history of the question, the immediate cause of the discussion, definitions and explanations, and any limitations upon the scope of the question which will affect the issues to be debated. The first negative speaker may reinterpret the background if he thinks it incomplete or biased. The first speaker on each side may also outline for the audience the case for his side and present the arguments for the first contention. The second speaker on each side will offer the arguments for the remaining contentions, will use refutation as necessary, and will summarize the case.

The first rebuttal speech is given by the first negative speaker; the second rebuttal speech is given by the second affirmative speaker. Rebuttal is concluded by the second negative and first affirmative speakers. Frequently, ten minutes are assigned to each constructive speech and five minutes to each rebuttal. No new constructive argument is permitted in a rebuttal speech. If the negative offers an alternative plan in addition to their arguments against the plan proposed by the affirmative, the burden of proof, which rests on the affirmative at the outset, will shift to the negative. Each side then has the responsibility of persuading the audience that its plan is the more desirable.

REQUIREMENTS FOR WORDING THE PROPOSITION

The proposition determines the scope and the limits of a debate. Depending upon the type of debate it is to serve, a proposition may be a motion, a resolution, or a bill calling for action by a parliamentary assembly; a statement of affirmative position on a controversial issue for cross-examination debating; or a declaration of opinion on fact, value, or policy for formal debating. For intercollegiate debating, the best propositions are usually those concerned with public policies of current interest. A persistent proposition for intercollegiate debate on public policy is the following:

Resolved: That a year of military training should be required before the age of twenty-one of every male citizen fit for military service.

For any type of debate the proposition should be a simple, clear, and concise affirmation stating a single, specific proposal without bias and with the burden of proof on the affirmative. The speaker should check his proposition to be certain that it meets these requirements.

Simplicity. Complex propositions make analysis difficult. The simpler the statement the more useful the debate is likely to be. "Citizens should be required to vote" is more likely to produce an informative debate than "Unless special circumstances keep them from the polls, citizens should be required to vote." In the latter proposition too much attention will be focused upon the problem of "special circumstances."

Clarity. Vague statements offering various interpretations result in confused debating. "Voting should be considered a privilege as well as a duty" does not indicate any clear policy for definite action.

Conciseness. The fewest possible words should be used. Wordiness results in a cumbersome proposition and leads to misunderstanding. "All loyal American citizens should be permitted to exercise the exceptionally fine privilege the Constitution gives them, that of voting" may be reduced to "All loyal American citizens should be permitted to vote regularly."

Affirmative Wording. A negative proposition may seem to reverse the affirmative and negative positions. "Eighteen-year-olds should not be denied the vote" should be restated "Eighteen-year-olds should be permitted to vote."

Declarative Statement. An assertion is preferable to a question. A question is generally used for discussion because the purpose is inquiry: "How can more citizens be induced to vote?" A statement is needed for debate because the purpose is advocacy: "Citizens should be required to vote."

Unity. A single idea is enough for one debate. For example, the proposition, "The Legislature should make voting compulsory and should make registration permanent," contains two different debate subjects: compulsory voting and permanent registration.

Specific Proposal. General propositions result in diffused, unsatisfactory debates. "The American people should be made to realize the importance of going to the polls" can be made more specific by saying: "Every state should appropriate funds to inform American citizens about the reasons for voting."

Freedom from Bias. Prejudiced language introduces unjustified assumptions into the proposition. "Only intelligent native-born Americans should be allowed to vote" reveals a prejudiced attitude that must be excluded for a fair-minded debate. "Voters should be required to pass a literacy test" keeps the debate on an impartial basis.

Burden of Proof on the Affirmative. The proposition should be so worded that the affirmative will advocate a change. "Citizens should have the right to refrain from voting" forces the negative to advocate a new policy.

THE ISSUES

In order to discover the issues for a debate, the speaker should consider why the proposition is a matter for debate at this time, how the problem arose in the first place, and what has been its history and development. He must also define fully and accurately all terms in the proposition with reference to the immediate debate. He must decide what should be admitted, waived, or excluded as irrelevant.

The speaker should list in one column all major contentions that support the affirmative and in another column all major contentions that support the negative. Out of these contrasting contentions should arise questions to which the affirmative will answer "Yes" and the negative "No." These major questions will constitute the basic issues in the debate and will in turn lead to subordinate issues. Whenever the negative agrees with the affirmative on the answer to one of these basic questions, the question ceases to be an issue in the debate.

To propositions of policy, three stock issues are usually applicable: (1) Is a change needed? (2) Does the proposal offer the best possible change? (3) Does the proposal create evils greater than the anticipated benefits? If the negative agrees with the affirmative that a change is needed, then only the second and third questions are pertinent issues. The negative now becomes responsible for introducing an alternative remedy and showing its superiority over the affirmative remedy. Issues two and three apply to both proposed remedies.

PREPARATION OF A BRIEF

A brief records in sentence form the speaker's complete analysis of the proposition for debate with all supporting material for both the affirmative and the negative. It enables the speaker to test the thoroughness of his preparation, the soundness of his reasoning, and the adequacy of his evidence. If the brief is as searching as it should be, the speaker should have before him every aspect of the problem in exact relation to every other aspect of the problem. From it he should be able to derive constructive speeches and rebuttals as needed.

Each speaker should prepare his own affirmative and negative brief in order to know thoroughly the whole case for both sides. Members of a debating team may prepare their brief on a co-operative basis.

Form and Development. Throughout all parts of the brief the use of symbols is consistent, the order being: Roman numerals, capital letters, Arabic numerals, small letters. For the next steps the symbols are used in the same order in parentheses. Each symbol should be followed by one assertion setting forth only one idea.

In the introduction the relationship proceeds in steps from general to specific; in the body the relationship proceeds in steps from generalizations to reasons to evidence. All statements with the same order of symbols should be co-ordinate. In order to make the appearance of the brief neat and clear, all second and third lines of a statement should be indented evenly in block form, and all symbols of the same kind should be arranged exactly under one another. (See sample brief, page 76.)

Parts of a Brief. Development of the brief is systematic throughout. Its three parts are the introduction, the body, and the conclusion.

THE INTRODUCTION. Following the statement of the proposition in full, the introduction sets forth in complete sentence form the analysis of the proposition: (1) the immediate causes for the discussion, (2) the origin and history of the question, (3) definitions of terms, (4) irrelevant matter, (5) admitted matter, (6) waived matter, (7) major contentions of affirmative and of negative, (8) main issues, and (9) partition of the arguments of affirmative and of negative. Issues are presented as questions, but all other sentences are stated as assertions. (See sample brief.)

THE BODY. The body of the brief records the arguments and supporting evidence of the affirmative and the negative. The main arguments are the affirmative and negative answers to the issues. The affirmative section is set forth in full, followed by the negative section.

To test the relationship between each argument and its proof immediately below, the word *because* may be inserted after every statement in the body until the last statement in each argument is reached. In other words, each supporting statement will answer the question "Why?" with reference to the statement it supports. Since it is impossible to divide an argument without having at least two supporting ideas, there will be two or more supporting statements under every major statement until specific evidence is reached. Occasionally there will be only a single item of evidence available; this item is then incorporated as part of the statement it supports. If items of evidence have references to their sources, the brief has greater usefulness to the debater.

THE CONCLUSION. The conclusion of the brief recapitulates in sequence the main arguments in the form of "*since* clauses" followed by the proposition introduced by *therefore* as the main clause. The affirmative section and the negative section will each have its own conclusion, opposite in effect. (See sample brief.)

PREPARATION OF THE DEBATE SPEECHES

Debaters must prepare two different kinds of speeches: the constructive speech and the rebuttal speech. Both should be adjustable to the development of the debate and to the needs of the audience, but the rebuttal speech has to be more flexible.

The Constructive Speech. Each debate speaker must plan a constructive speech derived from the arguments and evidence in his brief and adapted both to the needs of his listeners and to the probable arguments of his opponents. When a team of two or more speakers share an affirmative or a negative case, they must first reach close agreement on the line of development and the division of arguments.

Speeches must be left flexible for the introduction of refutation when necessary and for continuous adjustment to the arguments advanced by the opposition. Since time for debate speeches is limited, the problems of selection and proportion in developing the case are major considerations. Thoughtful analysis of all elements in the situation should guide each speaker in determining the arguments to use, the ones to stress, the evidence that will be most persuasive, the general or special interests and beliefs of the listeners which can be utilized, and the order of ideas that will make the strongest appeal.

In language as well as in content, the debate speaker should consider the requirements of his listeners. Restatement and summary are especially important to keep the audience reminded of the progress of the argument. Common words should replace unfamiliar terms. Striking illustrations derived from the evidence relieve the strain of listening to elaborate reasoning. Even figurative analogies are useful in holding attention to an argument and in clarifying the thought, if they keep the thinking directed toward the proof of the proposition.

In order to meet all requirements for the preparation of his speech, the debate speaker should study both the argumentative and the persuasive problems. He will find all the essentials of thorough speech preparation indispensable in proving his case, in meeting the opposition, and in holding and persuading his audience. (See Chapters 3 and 5.)

The Rebuttal Speech. In rebuttal no new constructive arguments are permissible, but additional evidence to strengthen those already presented may be introduced in recapitulating the case. The rebuttal speaker should analyze his opponents' case, should refute the major arguments as effectively as possible, and should point out any weaknesses, inconsistencies, or shortcomings in the opponents' position. He should not make the mistake of trying to deal with every statement he would like to refute and of becoming bogged down with details.

No rebuttal is complete that fails to show the strength of the case as a whole. The speaker must conclude by refocusing the attention of the audience upon the major issues in the debate and by showing specifically how his proof answers those issues more satisfactorily than does the case of the opposition.

ATTITUDES AND TECHNIQUES IN DEBATING

Inexperienced debaters frequently antagonize their listeners by being contentious, belligerent, and positive. A debater can be modest, gracious, and friendly without losing force in his arguments. He should avoid overstating his case and using all-inclusive words and expressions that his evidence does not justify. Such expressions as "everybody knows," "it is generally accepted," and "beyond a shadow of a doubt" have no place in the closely reasoned arguments that debaters should use. Since they are dealing with probability and not certainty, they must make sure that they assume nothing the audience is not willing to accept and that they support all assertions with evidence.

Debaters should not allow themselves to be angered by sarcasm or insinuations of their opponents. Sharp thrusts of wit and humor are in order, but attacks upon the personalities of opponents are never justified. A devastating attack on the reasoning and evidence is the best answer to any imprudent remarks of opponents. A quiet, relaxed attitude with courtesy toward opponents and audience will make the best impression.

A debater may refer to a member of the opposite team as "My Opponent, the First Speaker," or as "The Gentleman of the Opposition," and to the audience as "Ladies and Gentlemen." Less formal address is in order when circumstances warrant it, but courtesy and consideration for others should never be sacrificed for informality. In any event the speaker must remember that his first requirement is direct, persuasive communication with his audience.

THE DECISION

In a legislative body the decision on a debate is the vote on the motion, resolution, or bill. In a political debate the decision is the election or defeat of the candidate. In a courtroom the decision is the verdict of the judge or jury. In business the decision is the retention or change of a policy.

In educational debates, however, decisions are of various types. In fact, some debates are conducted without an official decision.

Types of Decisions in Intercollegiate Debate. Decisions in intercollegiate debates may be made by a vote of the audience, of a committee of judges, or of a single judge who may also offer a critique.

Decision by the Audience. When a vote is cast by the listeners, they may be asked to express their opinions either on the proposition itself after considering the arguments on both sides, or on the merits of the debating, or on both. In order to find out how much the debaters have influenced the thinking of the listeners, a shift-of-opinion ballot may be used. On a ballot which provides spaces to indicate degrees of change of opinion either way, each listener is asked to record his opinion before and after the debate.

Decision by Judges. Since the listeners are not supposed to be experts on the techniques of debating, a decision on the merits of debating is better left to a judge or to a committee of judges who are expert on debate theory and practice. They may or may not confer in reaching a decision.

DECISION BY CRITIQUE. In recent times frequent use has been made of a critic judge. An expert on argumentation and debating is invited to give a decision on the debate and a critique on the work of the debaters. He analyzes in some detail how well each team has developed and presented its case and how effective each has been in rebuttal. He may also comment on various aspects of preparation and delivery.

Debates without Official Decision. Many colleges prefer debating without decision because they wish to focus attention upon informing the audience. If the formal debate is followed by a panel discussion with questions, the audience can learn a great deal more about the debate topic, and the debaters can learn a great deal more about the problems of adaptation to an audience than if the formal debate alone is held. The discussion will show the degree to which the debaters have persuaded their listeners, and the questions will reveal points that were not made clear and the arguments that were inadequately supported.

Importance of the Decision. Standards and practices of debating may be influenced by the effects decisions can have on the debaters. Unfair decisions by judges unfamiliar with debating techniques may easily discourage students who are trying to become intelligent speakers on public questions and who want to learn the ethical and professional standards for what is right and wrong in debating. Those responsible for arranging debates should choose competent and unbiased judges so that the decision will be fair and will further the objectives of a debate program. A variety of experience in having their abilities evaluated is probably desirable for most debaters. Overemphasis on decisions, however, will distort the debate program and make it a game.

THE DEBATE TOURNAMENT

As a means of giving debaters not only a great deal of practice on a single debate proposition but also an opportunity to try out their arguments on several different opposing teams, the debate tournament has some educational value. As a single exercise in a debate program it has merit, but as the only goal of a debate season it stresses the wrong objectives. The danger is that the participants will consider winning decisions the main criterion of success. Usually there is no audience, or a very small one, with the result that the speakers give their full attention to dealing with their opponents.

Procedure in Tournament Debating. The usual procedure for a tournament is that one of the competing colleges invites several institutions to send an affirmative and a negative debate team on an announced proposition to its campus. Pairings work out best if the number of colleges is a multiple of four. If there are sixteen colleges participating, each with an affirmative and a negative team, there will be sixteen debates in the first round. Each debate is usually decided by a single judge, either with or without a critique. The winners go on to the second round, and the process continues until the winning team is selected. Sometimes the eliminated teams are also paired a number of times, in order that all teams have as much practice as possible. When eliminated, speakers should join the audience for the remaining debates.

Problems in Tournament Debating. The chief problem is to find enough competent judges to give decisions and critiques that will be respected. Another problem is the endurance of all concerned when the arrangements call for continuous debating for several hours at a stretch. If the participants regard the procedure as a useful exercise and do not take the decisions too seriously, they may gain a great deal of valuable experience. On the other hand, if debaters think that tournament debating is the ultimate goal of their speaking careers as undergraduates, then the debate program should be re-examined and re-evaluated with that goal in mind.

STANDARDS IN DEBATE

If debate is to serve its true purpose, it must be advocacy at its best. All speakers should have a complete knowledge of the subject, competence in analysis, an understanding of the principles of argumentation, an appreciation of the validity of evidence, an ability to detect fallacies in reasoning, skill in refutation, judgment in persuasion, and directness, fluency, and force in delivery.

SAMPLE BRIEF [1]

Resolved, That New York State should adopt the American Bar Association Plan for modification of the divorce laws.

Introduction

I. Immediate Cause for Discussion
   A. In 1953 for the first time both the Senate and the Assembly of New York State considered a bill to establish a commission to examine the state's divorce and family relationship laws.
   B. The New York State law on divorce is the strictest of any in the United States.
   C. Changes in the attitude toward divorce have focused attention on reasons for modification of existing legislation.
   D. What New York State does influences the policies of other states.

II. Origin and History of the Question
   A. Divorces were easy to obtain in ancient Greece and Rome.
   B. Primitive peoples permit a husband to divorce his wife in certain circumstances.
   C. Practically all countries allow divorces.
   D. The Roman Catholic Church sanctions nullification but not divorce.
   E. Grounds for divorce vary widely in the states of this country.
   F. More divorces are granted in western states where the required residence is short and where grounds for divorce are more liberal and numerous than in the Atlantic seaboard states including New York.
   G. The American Bar Association urges adoption of a uniform divorce law throughout the forty-eight states.

III. Definition of Terms
   A. "Divorce" means the legal dissolution of a valid marriage, usually granted only for causes arising after marriage.
   B. "Nullification" means the invalidation of a marriage for causes arising prior to marriage.

IV. Irrelevant Matter
   A. The doubling since 1915 of the percentage of divorces in the United States with relation to the population has no immediate bearing on the need for a change in the law.
   B. The decrease in divorces in the United States since 1946 also has no special significance in considering this problem.

V. Admitted Matter

---

[1] This brief is the revision and expansion of a brief on a similar proposition prepared by Miss Janice Roth while a senior in Queens College.

    A. Divorce laws should continue to be the province of the states.

    B. The divorce laws in some states make divorce too easy to obtain.

VI. Waived Matter

    A. The interpretation of religious beliefs on divorce will be waived.

    B. The citation of precedents from foreign countries for legislation on divorce will be waived.

VII. Major Contentions

    A. Of the Affirmative

       1. The present divorce law in New York State is unsatisfactory.

       2. The plan of the American Bar Association would eliminate the evils of the present law.

    B. Of the Negative

       1. The present divorce law in New York State is satisfactory.

       2. The plan of the American Bar Association is undesirable.

VIII. Main Issues

    A. Are there faults in the present divorce law of New York State?

    B. Would the plan of the American Bar Association be more desirable than the present divorce law?

IX. Partition of the Arguments

    A. Of the Affirmative

       1. The first affirmative speaker will present the introduction and the first main argument.

       2. The second affirmative speaker will present the second main argument.

    B. Of the Negative

       1. The first negative speaker will present the first main argument.

       2. The second negative speaker will present the second main argument.

Affirmative Brief

I. The present divorce law in New York State is unsatisfactory.

    A. It is obsolete in that adultery is the only ground for divorce.

       1. It was adopted in 1787 to meet conditions of that time.

          a. Adultery was a criminal offense punishable by imprisonment.

          b. A social stigma fell upon a person accused of adultery.

       2. Adultery is no longer prosecuted as a criminal offense.

    B. It is easily evaded.

       1. A fraudulent charge of adultery is sufficient.

          a. In 1907 the Kerr case established a precedent that inclination and opportunity prove adultery.

      b. Registration as man and wife in a hotel, by a husband
         and a woman not his wife, provides sufficient evidence
         of adultery for a legal divorce.
   2. A short residence in a state with more liberal divorce
     laws makes a divorce possible.
      a. Seven states require only six months or less.
         (I.) Nevada requires only six weeks.
         (II.) Florida requires only ninety days.
         (III.) Wyoming requires only sixty days.
      b. Many states accept more grounds for divorce.
         (I.) All but North Carolina accept cruelty.
         (II.) All but North Carolina accept desertion.
         (III.) All but North Carolina accept alcoholism.
         (IV.) Four accept non-support.
      c. Compliance with the residence requirement of the
         state granting the decree of divorce makes the decree
         valid in New York.
C. It is unfair.
   1. Divorce is easy for those who have no scruples about a
     trumped-up charge of adultery or who can afford to move
     to another state.
   2. Divorce is impossible for those who are scrupulous and
     poor.
   3. The law assigns guilt to one partner.
      a. Proof must be submitted that one partner has com-
         mitted adultery.
      b. If both spouses have committed adultery, the law
         will not permit them to obtain a divorce.

The plan of the American Bar Association would eliminate the
faults of the present law.
A. The plan is based upon sound principles and practices.
   1. The authors of the plan have the highest integrity and
     competence.
      a. The commission includes experts on the problems of
         divorce: a lawyer, a psychologist, a psychiatrist, and
         a sociologist.
      b. The commission also includes religious leaders: a
         rabbi, a Catholic bishop, and a Protestant dean.
   2. The sponsor of the plan is the Interprofessional Council
     on Marriage and Divorce Laws of the American Bar
     Association.
   3. The plan adapts to divorce the philosophy of the ju-
     venile court.
      a. Use of this philosophy would discard guilt by one
         partner as the requisite of divorce.
         (I.) The plaintiff and the defendant would be elimi-
            nated.
         (II.) The sensational public trial would be eliminated.

           (III.) Instead of "Jane Doe vs. John Doe" the title would be "In the Interest of the John Doe Family."

      b. It substitutes an impartial investigation designed to determine what is best for the family and hence best for society.

   4. The plan also applies to divorce the implementation and technique of the juvenile court.

      a. The court's specialists undertake the impartial investigation.

         (I.) The court's specialists include a social worker, a psychiatrist, and leaders in education and religion.

         (II.) The specialists make recommendation for treatment where indicated.

            (A.) The treatment is designed to help the couple gain insight into their problems through psychiatric and sociological aid.

            (B.) The treatment is given at the discretion of the court specialists.

      b. When possible the family is reunited.

      c. When necessary a final divorce decree is issued.

         (I.) Both judicial inquiry and the investigation of specialists may indicate that the marriage is unworkable.

         (II.) The court may conclude that investigation and treatment show that the marriage is no longer useful to the spouse, the children, or the state.

   5. The plan includes provisions designed to decrease the number of out-of-state divorces.

      a. Residence of a year or more in the state granting the divorce would be required for recognition of an out-of-state divorce.

      b. Without compelling evidence to the contrary, a person residing outside of New York for less than a year would still be legally a resident of New York.

B. The plan is workable.

   1. It has been used successfully in the juvenile courts.

      a. It has helped to redirect hundreds of misguided youngsters.

      b. It has saved youngsters from the stigma of guilt.

   2. It has been used successfully in the New York Domestic Relations Court.

      a. It has dealt with the problems of many unhappy marriages.

      b. It has saved a large percentage of these marriages.

   3. Church leaders have shown interest in the plan.

      a. The Reverend Robert F. Duncan, S.J., closes a searching study reprinted in *The Catholic Mind* of March,

1951 with the statement: "The American Bar Association plan, then, merits a conditional approbation pending its more specific clarification and its actual mode of operation."

b. The Federal Council of Churches on October 23, 1950 issued a statement which "endorses the efforts of the American Bar Association to have divorce courts conducted as juvenile courts now are, with expert counselling to aid the presiding judge in bringing about reconciliation."

Conclusion of the Affirmative

Since the present divorce law in New York State is unsatisfactory and since the plan of the American Bar Association would eliminate the faults of the present law, therefore New York State should adopt the American Bar Association plan for modification of the divorce laws.

Negative Brief

I. The present divorce law in New York State is satisfactory.
  A. It is adequate in its basic provision.
    1. Adultery is the only ground serious enough to justify divorce.
    2. The grounds accepted in other states lead to serious abuses.
      a. When divorce is easy, families are broken up unnecessarily.
      b. Divorce courts in some states make a mockery of the marriage vows.
  B. It can be amended to prevent evasion.
    1. Fraudulent charges of adultery can be eliminated as a basis for a decree of divorce.
    2. The validity of an out-of-state divorce can be based upon refusal to consider less than a year of residence in another state as proof of intention to relinquish residence in New York State.
  C. It places the stigma on divorce that it should have.
    1. The sacrament of matrimony should be considered sacred.
    2. Marriage should establish the family as a life-long institution.
    3. The obligations of husband and wife, father and mother, should not be subject to reconsideration.
II. The plan of the American Bar Association is undesirable.
  A. Any plan that makes divorce easier will increase the number of divorces.
    1. No matter how deliberate the procedure may be, the result of the plan will be more broken families.

2. No matter how many "experts" are involved, more divorces will be granted than at present.

B. More divorces will lead to more social problems.
   1. Divorces are responsible for much juvenile delinquency.
   2. Divorces are responsible for mental disorders of both adults and children.

C. The proposed plan is highly theoretical.
   1. It assumes that the "experts" will be competent to deal with marriage problems.
   2. It assumes that the parties concerned will welcome the investigation of "experts" into their personal affairs.
   3. It assumes that the methods that work with children will work with adults.

D. The proposed plan is expensive.
   1. It is costly to the taxpayer.
      a. It creates many jobs to be paid for.
      b. It would increase the overhead of the courts.
   2. It is costly to the litigants.
      a. It prolongs the services of lawyers.
      b. It involves more incidental expenses.

E. The proposed plan has not received enthusiastic endorsement.
   1. The provisional endorsement of a Catholic priest does not represent the endorsement of the Catholic Church.
   2. Those who have expressed an interest in the plan recognize that it has not yet been tested.

F. Some lawyers may have a selfish interest in the plan.
   1. It would create positions for them.
   2. It would expand the work of courts.

Conclusion of the Negative

Since the present divorce law in New York State is satisfactory and since the plan of the American Bar Association is undesirable, therefore New York State should not adopt the American Bar Association plan for modification of the divorce laws.

Selected References for Brief

1. "Albany Hearing Set on Divorce Measure," *The New York Times,* February 27, 1953, p. 16. Explains the status of divorce legislation in the State Legislature.
2. Alexander, Paul William. "Divorce without Guilt or Sin," *The New York Times Magazine,* July 1, 1951, pp. 14–16. Explains the plan of the American Bar Association.
3. Alexander, Paul William. "Our Legal Horror—Divorce," *The Ladies' Home Journal* (October, 1949) 66:65. Presents striking illustrations showing the need for the new plan.
4. "Divorce: A Re-examination of Basic Concepts," *A Symposium:*

Law and Contemporary Problems, Vol. 18, No. 1, Duke University Law School, 1953. Offers a recent evaluation of problems of marriage and divorce.

5. "Divorce," *The Encyclopedia Americana,* IX (1938), pp. 206–208. Gives facts about divorce in the United States and in foreign countries.

6. Ernst, Morris Leopold. *For Better or Worse.* New York: Harper, 1952. Pp. 245. Presents a new approach to marriage and divorce.

7. "Federal Council Supports Bar Association on Divorce," *Christian Century* (November 8, 1950), 67:1316. States the position taken by the Federal Council of Churches on the American Bar Association plan.

8. Lichtenberger, James Pendelton. *Divorce: A Social Interpretation.* New York: Whittlesey House, McGraw-Hill Book Co., 1931. xii + Pp. 472. Treats marriage and divorce from the point of view of society.

9. "Marriages, Divorces and Rates in the United States" and "Grounds for Divorce," *The World Almanac and Book of Facts for 1953.* New York: *New York World-Telegram and Sun,* 1953, pp. 437 and 439. Presents recent statistics concerning divorce.

10. Mowrer, Ernest Russell. *Family Disorganization.* Chicago: The University of Chicago Press, 1927, xvii + Pp. 317. Introduces a sociological analysis.

11. Vernier, Chester Garfield. *American Family Laws,* 5 vol., Palo Alto, California: Stanford University Press, 1931–38. Makes a comparative study of the family law of the forty-eight American states, Alaska, the District of Columbia, and Hawaii.

12. Wels, Richard H., "Argument for a New Divorce Law in New York," *The New York Times Magazine,* December 19, 1948, p. 10. Points out the faults in the present law and indicates the changes needed.

Exercises

1. How does debate differ from discussion?
2. How are the issues in a debate determined?
3. What are the requirements for a debate proposition?
4. Prepare an acceptable proposition for debate for each of the following topics:
   a. A change in the type of city government.
   b. Revisions in college curriculum.
   c. The abolition of tipping.
5. Prepare a complete brief on one of the propositions developed in answer to question 4.

7

Parliamentary Procedure

Parliamentary procedure is more than a collection of rules to aid in the transaction of business. It is an expression of the philosophy involved in democratic ideology as that ideology has developed in the course of hundreds of years in England and America.

The basic assumptions underlying parliamentary procedure include: (1) Parliamentary procedure aids rather than hinders the harmonious transaction of business. (2) The majority rules. (3) All members of a meeting have equal rights and privileges, but also equal duties and obligations. (4) The rights of both majority and minority groups are safeguarded. (5) Complete discussion of every proposition presented for decision is an established right subject to any provision in the constitution or by-laws of the assembly, and to the following limitations: (a) a motion to close debate requires a two-thirds vote; and (b) a motion to limit debate requires a two-thirds vote. (6) The most direct method for accomplishing a purpose should be followed. (7) Motions have a definite and logical order of precedence. (8) Every member has the right to know what question is before the group at any time and what its effect will be. (9) Only one question can be considered at a time. (10) Power must be delegated only through democratic processes, that is, by majority vote. (11) The presiding officer should exercise his authority with fairness, judgment, and a high degree of responsibility. (12) For the information of all members, a record is kept of all actions taken.

PROCEDURE FOR STARTING A CLUB

Organizations are divided into two types: temporary or permanent. A temporary organization may last for one meeting or several, depending upon the length of time required to accomplish its purpose. A permanent organization is one that is formed with the expectation that it will function over a long period of time, or perhaps indefinitely.

The founders of either type of organization should meet in a committee or small group to discuss important preliminary questions, such as the purpose of the proposed organization; the manner in which that purpose is to be accomplished; financial arrangements; nature and types of membership; policies; affiliations with a larger or national organization; and temporary officers.

After they have reached agreement upon such basic problems, the committee should consider plans for an initial meeting. They will need to decide on the type of meeting as well as the time and place. They will have to adopt a method for notifying proposed members. They will also have to decide who is to call the meeting to order; who is to be nominated for chairman; who is to nominate the chairman; who is to explain the purpose of the meeting; and who is to write the resolutions or bylaws to be voted upon.

The group may be established as an organization when these questions have been satisfactorily answered. If the organization is to be a permanent one, a set of bylaws may be drafted. When all this preliminary organization has been completed, the founders are ready to call the first meeting.

The First Meeting. The first meeting of an organization is called to order by a member previously selected for the task. He then *moves,* that is, suggests, that the person previously chosen to be nominated as chairman be elected. After the motion has been *seconded,* it is put to a vote. The member then says: "Those in favor of Mr. X for temporary chairman say 'Aye.' Those opposed say 'No.'" The affirmative votes are counted, and the same process is repeated for the negative votes. If the majority vote is in the affirmative, the chairman says, "A majority having voted for Mr. X, he is elected temporary chairman. Mr. X will please take the chair." If the motion is defeated, the chairman will say, "The noes have it, and the motion is lost. Another motion is in order."

Ordinarily only one person is nominated for temporary chairman, but if additional persons are nominated, a vote is taken on each name, in the order of nomination, until one candidate receives a majority. This candidate is then declared elected and becomes the presiding officer. The presiding officer then opens nominations for a temporary secretary, who is selected in the same manner as the temporary chairman.

After the election of the temporary secretary, the chairman calls upon one of the founding members to explain the purpose of the meeting. This member should present the previously phrased motion or resolution, namely, that the assembly form itself into an organization. If this motion or resolution receives a majority vote, some member should then move to appoint a committee to draft a constitution and bylaws. If these have been previously drafted, the group responsible for the task is asked to report.

The Constitution and Bylaws. A constitution consists of at least seven basic provisions, which should be set forth briefly and clearly in separate articles: (1) the name of the organization; (2) the purposes and powers of the organization; (3) qualifications for membership; (4) officers of the organization and their duties and the length of their term of office; (5) a board of directors or governing board or an executive committee, and the method of selection; (6) the time for regular meetings and a method for calling special meetings; (7) the method of amending the constitution.

The bylaws contain all of the details necessary to carry out the provisions of the constitution. Ordinarily they include the following: kinds of membership; requirements for membership; method of admission of members; dues; powers and duties of officers; powers and duties of committees; method of election of officers and committees; provisions for calling and conducting meetings; parliamentary authority; number constituting a quorum; and procedure for amending bylaws.

DUTIES OF OFFICERS

The success of a club depends in part upon the competent and conscientious performance of its elected officers, who have the special obligation of conducting the affairs of the assembly in a fair and objective manner. The number of officers may vary according to the organization, but most of the duties and responsibilities for guiding the club are handled by the chairman or president, the vice-president, the secretary, and the treasurer.

Duties of the Chairman. The main duty of the chairman or president is to preserve order at meetings. He usually stands when addressing the group and refers to himself as *The Chair* and never as *I*. To avoid confusion, members must address the chair and be recognized by the chair before speaking to the group. The chairman votes only in cases of tie and may enter the discussion and speak from the floor only after he has designated a substitute or "pro-tempore" chairman to take his place.

In addition, the chairman may be given appointive powers. For example, he may name some committee and minor officers. Implicit in all his official duties is the necessity for seeing that the business of the group is carried on fairly and with a maximum of efficiency.

Duties of the Vice-President. In the absence of the president, the vice-president serves as chairman. He is frequently chairman of important groups and an ex-officio member of most committees.

Duties of the Secretary. The secretary is the recording officer of the assembly and the keeper of its minutes and records, except those (the treasurer's books, for example) assigned to others. Duties of the secretary are: (1) to keep a register of the members and to call the roll when necessary; (2) to officially notify officers, committees, and delegates of their appointment; (3) to furnish committees with all papers referred to them; (4) to supply delegates with credentials; and (5) to sign with the president all orders on the treasury authorized by the group, unless otherwise specified in the bylaws.

He should keep one book in which the constitution, bylaws, rules of order, and standing rules are all written, leaving every other page blank, so that amendments may be entered on the page opposite the article amended, with a reference in red ink to the date and page of the minutes where each amendment is recorded. He should also provide the presiding officer with a detailed memorandum of every item to come up under each section of the order of business.

Furthermore, when there is only one secretary, he must send out notices of all called meetings, and of other meetings when necessary, and conduct the correspondence of the society, unless there are other provisions. If there is a "corresponding secretary," these and other duties indicated in the bylaws devolve on him. The word *secretary* refers always to the recording secretary if there is more than one.

Duties of the Treasurer. The treasurer is in charge of the club's finances. He collects dues, writes receipts, pays bills, and makes detailed reports at specific intervals or upon request at a meeting.

THE MINUTES

It is the duty of the secretary to record the minutes of the meetings of an assembly. The minutes of each meeting should indicate: (1) the kind of meeting, i.e., regular or special; (2) the name of the group; (3) the date and time of meeting as well as the place, unless it is always in the same place; (4) the presence of the presiding officer and the secretary or, in their absence, the names of their substitutes; (5) the action that was taken on minutes of the previous meeting; (6) each main motion except for those withdrawn, with the name of the member who introduced it and the action taken; (7) points of order and appeals, whether sustained or lost, and all other motions not defeated or withdrawn; (8) the total attendance and, sometimes, the names of absentees; (9) the program, if any; and (10) time of adjournment.

THE ORDER OF BUSINESS

Practically every organization has a specific order of business to be followed at every meeting. If there is no set order, the following one, or whatever modifications of it are preferred, may be used: (1) call to order by presiding officer, (2) roll call by secretary, (3) reading and correction or disposition of minutes of previous meeting, (4) reports of officers, (5) reports of boards and standing committees, (6) reports of special committees, (7) unfinished business, (8) new business, (9) announcements, (10) program, and (11) adjournment.

It may not be necessary to go into all the items listed above unless the agenda indicates that an item is to come up under each of these headings. If a chairman does not adhere to the schedule, someone in the group may call for the "orders of the day." The chairman must then follow the regular schedule of business.

If a specific order of business is stated in the constitution or bylaws and if the assembly wishes to change the order, it may do so by a motion to suspend the rules. Changes in the order of business are frequently made by unanimous consent.

PRESENTATION OF A MOTION

A motion is the formal statement of a proposal or question for consideration and action by a group. It presents an item of business for decision. It may also be referred to as a "question" or "proposition."

The presentation of a motion requires the following successive steps:

1. A member rises and addresses the presiding officer.
2. The presiding officer grants the floor by stating the member's name.
3. The member proposes a motion.
4. Another member seconds the motion.
5. The presiding officer states the motion to the group.

How to Address the Chair. Except when he is presiding, any member has the right to present a motion. To do this, the member rises and addresses the presiding officer by his official title, for example, "Mr. President," "Madam Chairman," or "Mr. Moderator." If the presiding officer has no official title, it is correct to use "Mr. Chairman," or if the presiding officer is a woman, "Madam Chairman." This form of address signifies to the presiding officer that the member wishes to have the right to speak or to present a motion. After addressing the presiding officer, the member waits for recognition.

How to Accord Recognition. Ordinarily, the first person who rises and asks for recognition is entitled to speak. The chairman recognizes a member by announcing his name, addressing him as "Mr. Member," or in some other way designating him as the speaker selected. In large groups where the chairman may not know the names of all members, the member, when he is recognized, should state his name and the organization or district which he represents.

If several members speak at the same time, the following rules will help the chairman to decide to whom to grant recognition first: [1]

1. Preference is given to the proposer of a motion (or a committee chairman who has presented a report) to have the first opportunity to explain the motion or report.
2. A member who has not spoken has prior claim over one who has already discussed the question. Also, a member who rarely speaks is given preference over one who frequently claims the attention of the group.
3. Whenever he can, the chairman alternates between proponents and opponents of a motion. Where there are opposing opinions, the chairman may inquire of a speaker on which side he intends to speak and thus more fairly divide the opportunities to address the group.

How to Propose a Motion. A motion is a recommendation that the group take certain action or express certain sentiments. The speaker should introduce his statement with the words "I move that," which simply mean "I propose that." For example, the statement, "I move that this organization approve plans for a Scholarship Loan Fund," is correctly phrased. If the motion is lengthy, the proposer should put it in writing before proposing it; otherwise, the chairman may request him to do so for the convenience of the secretary.

How to Second a Motion. After a member has stated his motion, he resumes his seat. Another member may then second the motion by saying, without waiting for recognition, "I second the motion." Seconding a motion shows that the member wishes the matter to receive consideration by the assembly, but does not commit him to vote in favor of it.

When a motion has been properly moved and seconded, the chairman should formally restate it to the group as clearly and as concisely as possible. Any change in wording must be made only with the consent of the mover. It then belongs to the organization and is no longer under the control of its sponsor. From the time when it is formally stated by the presiding officer until it is voted upon or otherwise disposed of by the assembly, it is open to debate and is known as the *pending question*.

If a motion is not promptly seconded, the chairman should

[1] Cf. Alice F. Sturgis, *Standard Code of Parliamentary Procedure* (New York: McGraw-Hill Book Co., Inc., 1950), p. 19.

state the motion again and ask if there is a second. If there is no response, he may state, "The motion is lost for want of a second," and proceed to other business.

METHODS OF VOTING

Members of any democratic organization should have a voice in determining the will of the group. This effect is accomplished through the process of voting.

The most frequent method of voting is the *viva voce* or *voice method,* in which those in favor of a motion say "Aye" and those opposed say "No" in response to the chairman's question. The chairman determines the outcome of the vote by the volume of voices. If the voice vote is indecisive, the members may be asked to stand or to raise their hands to indicate their vote. These methods are known as the *rising vote* and vote by *show of hands* methods.

Still another system is the *roll-call* vote, in which the names of those entitled to vote are called either in alphabetical order or by districts. Members vote by saying "Yes" or "No." If a secret vote is desired, or if several candidates or questions are to be voted upon at one time, the *ballot* method may be used. In some organizations, *voting by mail* is permitted, but this method must be specifically authorized by the constitution and bylaws.

KINDS OF MOTIONS

If a member of a group wishes to propose a course of action for the assembly, he must do so in the form of a motion. This motion is then regarded as a *main* motion, but since consideration of it by the group may be delayed by the introduction of other motions which have *precedence,* the types of motion should be learned according to their order of precedence or rank. Motions are classified in order of precedence as (1) privileged, (2) subsidiary, and (3) main.

Privileged Motions. Privileged motions have no direct connection with the main motion before the group, but are of such urgency that they are entitled to immediate consideration. They are considered as privileged only when other business is before the group. If made when there is no motion or proposal before the assembly, they are treated as main motions. Privileged motions are listed here in order of their rank: (1) fixing of time to which to adjourn, (2) adjourning, (3) taking a recess, (4) raising a question of privilege, and (5) calling for the orders of the day.

FIXING OF TIME TO WHICH TO ADJOURN. The purpose of this motion is not to end the present meeting, but to set the time of the next one. The usual form of the motion is: "I move that when we adjourn, we adjourn until [specified hour A.M. or P.M.]," and the day and date are specified.

ADJOURNING. A motion to adjourn signifies the formal end of a meeting, convention, or conference. In declaring any meeting adjourned, the presiding officer should state the time and place for reconvening. The motion to adjourn is neither debatable nor amendable and requires a majority vote.

TAKING A RECESS. A motion to recess is used to permit an intermission during a meeting. It requires a majority vote, is not debatable, but can be amended.

RAISING A QUESTION OF PRIVILEGE. Any member may secure immediate action upon a matter concerning himself, another member, or the organization itself through a question of privilege. This motion, which is decided by the chairman, provides opportunity for immediate action on such matters as heating, lighting, ventilation, or any similar convenience. A question of privilege is neither debatable nor amendable.

CALLING FOR THE ORDERS OF THE DAY. The purpose of a call for the orders of the day is to draw the attention of the chairman to an omission of a scheduled event or to a mistake in the sequence of business planned for the meeting. For example, if the chairman had forgotten a previously agreed upon recess time, a member could call for the orders of the day in order to remind him.

Subsidiary Motions. Subsidiary motions, so called because they are subsidiary to the main motion and depend upon it for existence, are used to modify or dispose of the main motion. They are alternative aids in considering, acting upon, and disposing of the main motion. Because they relate to the main motion, it is "in order," that is, correct from a parliamentary standpoint, to propose them when a main motion is pending before the group.

The following subsidiary motions should be learned in the order of precedence in which they are listed: (1) postpone temporarily (lay on the table), (2) vote immediately (previous question), (3) limit or extend the limits of debate, (4) postpone definitely, (5) refer to a committee, (6) amend, and (7) postpone indefinitely.

POSTPONE TEMPORARILY. To postpone a motion temporarily, or "to lay it on the table," means to set it aside until a later time or date. This subsidiary motion is neither amendable nor debatable and requires a majority vote for passage.

VOTE IMMEDIATELY. The purpose of the motion to vote immediately is to stop all discussion on the question before the group or to prevent the proposal of subsidiary motions, and to bring the question to a vote immediately. Because this motion is the most drastic of those used to control debate, a two-thirds vote is necessary to order an immediate vote.

LIMIT DEBATE. The purpose of the motion to limit debate is to restrict the length of time to be devoted to discussion. The reverse may also be moved, that is, a motion may be made to extend the limits of debate by removing restrictions already imposed in order to increase the time given to debate. This motion requires a two-thirds vote because it restricts freedom of the assembly to discuss the main motion. The motion is not debatable.

A motion curtailing or extending the limits of debate is in force only during the meeting at which it was adopted. If the main motion is postponed until another meeting, the order which limited the debate loses its force.

POSTPONE DEFINITELY. The purpose of the motion to postpone definitely, or to a certain time, is to postpone consideration of a motion to a later time and to fix a definite time for consideration or for further consideration of the motion. It provides a satisfactory way of fixing in advance the day or the time when a question will come up for consideration. This motion, which is debatable and amendable, requires a majority vote.

REFER TO A COMMITTEE. A motion to refer to a committee may be used for a number of reasons:

(a) To secure more information about a matter and recommendations on it;

(b) To ensure privacy when considering a delicate matter;

(c) To secure study by a smaller group so that more thorough and efficient study may be given;

(d) To permit informal consideration;
(e) To delay a proposal or to defeat it by referring it to an unfriendly committee.

This motion is debatable and amendable and requires a majority vote.

AMEND. The purpose of the motion to amend is to modify or change a motion that is being considered by the group so that it will express the will of the group more accurately.

There are two limitations on the number of pending amendments. Amendments applied to the original motion are amendments of the first rank, and amendments to the proposed amendment are amendments of the second rank. Only one amendment may be under consideration at a time. Since the amendment may not be satisfactory to the majority of the group, it is possible to amend the amendment before it is adopted.

Amendments may be made in one of three ways: (1) by adding or inserting something which the motion did not contain originally; (2) by eliminating or striking out something from the motion which was a part of it originally; (3) by substituting something for a part of the motion that is to be eliminated.

The motion to amend requires a majority vote, even though the motion to which it applies requires a two-thirds vote.

POSTPONE INDEFINITELY. The purpose of the motion to postpone indefinitely is to suppress the question before the group, without permitting it to come to a vote. Its purpose is not to postpone, but rather to kill the question without bringing it to a direct vote. This motion, which is debatable but not amendable, requires a majority vote. Through a new motion, the matter may come up again after other business has been concluded.

Main Motions. Main motions constitute the most important group. They are used to introduce subjects for discussion and action and may deal with any topic which a member may properly bring before the group.

There are several specialized motions sometimes referred to as *specific main motions* to indicate that they are classified as main, although they are known by specific names.[2] These are: (1) reconsider, (2) rescind, (3) create orders, and (4) resume consideration.

[2] Alice F. Sturgis, op. cit., p. 159.

RECONSIDER. The purpose of the motion to reconsider is to reintroduce a motion that has been previously decided. This proposal can be made only by a member who voted with the prevailing side. It requires a second and is debatable only if the motion to which it is applied is debatable. The motion to reconsider is not amendable and requires a majority vote. Reconsideration is not a repeal, but a method of reopening a question that has been closed.

RESCIND. The purpose of the motion to rescind is to nullify an action taken on a previous motion. A vote may be rescinded by a majority if previous notice has been given; otherwise, a two-thirds vote of those present, or a majority vote of the entire membership, is required. The motion to rescind cannot be renewed at the same meeting.

RECONSIDER AND ENTER ON THE MINUTES. The motion to reconsider and enter on the minutes exists only when specifically set forth in the bylaws or rules. It is a device used to protect an organization from the action of an organized minority that may have control of a meeting because of absentees. One person makes a motion and another seconds it, thereby postponing business, no matter how urgent, until the next meeting, even though it be weeks or months away.

TAKE FROM THE TABLE. The purpose of the motion to resume consideration is to take from the table or bring up for consideration a motion previously laid on the table. A majority vote is required. If the motion is defeated, it may be renewed later in the same meeting if there is time after other business has been considered.

Incidental Motions. Incidental motions have few characteristics in common except that they grow incidentally from the business before the group. There is no order of rank among them, but they do have precedence over the motion from which they arise.

Most incidental motions relate to the rights of members of the groups. The most frequently used incidental motions are: (1) appeal, (2) point of order, (3) parliamentary inquiry, (4) suspend rules, (5) withdraw a motion, (6) object to consideration, (7) division of the question, and (8) division of the assembly.

APPEAL. The purpose of an appeal from a decision of the chair is to enable a member who believes that the presiding officer has made a mistake or has been unfair in his decision, to have the group decide by vote whether or not the chairman's decision should be sustained.

A majority vote in the affirmative, or even a tie vote, sustains the chairman's ruling. Sometimes the motion is open to limited discussion, but it is not amendable.

POINT OF ORDER. The purpose of a point of order is to call attention to a violation of the rules, an omission or mistake in procedure, or a departure from the motion or question under discussion. Point of order may be used to insist on strict compliance with the rules or merely to raise a question concerning their application.

If the point of order is held to be "well taken," the chairman orders the mistake corrected. If the point of order is held to be "not well taken," business is resumed at the point where it was interrupted.

PARLIAMENTARY INQUIRY. Questions of procedure regarding a motion before the group or one soon to be introduced may be directed to the presiding officer. He will give the information requested or call upon the parliamentarian to answer the inquiry.

SUSPEND RULES. The motion to suspend rules is used to set aside temporarily certain practices, such as those relating to the order of business. This motion cannot be used to suspend the provisions of the constitution or bylaws and is neither amendable nor debatable. A two-thirds vote is required for its adoption.

WITHDRAW A MOTION. Before a motion is stated by the chairman, it may be withdrawn by the proposer, with the consent of the second. If anyone objects, the motion granting permission to withdraw or modify is formally presented. Leave to withdraw a motion does not require a second; the motion is neither debatable nor amendable but does require a majority vote. Once the motion has been stated by the chairman, however, it may be withdrawn or modified only by general consent.[3]

OBJECT TO CONSIDERATION. If a member of a group objects to an original main motion, he may so state, provided he does so before any subsidiary motion is stated or any debate occurs. The purpose of objection to consideration is to avoid the discussion of any question which the assembly believes to be embarrassing, unprofitable, or inopportune. It is neither debatable nor amendable and requires a two-thirds vote to sustain the objection.

[3] For further details regarding motions, see the accompanying three tables of Parliamentary Motions on pages 96–98.

TABLE I*

A CONDENSED TABLE OF COMMONLY USED
PARLIAMENTARY MOTIONS

The following summary of motions is designed for those just beginning the study of parliamentary procedure.

The capital letters appearing after certain of the motions below indicate essential facts to know about the motion. *A* means that the motion can be amended; *D* means that the motion can be debated; "⅔" or "no vote" indicates the vote required. Absence of an *A* means that the motion is not amendable; absence of a *D* means that it is not debatable; absence of "⅔" or "no vote" means that the customary majority vote is required. See footnotes 1 and 2, this page, for further explanation.

The numbering of the motions is significant. Certain motions take rank or precedence over others: motion number 1 ("Fix the time to which to adjourn") takes precedence over all others. Motion number 10 ("Refer to a committee") takes precedence over number 11, number 12, and number 13, but is itself outranked by motions numbered from 1 through 9.

PRIVILEGED MOTIONS

1. Fix the time to which to adjourn (*A*) [1]
2. Adjourn [2]
3. Take a recess (*A*)
4. Question of privilege (no vote)
5. Call for orders of the day (no vote)

SUBSIDIARY MOTIONS

6. Lay on the table
7. Previous question (⅔)
8. Limit or extend debate (*A*)⅔
9. Postpone to a definite time (*A*)(*D*)
10. Refer to a committee (*A*)(*D*)
11. Amend (*A*)(*D*)
12. Postpone indefinitely (*D*)
　　　　All of the foregoing take precedence over
13. The main motion (*A*)(*D*)

For a complete table of all parliamentary motions, arranged in alphabetical order, see Table II, page 97. For the same table, rearranged and classified according to motions, see Table III, page 98.

* Tables I, II, and III reprinted with adaptations with the permission of publisher and authors from *The Fundamentals of Speaking* by Wilbur E. Gilman, Bower Aly, and Loren D. Reid, published by The Macmillan Co., 1951, pages 571–73.

[1] To be interpreted thus: "Amendable, not debatable, majority vote."
[2] To be interpreted thus: "Not amendable, not debatable, majority vote."

TABLE II

TABLE OF PARLIAMENTARY MOTIONS*

(Arranged in Alphabetical Order)

Type of motion	Precedence of motion	Motion	In order when another has floor?	Requires a second?	Debat-able?	Amend-able?	Vote required?	Can it be reconsidered?
P	2	Adjourn (when privileged)	No	Yes	No	No	Maj.	No
IS	11	Amend	No	Yes	Yes[3]	Yes	Maj.	Yes
P		Appeal	Yes[1]	Yes	Yes	No	Maj.	Yes
I	5	Call for orders of the day	Yes	No	No	No	None	No
I		Closing nominations	No	Yes	No	Yes	2/3	No
I		Division of assembly	Yes[1]	No	No	No	None	No
P		Division of question	Yes[2]	No[2]	No	Yes	None[2]	No
	1	Fix time to which to adjourn	No	Yes	No[4]	Yes	Maj.	Yes
S	6	Lay on table	No	Yes	No	No	Maj.	No
S	8	Limit or extend debate	No	Yes	No	Yes	2/3	Yes
M	13	Main motion	No	Yes	Yes	Yes	Maj.	Yes
I		Objection to consideration	Yes	No	No	No	2/3	Yes[8]
I		Parliamentary inquiry	Yes	No	No	No	None	No
S	9	Postpone to definite time	No	Yes	Yes	Yes	Maj.	Yes
S	12	Postpone indefinitely	No	Yes	Yes	No	Maj.	Yes[8]
S	7	Previous question	No	Yes	No	No	2/3	Yes[9]
I		Questions of order	Yes	No	No	No	None	No
P	4	Questions of privilege	Yes	No	No	No	None	No
SM		Reconsider	Yes	Yes	Yes[5]	No	Maj.	No
SM		Reconsider and enter on minutes	Yes	Yes	No	No	None	No
S	10	Refer to a committee	No	Yes	Yes	Yes	Maj.	Yes[10]
I		Reopening nominations	No	Yes	No	Yes	Maj.	Yes[11]
SM		Rescind	No	Yes	Yes	Yes	2/3[6]	Yes[11]
I		Suspension of the rules	No	Yes	No	No	2/3[7]	No
P	3	Take a recess (when privileged)	No	Yes	No[4]	Yes	Maj.	No
SM		Take from the table	No	Yes	No	No	Maj.	No
I		Voting, motions relating to	No	Yes	No	Yes	Maj.	Yes
I		Withdraw a motion, leave to	No	No	No	No	Maj.	Yes[11]

* Explanation of abbreviations in column 1: *P*–privileged; *S*–subsidiary; *I*–incidental; *SM*–specific main; *M*–main motion. The numbers in column 2 indicate that motions have different degrees of precedence. Highest precedence is indicated by 1, next highest by 2, etc. Motions for which no number is given have no precedence established.

[1] Can not, however, interrupt speaker. [2] If motion relates to different subjects which are independent of each other. [3] Not debatable when motion being amended is not debatable. [4] Not debatable when another question is before the assembly. [5] Not debatable when motion being reconsidered is not debatable. [6] If previous notice has been given to all members, a majority vote suffices. A majority vote of the entire membership may rescind without previous notice. [7] Except certain standing rules, such as those governing time and place of meeting, which may be suspended by majority vote. [8] Negative vote can not be reconsidered. [9] Can not be reconsidered after it has been voted upon. [10] Can not be reconsidered after committee has taken up the subject. But a 2/3 vote will discharge committee. [11] Affirmative vote can not be reconsidered.

TABLE III

TABLE OF PARLIAMENTARY MOTIONS

(Classified According to Types and Showing Order of Precedence)

Rank	Name and type of motion	In order when another has floor?	Requires a second?	Debatable?	Amendable?	Vote required?	Can it be reconsidered?
	Privileged Motions						
1	Fix time to which to adjourn	No	Yes	No[4]	Yes	Maj.	Yes
2	Adjourn (when privileged)	No	Yes	No	No	Maj.	No
3	Take a recess (when privileged)	No	Yes	No[4]	Yes	Maj.	No
4	Questions of privilege	Yes	No	No	No	None	No
5	Call for orders of the day	Yes	No	No	No	None	No
	Incidental Motions (These motions have no rank among themselves, but grow out of other motions.)						
	Appeal	Yes[1]	Yes	Yes	No	Maj.	Yes
	Closing nominations	No	Yes	No	Yes	2/3	No
	Division of assembly	Yes[1]	No	No	No	None	No
	Division of question	Yes[2]	No[2]	No	Yes	None[2]	No
	Objection to consideration	Yes	No	No	No	2/3	Yes[8]
	Parliamentary inquiry	Yes	No	No	No	None	No
	Questions of order	Yes	No	No	No	None	No
	Reopening nominations	No	Yes	No	Yes	Maj.	Yes[11]
	Suspension of the rules	No	Yes	No	No	2/3[7]	No
	Voting, motions relating to	No	Yes	No	Yes	Maj.	Yes
	Withdraw a motion, leave to	No	No	No	No	Maj.	Yes[11]
	Subsidiary Motions						
6	Lay on table	No	Yes	No	No	Maj.	No
7	Previous question	No	Yes	No	No	2/3	Yes[9]
8	Limit or extend debate	No	Yes	No	Yes	2/3	Yes
9	Postpone to definite time	No	Yes	Yes	Yes	Maj.	Yes
10	Refer to a committee	No	Yes	Yes	Yes	Maj.	Yes[10]
11	Amend	No	Yes	Yes[3]	Yes	Maj.	Yes
12	Postpone indefinitely	No	Yes	Yes	No	Maj.	Yes[8]
	Specific Main Motions						
	Reconsider	Yes	Yes	Yes[5]	No	Maj.	No
	Reconsider and enter on minutes	Yes	Yes	No	No	None	No
	Rescind	No	Yes	Yes	Yes	2/3[6]	Yes[11]
	Take from the table	No	Yes	No	No	Maj.	No
13	Main motion	No	Yes	Yes	Yes	Maj.	Yes

[1] Can not, however, interrupt speaker. [2] If motion relates to different subjects which are independent of each other. [3] Not debatable when motion being amended is not debatable. [4] Not debatable when another question is before the assembly. [5] Not debatable when motion being reconsidered is not debatable. [6] If previous notice has been given to all members, a majority vote suffices. A majority vote of the entire membership may rescind without previous notice. [7] Except certain standing rules, such as those governing time and place of meeting, which may be suspended by majority vote. [8] Negative vote can not be reconsidered. [9] Can not be reconsidered after it has been voted upon. [10] Can not be reconsidered after committee has taken up the subject. But a 2/3 vote will discharge committee. [11] Affirmative vote can not be reconsidered.

Division of the Question. The purpose of a demand for division of a question is to enable the assembly to divide a motion which is composed of two or more independent parts or ideas so that each part may be considered and voted upon separately. Ordinarily, this matter is decided by the chairman and requires no vote. If a formal vote becomes necessary, a majority decision will decide the question.

Division of the Assembly. This motion is used to obtain an accurate vote. For example, it may be used to verify a viva-voce vote by requiring the voters to rise to be counted.

RULES OF PRECEDENCE

There are two basic rules of precedence. The first rule is that when a motion is pending, any motion of higher precedence may be proposed, but no motion of lower precedence may be proposed. The second rule is that motions are considered and voted upon in inverse order to their proposal, the last proposed being considered and disposed of first. If, for example, motions 10, 8, 6, and 4 on page 96 were proposed in that order and were all pending, they would be taken up for consideration in the inverse order: 4, 6, 8, 10, and 13.

Exercises

1. Observe the uses and breaches of parliamentary procedure at a meeting of some club to which you belong.

2. Visit a business meeting of a convention or a large organization. Observe the uses of parliamentary procedure.

3. Formulate three rules for avoiding confusion concerning the forms and degrees of amendments.

4. Interview as many officers as you can of some club or civic group. Find out from them what they would like members to know of parliamentary procedure.

5. Assume that you have been asked to be chairman of a new civic group in your community. Indicate what you think would be the minimum of parliamentary procedure you would need to know to perform your duties efficiently.

8

Oral Interpretation of Literature

Differences between oral interpretation of literature and other forms of communication are many and varied. For example, when a speaker converses, makes a public address, or joins in a group discussion, he is expressing his own ideas. He is free to alter his prepared material to suit the reactions of his audience. The effective speaker can detect the fatigue, boredom, or hostility of his group. If he is wise, he will inject one or two sentences or include a story to clarify a point or to change the mood of his audience.

The oral reader has no such latitude. He may use only the thoughts provided by the author. He may heighten the author's meaning by his own skillful use of technique, or by the vibrancy of his voice, or by the artistic re-creation of the essential mood. Substantially, however, he is limited by the thoughts of the author and by the words the author has used to express himself.

SELECTION OF THE MATERIAL

In order to make a wise choice of material for oral interpretation, a reader must have in mind some criteria for selection. He should prepare a list of available readings of various types and check them against the required standards.

Criteria for Selection. In addition to the obvious factor of the limitations of the time allotted for the presentation, at least four other criteria must be considered in choosing material for oral reading. The selection must be: adaptable to oral interpretation; suitable to the occasion; suitable to the audience; and within the reader's intellectual and interpretative abilities.

SUITABILITY FOR ORAL RENDITION. The material must lend itself to oral reading. Highly statistical data, too many abstract statements without sufficient concrete examples, or long, involved sentences are likely to be difficult to interpret orally. The reader should select material that is sufficiently concrete, with a style and with combinations of sounds that help rather than hinder interpretation.

SUITABILITY TO THE OCCASION. If the selection is too serious for a festive occasion, or too gay for a solemn one; too ponderous for an informal meeting, or too humorous for a formal one; too lengthy for a short program or too short for a lengthy one, the reader will have difficulty in establishing and maintaining the proper mood.

SUITABILITY TO THE AUDIENCE. Still another criterion for selecting material for oral interpretation is the type of audience. The reader should know as much as possible about the members of the group he is to address. For example, he should know their approximate range in ages, their interests, abilities, and tastes. After he has considered the type of prospective audience, and the nature of the occasion that has brought them together, he can best decide on the literary level of his material and whether to read poetry or prose, serious or humorous selections.

SUITABILITY TO THE READER's CAPACITIES. The reader should select material that he himself enjoys and which he has the ability to interpret. If he chooses a selection that is too difficult for his own comprehension, he can hardly expect to convey its meaning to the audience. If he selects one which bores him, he cannot expect to keep his audience interested. If he decides on material that is too varied for his voice range, he will be unable to communicate the ideas in the selection effectively.

The Reader's Notebook and Record Library. Each reader should compile for oral reading material that interests him personally. This may be kept in a looseleaf notebook and classified according to form, i.e., prose, poetry, or drama, or according to subject matter. It is likely that a reader will discover that his tastes change and that selections he liked a year ago no longer interest him. Such selections should be replaced with some of current interest.

Collecting a record library of professional readings will also prove helpful. The objective of listening to records is to learn as much as possible about the style of professional readers. The professionals, however, should not be thought of as a source of imitation. On the contrary, the reading of the same excerpt by several persons should reinforce the fact that oral interpretation is a highly personal art and should be developed as such.

PREPARATION OF THE MATERIAL

The steps involved in preparing material for oral presentation include: (1) a study of the complete selection, as well as an analysis of the devices and techniques used by the writer to create a mood or impression; (2) a synthesis or unification of the entire selection after a detailed study of its component parts; and (3) practice in reading the material aloud, first in sections and then in its entirety.

Preliminary Study. Perhaps the best preparation for oral reading is thoughtful and analytical silent reading. Here the reader must ascertain that he knows the exact definition and connotation of every word in the selection, that he fully understands any allusions or references to the Bible, to mythology, or to other literary works, and that he is correctly interpreting the material in light of the customs and habits at the time and place it was written.

UNDERSTANDING ALL THE WORDS. Many readers believe that they get the "feeling" of a phrase when they really have no clear idea of what the individual words mean. A group that had just read Poe's *The Fall of the House of Usher,* for example, was unable to define accurately the word *ennuyé* in the phrase "*ennuyé man of the world.*" If the word is construed to mean "flamboyant" (as it was in one college group) or "sneering" (as it was in another), rather than "bored," a highly distorted picture of Usher is likely to result.

UNDERSTANDING THE FIGURES OF SPEECH AND THE ALLUSIONS. All unfamiliar references should be checked carefully for meaning and for their special connotation. A detailed study of figures of speech and allusions is particularly important in the reading of poetry, which is likely to contain more allusions than prose since the poet may use a more imaginative vocabulary.

The most effective means of creating images is through the use of figures of speech. The three most often used are the *simile,* the *metaphor,* and the *analogy,* all of which express or imply comparison.

A *simile* expresses a comparison, usually by using the words *as* or *like.* Notice the use of simile in these lines from Keats' sonnet *On First Looking into Chapman's Homer:*

> Then felt I like some watcher of the skies
> When a new planet swims into his ken;
> Or like stout Cortez when with eagle eyes
> He star'd at the Pacific—

A *metaphor* implies comparison and omits the words *as* or *like,* as in these lines from *Barren Spring* by Dante Gabriel Rossetti:

> Behold, this crocus is a withering flame;
> This snowdrop, snow.

Analogy is an expression of likeness or similarity between two objects regarding particular attributes, circumstances, or effects. Shakespeare's *Sonnet 18* compares a loved one with a summer's day, as shown by these opening lines:

> Shall I compare thee to a summer's day?
> Thou art more lovely and more temperate:

Hyperbole is extravagant exaggeration by which something is represented as much greater or less, better or worse, than in reality, as in these lines from Shakespeare's *Troilus and Cressida:*

> Is she worth keeping? Why, she is a pearl,
> Whose price hath launch'd above a thousand ships,
> And turn'd crown'd kings to merchants.

Metonymy refers to the use of one word for a related object which it suggests or calls to mind, as the use of *scepter* for *sovereignty, gray hairs* for *old age. Synecdoche* is the use of a part for the whole, as *fifty head* for *cattle* or the whole for a part, as *smiling year* for *spring.*

Irony is the use of a word whose literal meaning is the opposite of the intended implication in the context, as shown by this line by Antony from *Julius Caesar:* "For Brutus is an honorable [meaning dishonorable] man."

Personification is the attributing of human qualities to inanimate objects. In *Ode to the West Wind,* for example, Shelley treats the wind as a living spirit:

> O wild West Wind, thou breath of Autumn's being,
> Thou, from whose unseen presence the leaves dead
> Are driven, like ghosts from an enchanter fleeing. . . .

Apostrophe refers to the addressing of an abstract idea or imaginary object, or a deceased or absent person as though he were alive or present. The opening lines of Wordsworth's sonnet *To Milton* illustrate the use of apostrophe:

> Milton! thou shouldst be living at this hour:
> England hath need of thee:—

Apart from the figures of speech that may be easily defined, there may be Biblical, mythological, historical, or literary allusions and references that are not clear at first reading. Since such allusions may contribute substantially to the meaning of the selection, it is well for the reader to know as much about them as necessary for an accurate interpretation of his material. Dictionaries, encyclopedias, and other reference works will usually provide the needed information.

UNDERSTANDING THE LITERARY BACKGROUND. Although it is not essential to know everything about an author or to read all his works in order to interpret one relatively short selection, a knowledge of his life and an awareness of his times in so far as they affected his writings may be essential for a full appreciation of the man and an accurate interpretation of his work. To know something of Dickens' childhood experiences in a blacking warehouse or of Melville's life on the sea would give the interpreter a clearer insight into the works of both authors and thereby enrich his presentation.

Analysis of the Author's Thought. After the reader is sure he thoroughly understands all the words and allusions, he must analyze the contents for the significance of the work. Is the material to be interpreted literally or figuratively? The reader must understand the theme, significance, or moral of the selection, and the devices and techniques used by the author to substantiate and build up the theme.

GRASPING THE KEY THOUGHT. If the material is a narrative or a lyric poem, the main idea or key thought may be restated with relative ease. If, however, the selection is an essay on science or philosophy, extensive research may be necessary before an accurate rephrasing of the author's idea or theme can be made.

There are two tests to apply to the analysis of a selection. First, the reader should be able to state the main idea, preferably in a sentence or two; and second, he should be able to summarize the contents, giving each idea in its proper relation to the rest of the selection.

UNDERSTANDING THE THOUGHT PROGRESSION. The next step in preparation is determining the development of the author's thoughts. Analysis of both form and content is required for a thorough interpretation.

In a story or narrative poem, for example, the reader should know how the action proceeds to the climax of the story. How is the main character built up? How are subordinate characters used? How is dialogue employed? What is the climax of the story? What are the steps the author takes to draw the story to a conclusion?

If the selection is an essay, the subordinate ideas should be clear in the mind of the reader. He should also note the order of presentation of the writer's views and opinions and should analyze the method used in correlating these concepts.

If the selection is a poem, the reader should know who is speaking, the author or a character. He should know the characteristics of the speaker, whether he is young or old, rich or poor. He should know to whom the speaker is addressing his remarks and where the action of the poem is taking place.

This knowledge will determine the tone of the reader's voice, his volume, pitch, tempo, and the over-all mood he sets up. The calm meditative quality of Matthew Arnold's *Dover Beach* will require quite a different approach from the rueful note of A. E. Housman's *When I Was One-and-Twenty*.

SEPARATING THE THOUGHTS INTO PHRASES. Each phrase contains an idea expressed in a word or words that carry the meaning. Each phrase should be separated by a short or long pause from every other phrase so that the meaning of the passage is not obscured. This separation is as important as it is in musical phrases, for, as in music, the phrase represents a unit of thought. Those who have not had a great deal of experience in reading aloud are sometimes helped by using a visual method of indicating the phrase and the kind of pause (see page 110). This method is not meant to be an arbitrary one; it is suggested to help the reader understand sentence relationships and the value of the pause.

Analysis of the Author's Means of Emphasis. In order to understand the writer's thoughts and to interpret them to others, the reader must study each selection to observe the methods used by the author to stress words, phrases, or sentences in order to emphasize some ideas and to subordinate others. He may emphasize a thought by stating it in the first or topic sentence. He may rely on repetition, invert the normal word order, use contrast, or utilize the techniques of onomatopoeia and alliteration to affect the sounds of the words he uses.

TOPIC SENTENCES. A topic sentence is one which expresses the central idea of a paragraph. Its position in the paragraph may vary, but it is usually the first sentence. The general idea contained in the topic sentence may then be developed by using definitions, by explaining particulars and details, by giving examples or typical instances, or by offering analogies and comparisons.

REPETITION. Examples of emphasis by repetition may be seen in the use of the word *bells* in Poe's poem *The Bells* or in these lines spoken by Shylock in Shakespeare's *Merchant of Venice:*

> I'll have my bond; speak not against my bond:
> I have sworn an oath that I will have my bond.
>
> I'll have my bond; I will not hear thee speak:
> I'll have my bond; and therefore speak no more.
>
> I'll have no speaking: I will have my bond.

WORD ORDER. Changing the usual word order of subject, verb, and object will also accentuate an idea. An effective use of this type of emphasis is found in these lines from *Snow-Flakes* by Henry Wadsworth Longfellow:

> Over the woodlands brown and bare,
> Over the harvest-fields forsaken,
> Silent, and soft, and slow
> Descends the snow.

ONOMATOPOEIA AND ALLITERATION. *Onomatopoeia* refers to the use of words, such as *buzz, hiss, cuckoo,* and *whippoorwill,* whose sounds suggest their meanings. The ice in *The Rime of the Ancient Mariner* "cracked and growled, and roared and howled." *Alliteration* refers to the repetition of the same sounds at the beginning of two or more successive words. Frank Dempster Sherman's "Who makes this mimic din in this mimic meadow inn?" is an example of alliteration.

CONTRAST. Emphasis may be achieved by pointing out the opposite or negative aspects. In the opening lines of *A Tale of Two Cities,* Dickens used contrast to dramatize the setting for his story:

> It was the best of times, it was the worst of times, it was the age of wisdom, it was the age of foolishness, it was the epoch of belief, it was the epoch of incredulity, it was the season of Light, it was the season of Darkness, it was the spring of hope, it was the winter of despair, we had everything before us, we had nothing before us. . . .

Analysis of the Author's Mood. The mood of a selection may depend upon the rhythm of the author's words or sentences, and his choice of words to emphasize particular sounds. However, in order to capture the mood of the material, the oral reader must transcend the literal definitions of words and the careful planning of phrases and emphasis. He must understand and appreciate the emotional, spiritual, and psychological aspects of the work he seeks to interpret. Oral reading, like music, is a highly creative art, representing a synthesis of intellect and imagination. The end result of effective oral interpretation is the projection of the author's thoughts, heightened by the reader's ability to penetrate into the inner recesses of the author's mood.

USE OF RHYTHM. The author may achieve a specific mood in either poetry or prose by the rhythm of his words and sentences. A mood of suppressed rage permeates the rhythm as well as the imagery of *The Mirror of the Sea* by Conrad:

> Awful and threatening scowls darken the face of the West Wind in his clouded, south-west mood; and from the King's throne-hall in the western board stronger gusts reach you, like the fierce shouts of raving fury to which only the gloomy grandeur of the scene imparts a saving dignity. A shower pelts the deck and the sails of the ship as if flung with a scream by an angry hand, and when the night closes in, the night of a south-westerly gale, it seems more hopeless than the shades of Hades. The south-westerly mood of the great West Wind is a lightless mood, without sun, moon, or stars, with no gleam of light but the phosphorescent flashes of the great sheets of foam that, boiling up on each side of

the ship, fling bluish gleams upon her dark and narrow hull, rolling as she runs, chased by enormous seas, distracted in the tumult.[1]

In the following excerpt from Arthur O'Shaughnessy's *Ode,* there is a glimpse of inspiration in the rhythmic pattern:

> And out of a fabulous story
> We fashion an empire's glory:
> One man with a dream, at pleasure,
> Shall go forth and conquer a crown;
> And three with a new song's measure
> Can trample an empire down.

Note the somber effect of rhythm in I Corinthians 13:1–2:

> Though I speak with the tongues of men and of angels, and have not charity, I am become as sounding brass, or a tinkling cymbal. And though I have the gift of prophecy, and understand all mysteries, and all knowledge; and though I have all faith, so that I could remove mountains, and have not charity, I am nothing.

The essential rhythm or meter of a selection cannot be separated from the dominant mood. The reader should feel the rhythm as he studies his selection for colorful words, imaginative symbols, and skillful use of sounds.

CHOICE OF WORDS. Arthur Machen, in his novel *The Hill of Dreams,* has shown, in a brief but highly concentrated paragraph, the task of the author. He writes of his protagonist, Lucian:

> Language, he understood, was chiefly important for the beauty of its sound, by its possession of words resonant, glorious to the ear, by its capacity, when exquisitely arranged, of suggesting wonderful and indefinable impressions, perhaps more ravishing and further removed from the domain of strict thought than the impressions excited by music itself. Here lay hidden the secret of suggestion, the art of causing sensation by the use of words.

If the task of the writer is to "cause sensation by the use of words," the duty of the oral reader is overwhelmingly to share these sensations and, if possible, to heighten them by the effectiveness of his communication.

[1] Joseph Conrad, *The Mirror of the Sea* (Doubleday & Co., 1928), p. 85.

In preparing a selection, the reader should note not only the words the author has used but also the sounds that recur and help to create a mood. Long vowels and long diphthongs as well as continuant consonants are especially effective in creating and sustaining mood. In Shelley's *A Dirge* the recurrent continuants conjure up a mood of melancholy which may have been induced primarily by the title:

> Rough wind, that moanest loud
>   Grief too sad for song;
> Wild wind, when sullen cloud
>   Knells all the night long;
> Sad storm, whose tears are vain,
> Bare woods, whose branches strain,
> Deep caves and dreary main,—
>   Wail, for the world's wrong!

The following excerpt from *The Princess* by Tennyson also makes marked use of continuant consonants, long vowels, and long consonants. The mood is subdued, but not actually one of melancholy. There is a quality of grandeur present.

> The splendor falls on castle walls
>   And snowy summits old in story:
> The long light shakes across the lakes,
>   And the wild cataract leaps in glory.
> Blow, bugle, blow, set the wild echoes flying,
> Blow, bugle; answer, echoes, dying, dying, dying.

Methods for Indicating Pause and Stress. Punctuation, of course, serves as one guide for phrasing in oral presentation, but visual devices, especially in the early stages of preparation of the material, are helpful in telling the reader where to pause and which words to stress.

Since the long double bar (‖) is the symbol used in music to indicate a long pause, it may also be used to indicate a long pause in reading. A short double bar (‖) may then be used to indicate a short pause. A variety of methods may be used to indicate stress. The underlining of words is one effective guide. If a single line is used for ordinary stress, a double line may be used for very strong stress. Some readers prefer to place a mark over the stressed word rather than under it. Whichever method is decided upon should be used consistently, but no method should be a mechanical substitute for thinking of the meaning at the moment of reading the passage.

The following paragraph from Shelley's *Defense of Poetry* is marked to indicate pauses and stress. In preparing a manuscript for oral presentation, the reader may find it helpful to double or triple space so that sentence relationships may be seen clearly.

"Poetry is not like reasoning, || a power to be exerted || according to the determination of the will. || A man cannot say, || 'I will compose poetry.' || The greatest poet even cannot say it; || for the mind in creation is as a fading coal || which some invisible influence, || like an inconstant wind, || awakens to transitory brightness; || this power arises from within, || like the colour of a flower || which fades and changes as it is developed, || and the conscious portions of our nature are unprophetic || either of its approach or its departure. || Could this influence be durable || in its original purity and force, || it is impossible to predict the greatness of the results; || but when composition begins, || inspiration is already on the decline, || and the most glorious poetry that has ever been communicated to the world || is probably a feeble shadow || of the original conceptions of the poet." ||

PRESENTATION OF THE MATERIAL

The present chapter, so far, has placed emphasis upon the preparation of material—upon the necessity of understanding the author's words, of analyzing his thoughts, and of feeling his mood. Actual presentation of the material before an audience is not merely a matter of reading aloud. In addition to the vocal requirements and techniques for effective reading, oral interpretation may involve the use of physical aids, such as lighting, special clothes (some readers use costumes and make-up to help to create atmosphere), gestures, and stage props.

Vocal Aids to Oral Interpretation. The reader's skillful use of the pause and stress, and the variety of the pitch and intonation of his voice will help immeasurably to convey the mood and meaning of the material. Tempo, pitch, volume, and quality should be varied to suit the character. Obviously, the vocal quality used for a character must be consistent throughout the reading, especially in the reading of dialogue.

THE PAUSE. The main purposes of the pause are to indicate units of thought to the listeners and to give the oral reader an opportunity to get sufficient breath to continue and to attain a full understanding of the next unit of thought. There are other reasons for the pause, but they are concerned primarily with the audience rather than with the reader.

Kinds of Pauses. There are many different kinds of pauses. Some of the most widely used varieties follow. The pause that gives the listener an opportunity to think, the "meditative pause," an example of which occurs in these lines by King Richard in Shakespeare's *Richard II:*

> I wasted time, ‖ and now doth Time waste me; ‖
> For now hath Time made me his numbering clock. ‖

The "logical pause," which separates one thought from another, as in these lines by Brutus in Shakespeare's *Julius Caesar:*

> You shall not in your funeral speech blame us, ‖
> But speak all good you can devise of Caesar, ‖
> And say you do't by our permission; ‖

Another kind of pause is the one used with parenthetical material which requires a pause before and after the parenthesis to set the information apart. A parenthesis may be a single, relatively unimportant word, or it may be a phrase or sentence the author uses to heighten the effect of his material. The pause used around the parenthesis, therefore, may vary from logical ones before and after a word like *however* to "dramatic pauses" as in the following lines of Antony from *Julius Caesar:*

> Over thy wounds now do I prophesy, ‖
> Which, ‖ like dumb mouths, ‖ do ope their ruby lips, ‖
> To beg the voice and utterance of my tongue: ‖

There is still another pause, generally of an impressive nature, found in the following lines from Kipling's *Recessional:*

> Lord God of hosts, ‖ be with us yet, ‖
> Lest we forget ‖ —lest we forget! ‖

Length of Pauses. To give rules governing the exact length of pauses is impossible. Pauses vary with the rate of the speaker's speech and with the type of material he is reading. In poetry where there is a definite rhyme scheme, pauses must naturally follow the rhythm of the line. In prose and in poetry that does not have a definite rhythmic pattern, pauses must be used at the discretion of the reader. Too frequent or overlong pauses should be avoided. They tend to make reading monotonous; whereas variety in pause vitalizes the material.

The pause in reading may be compared with the one in music. When an organist is playing, the listener knows that more music is coming even when no note is actually being played. This type may be called a *live* pause. If, however, a speaker pauses and the audience decides he has finished, although he had no intention of stopping, the pause is called a *dead* pause—a detriment to any reader. The careful planning of pauses and the effective use of breath will help to keep pauses alive and audiences aware that something more is coming.

EMPHASIS. One of the most important tools in oral reading is proper emphasis. In preparatory reading words should be selected for stress in oral presentation. When words are strongly accentuated, they have *primary* stress; when they are slightly emphasized, they have *secondary* stress. There must, of course, be a corresponding weakening of unimportant words such as articles, conjunctions, pronouns, prepositions, and connectives.

Emphasis may be achieved by varying the force or volume of voice. In the famous speech of Marullus in *Julius Caesar,* for example, there is great variety between the opening explosive questions:

> Wherefore rejoice? What conquest brings he home?
> What tributaries follow him to Rome
> To grace in captive bonds his chariot-wheels?

and the closing lines, hushed with awe at the magnitude of the perfidy of the people:

> Run to your houses, fall upon your knees,
> Pray to the gods to intermit the plague
> That needs must light on this ingratitude.

PITCH. Another device that aids in communicating ideas and emotions is change of pitch. While there is a dominant pitch in every voice, there is also sufficient range in each voice so that adaptations may be made, depending upon the material to be read. The expression of grief, for example, would demand a lower pitch than that of joy or patriotism. Low pitch usually denotes sadness, meditation, or a solemn occasion, while high pitch indicates fear or hysteria. Gaiety is expressed by varied pitch which runs the whole range of the speaker's voice and has the effect of laughter.

Pitch should provide the clue to the mood in all reading, as it does in conversation. Whether the speaker is angry, scornful, cheerful, or argumentative, the pitch of his voice should convey the emotion, even if the words he is saying cannot actually be heard.

INTONATION. The glide of a voice from one pitch to another, intonation, is an important factor in communication. There are three kinds of intonation: rising, falling, and circumflex. (Examples of these patterns appear on pages 182–183.)

Physical Aids to Oral Presentation. The use of physical aids depends upon the selection to be read, the type of stage, and the personality of the reader.

FACIAL EXPRESSION. The facial expression of the oral reader should be in accordance with the nature of his material. A serious or tragic excerpt should not be read with a smiling or cheerful countenance, nor should a gay or humorous selection be read with a serious expression. The raising of the eyebrows, or the movement of the eyes and lips may be very effective in conveying emotions. The inexperienced reader would do well to practice in front of a mirror. It should be noted, however, that the use of facial mannerisms may interfere with the communication of the idea he is striving to convey if they are inappropriate or exaggerated.

GESTURES. Bodily action should be kept at a minimum. Actors or impersonators may make full use of bodily action, but oral readers must depend primarily on the voice for interpretation. A general rule to observe in connection with gestures is to use them only when they grow out of the material and when the reader feels at ease in using them. If he is self-conscious about using gestures, he will cease to communicate effectively, and his audience will immediately sense this break in his trend of thought.

READING STAND. If a lectern, or reading stand, makes reading easier and provides better lighting, one should be used. If the reader feels uncomfortable with a lectern, he should dispense with it. He should, however, practice working with and without a lectern, since one will not always be available with every stage or for every type of audience situation.

STANCE. The kind of occasion and the seating arrangement of the audience will indicate whether the reader should stand or remain seated during the reading. Audibility is the first criterion. If he can project his voice sufficiently and is more comfortable when seated, he may remain seated.

Whether he stands or is seated, he should hold his material high enough to read over it with ease and without distracting his audience. He should avoid turning pages noisily or fumbling with them, especially if he uses a loud speaker, which will accentuate each sound.

Exercises

1. Assume that you have been asked to prepare an hour program of oral readings for a club or group of which you are a member. Indicate your selections; justify your choices in the light of your prospective audience.

2. Make a list of the words and allusions that you will need to investigate from the materials selected in the preceding exercise.

3. After you are satisfied that you know the denotation and connotation of the words, prepare the material for oral reading, indicating stress and pauses.

4. Discuss the methods the authors used to achieve clarity in communicating their ideas.

5. Analyze the methods used to build up moods in the respective selections.

9

Dramatics

This chapter purposes to inform amateur acting groups about some of the problems involved in play production and to aid them in organizing efficiently their time and efforts. It is divided into two parts, one on full-scale stage production, the other on group play reading.

VOCAL TRAINING FOR DRAMATICS

The role of voice and speech in acting cannot be overestimated. The actor must transmit the actual words of the dramatist to his audience; indicate subtle and significant meanings through inflections; convey the age, social position, mood, and any other essential qualities about the character; set the mood the dramatist wants to permeate his work; and provide sufficient variety to portray changes in character and mood through control of voice and accuracy of speech.

Accurate production of sounds is not satisfactory unless these sounds can be heard. The exercises for breathing in Chapter 12 are especially important to increase volume and to provide variety in range and pitch. Other essential exercises in the same chapter include those for flexibility of the lips, tongue, and palate.

In order to modify his own speech or to prepare for dialect parts, the actor will find a thorough study of the sounds of English indispensable to his craft. (An analysis of English sounds will be found in Chapters 13 through 17.) Depending on the degree to which he wishes to utilize foreign languages for dialect purposes, a study of comparative phonetics will likewise be extremely useful. Narrow transcription is recommended for this purpose.

STAGE PRODUCTION

A dramatic production, no matter how simple, is the result of group activity and collaboration. Every production requires a vast number of decisions, ranging from the placement of furniture to the interpretation of the play as a whole. In order to ensure a maximum of efficiency, the dramatics group should establish some kind of working organization among the members as soon as possible.

The Dramatic Group and Its Organization. In actual practice, especially in amateur dramatics, one person may perform many functions, such as acting, designing part of the scenery, and helping with the publicity—all for the same play. Such duties will usually be assigned by members of the production staff.

THE PRODUCTION STAFF. The following organization plan is flexible and may be changed to conform with a large or small production. A three-act play with several scenes would naturally involve a larger production staff than a one-act play with no change in scene. Regardless of the size of the show, a detailed plan of procedure is feasible in that it ensures production efficiency and gives tasks to those who have no desire to act or for whom suitable parts are unavailable.

The Director. The director is responsible for the ultimate production of the play. All final authority concerning rehearsals and the performance is vested in him. During rehearsals, he should check all speech, noting especially the uniform pronunciation of proper names occurring in the text. He should also verify the consistency of dialects throughout the play.

Assistant Directors. The elaborateness of the production naturally determines the number of assistants. Their duties are dictated by the director.

Business Manager. The business manager handles advertising, programs, tickets, and funds.

Stage Manager. Mechanical aspects of the production are under the supervision of the stage manager. He is in charge of the stage crew, which ordinarily includes carpenters, electricians, scenery movers, and curtain men.

Property Man. The property and material used in furnishing the stage are under the control of the property man. He is also responsible for the return of all such equipment to the proper places.

Wardrobe Custodian. All costumes are issued by, and returned to, the wardrobe custodian.

Script Holder. The task of the script holder is to prompt the actors if they forget their lines.

Make-up Man. While many professional actors make themselves up, amateur groups frequently employ the services of a make-up man, especially for character make-up.

COMMITTEE ORGANIZATION. Sometimes all the members of a dramatics group may be included in a production. In order to utilize as many participants as possible, some kind of committee organization should be instituted as early as possible to take care of all details.

Such an organization would include separate committees to handle various production problems. There might be a tryout committee to aid in selecting the cast; another to keep players informed of rehearsal schedules; and a third in charge of lighting. A committee could also be formed to submit plans for costumes and scenery, with a subsidiary group assigned the responsibility for rented or borrowed costumes and property. Other members might be assigned to be in charge of the wardrobe, make-up, publicity, or other backstage duties.

Selection of a Play. One of the most difficult problems facing the amateur dramatics group is the selection of a play. There are many factors to be considered. Is the play worth producing? Is the theme a worthy one? Will it have sufficient appeal to the potential audience? If the play is to be one of a series, where will it fit in most effectively, and what will be its relation to the other plays being produced the same year? Can it be financed within the prospective budget?

Variety is important, especially for amateur groups. A program too heavy in tragic works or plays of social consciousness might well discourage subscribers. An audience that would be charmed by Zona Gale's *Miss Lulu Bett* or Sir James Barrie's *What Every Woman Knows,* or Campbell's adaptation of *The Enchanted April* might have little interest in Maxim Gorki's *The Lower Depths,* Gerhart Hauptmann's *The Weavers,* or Eugene O'Neill's *The Iceman Cometh,* especially if such plays were not well interspersed with comedy, farce, or melodrama.

SUITABILITY TO THE GROUP. After a play has been tentatively selected for the benefit of the audience, it must meet at least two tests before it is finally agreed upon as the best vehicle for a specific dramatics group. The director must understand and like the play or he will not be able to do justice to it. There should be at least one possible actor for each role. Miscasting of even one important role can do much to interfere with the success of a play.

PROBLEMS OF STAGE SETS. A play having a number of shifts of scene may be impractical from two points of view: first, the changes of set are too expensive; second, too much time is required to shift the sets, even if the problem of expense were overcome. An unduly long wait between scenes or acts is sure to lessen audience interest.

Cycloramas, or draped backgrounds, may help to cut the cost of sets and to improve generally the efficiency of scene shifting. From a point of view of expenditure of time, effort, and money, plays with but one set throughout may be more desirable than those with many changes.

PROBLEMS OF ROYALTIES. Before a production is finally decided upon, it is well to find out the cost of the royalty. In general, authors and dramatic agents are sympathetic toward amateur productions, and a reasonable consideration may be granted if extensive royalties cannot be paid. Public performance of a play without permission of the copyright owner constitutes copyright infringement and subjects the unauthorized performer to a claim of damages. Copyright in the United States protects the author for twenty-eight years and may be renewed only once. After the copyright has expired, the play goes into public domain; that is, it may be appropriated by anyone for use without the payment of a royalty fee.

The unexpectedness of royalty charges can be very disconcerting. Prices for the use of works by some authors may be consistently forbiddingly high, as in the case of George Bernard Shaw. Other authors vary tremendously in their fees. Sometimes, a well-known play is easily obtainable at no cost whatever, whereas an obscure play by the same author may be very expensive.

Details of royalty charge and payment should be ascertained from the publisher very early in the consideration of a play. If the matter is put off until rehearsals have started and everyone is eager to produce the play in question, the disappointment will be great if the royalty rate turns out to be prohibitive. To withdraw from the enterprise after publicity has been arranged presents an even more difficult problem.

THE VALUE OF ONE-ACT PLAYS. For amateur groups especially, one-act plays offer many advantages. Because of their brevity, two to four one-act plays may be presented in the time usually required for one full-length play. Such a program provides variety for the audience as well as for the acting group. More actors can be given parts in an evening of one-act plays than in the usual three-act play.

Actors may play roles for which they are best suited. If, for example, an actor likes to play tragedy, he may find a suitable part in a one-act play, whereas if his group is producing a three-act comedy, he may have to wait for another selection or play a role in which he is not primarily interested. Moreover, actors who wish to develop a range in acting and voice may do so most advantageously by playing in a variety of one-act plays.

THE VALUE OF CLASSICS AND OLD FAVORITES. Amateur dramatics groups would do well to consider Shakespearean plays as well as those of Sheridan and other authors in the public domain. There is probably no better source than Shakespeare for all kinds of speeches. Few authors provide such range in lines and such variety in emotions. The success several years ago of the modern-dress *Hamlet* and *The Taming of the Shrew* shows that Shakespeare is not dependent upon elaborate settings and costumes.

Participation in the plays of Shakespeare, of Sheridan, of the Greek dramatists (in translation), or of early Spanish dramatists such as Lope de Vega provides a richness of dramatic background that adds to the stature of the actor.

Preparation of the Text. Before rehearsals begin, the director should make all necessary changes in the text of the play. Plays that are overlong should be cut; objectionable scenes should be removed; lines that would antagonize a community or a local audience should be deleted. Occasionally, especially when plays have been cut, changes have to be made in the sequence of scenes. Such alterations should obviously be made well in advance so that the cast does not spend time in memorizing cues or in rehearsing material that is later changed or deleted.

Selection of the Cast. In some organizations the director alone selects the cast; in others, a committee of from three to five members, including the director, may make the final choice. For large amateur groups, the device of having a double cast is advantageous in that the casts may alternate in public performances. Because of the extra work involved for the director, an assistant director should be provided for the second cast.

Whether the cast is selected by a director or by a committee, the usual procedure is to call interested actors for tryouts. They are then assigned parts of the play to be interpreted. If sufficient time is given before the tryout, the actors may be required to memorize the part; if not, they may be asked to read selected parts.

CANDIDATE'S PHYSICAL SUITABILITY. In selecting a cast, the director or committee has to keep in mind more than the acting ability of the prospective actors. Height, weight, movement, and general appearance all enter into the suitability of an actor for a specific part. A girl who could be an excellent Juliet might lack the physical qualifications for a Lady Macbeth, while an actor who could play an acceptable Falstaff might be ludicrous as Abraham Lincoln.

CANDIDATE'S ACTING AND VOCAL ABILITIES. The candidate's acting and reading abilities should be revealed during the tryouts. If the role contains more than one mood, the candidate should be required to read a typical scene for each mood. Pantomime tests are sometimes given in order to test the candidate's power to express silently some particular emotion.

The actor's voice should conform to the role he is to play. He must be able to achieve variety in volume, pitch, tempo, and quality. Above all, he must be heard, not only in the first row of the orchestra but also in the last row of the balcony.

Analysis of the Play. Prior to rehearsals, there should be group studies of both characters and situations inherent in the play and of the relationships of the various characters to the plot. Such study and interpretation may require several meetings. As a rule, the author does not provide much character analysis. Instead, he shows the *effect* of characters on each other. Sometimes he shows the growth or development of characters, but he leaves to the actor the interpretation of their psychology. This technique makes many demands on the imagination of the actor. The character must be, from the minute the actor begins to interpret him until the final production of the play, as vivid as a close friend.

If the play is a historical one, the actor should check pictures and descriptions and legends about the character. In some plays of a highly imaginative nature, the actor must create the character from the statements other characters make about him without further help from the author. At any rate, if he is to re-create the character, the actor must be prepared to read and re-read the play as many times as are necessary to enlighten him about his specific part.

The Problem of Impersonation. After the the actor has analyzed the character he is to portray and has projected him imaginatively, he may begin his interpretation. The final problem involved here is one of impersonation. No other phase of speech activity calls on the resources of the speaker to the extent that impersonation does. This activity involves imagination, emotional response to a situation, and the ability to translate the attitudes, virtues, and faults of another into voice, posture, gestures, and even processes of thought.

THE NEED FOR UNDERSTANDING THE CHARACTER. An actor must have a very clear idea as to the appearance of the character he is impersonating, his mannerisms, and, in short, every aspect of his personality. He must know the age of the character; whether he is given to fatigue which affects his posture; how he walks; whether his facial expression is pleasant, gloomy, or sardonic; whether he is meek or domineering, shy or aggressive; the quality of his voice and the speed of his speech; his physical characteristics—whether he is tall or short, handsome or plain; whether he has any specific marks of identification, such as a physical handicap or a birthmark, and his reaction to these features.

While proper make-up well applied may help an actor in his appearance, the art of impersonation is more than merely appearing to be tall or short, halt or blind. The actor must perform in a certain way to give the illusion he wants to create about his character; he cannot rely on mere externals. For example, in order to appear short, he may assume poses in which he peers up at others in the cast.

THE NEED FOR "KEEPING IN CHARACTER." The phrase "keeping in character" is applied to the need for the actor to maintain all the traits of the character he is impersonating as long as he is in front of the audience. Frequently, even when the play is over and the cast comes out for a curtain call, actors manage to sustain the mood of the character until the final curtain has fallen.

An important point to remember in connection with impersonation is that the actor must keep in character during the entire play, whether or not he is speaking. Any unevenness in this regard will stamp him an amateur immediately. The inability to keep in character through the non-speaking moments of the play is a sign of inexperience and implies a lack of ability to project the character sufficiently. Sometimes a play seems to be good in spots but poor as a whole because the characters have not been able to sustain the mood of the impersonation.

Rehearsals. Although professional groups may prepare for public presentation in much less time, amateurs generally require from six to eight weeks for an ordinary full-length play. Regular rehearsals should each last three hours, if possible. Shorter periods are inefficient, and longer ones may prove too tiring, especially for amateurs. The number of rehearsals will depend on the complexity of the play and the experience of the cast. With amateurs, from twenty to thirty three-hour rehearsals will be necessary.

INITIAL REHEARSALS. Some directors like to devote time during the first and even sometimes during the second rehearsal to the reading of the play without any attempt at action. Other directors begin the first rehearsal with a detailed explanation of the set, showing sketches and ground plans and identifying each piece of furniture and each door and window. The actors then are grouped and read their lines, following any suggestions given them by the director. Not very much movement occurs during the first rehearsal.

About two-thirds of the first rehearsal should be devoted to the first act; during the last third of the time, the act should be run through again quickly. The purpose of this repetition is to fix in the actor's memory what he has learned. It also serves as an opportunity for the director to note and list the principal remaining problems. These he endeavors to solve by the time of the next rehearsal. The second rehearsal is devoted to the first act, with repetition toward the end of the rehearsal period.

By the time of the third rehearsal, actors are not permitted to use their scripts, no matter how much they have to be prompted.

Many amateurs make the mistake of memorizing immediately, sometimes before they are really clear on the exact interpretation of the lines. After they have once memorized lines, they may have difficulty in changing their interpretation.

By the time of the fourth rehearsal, actors should be expected to know all the lines of the first act and have an adequate idea of all action patterns. A similar process should be followed for rehearsals four through nine for the other acts, with intensive rehearsal of the especially difficult scenes, of mob scenes, and of mechanical aspects such as lighting, properties, and sets. In addition to these formal rehearsals, there will need to be private conferences with the director and rehearsals with individuals or small groups of the cast in order to ensure proper co-ordination of all members of the group.

LATER REHEARSALS. During the next three or four rehearsals, details are added in business and movement; groupings and poses are refined; dull scenes are enlivened; and any other unsatisfactory procedures are corrected.

Technical rehearsals may be necessary if the play involves many scene shifts or other technical problems. Some of the time of later rehearsals must be spent on technical problems such as those relating to costumes, make-up, light and sound cues, and the use of complicated props.

There are generally a few rehearsals devoted to the pacing of scenes. The director has usually noted where more speed is necessary, where different grouping will change effects, where increased numbers of actors or greater movement will accelerate the pace. Such additions cannot always be made until the play is running smoothly in rehearsal.

The last few rehearsals are run through without breaks except at intermissions. Between the acts, members of the cast are told of the latest criticisms and suggestions of the director. These rehearsals are called polishing rehearsals, as they give the play its final polish and do much to assure smooth performances.

DRESS REHEARSALS. At least two days before the final performance is scheduled, a dress rehearsal should be held with the sets, properties, and furnishings the same as they will be in the final performance. No detail should be unchecked. The dress rehearsal should not exceed five hours at any one time. At least two such rehearsals are necessary; three are better, and more may be desirable if the production presents special problems in lighting or scenery or costume changes.

Mechanics of Production. Various problems in the mechanics of production are fairly constant, no matter how simple or how elaborate the production is to be. In so far as possible, problems in mechanics should be worked out immediately after the play has been selected.

THE PROMPT BOOK. The prompt book is a necessity for the director and should contain everything that is said or done in the entire production. Some directors prefer two prompt books, one for diagrams of the sets and lighting plans, and one for lines.

Prompt books should be kept at hand during rehearsals so that if changes are decided upon, they may be entered immediately. The prompter must be trained as carefully as anyone in the cast, if he is to be relied on to cue efficiently.

The prompter checks each player a page in advance of his entrance. Any offstage business, such as distant thunder, is also indicated a page or so in advance in order that the proper signal may be given. When difficult scenes are involved, the wisest procedure is to have two or more prompters available.

COSTUMES. One of the principal ways of conveying to the audience the nature of the character, the situation, and the play is through the use of appropriate costumes. Not only should the costumes indicate whether the play is a romantic farce or a tragedy, but they should also show the relationships of the characters to the play and to one another. Opponents, for example, may contrast violently in costume, whereas other characters may show harmony by proper blending of color and line. Whenever a costume is selected or designed, it is important to keep in mind the nature of the character, his age, his social position, his emotional state, and his activity at any specific moment in the production.

Each actor should learn as much as possible about the texture and quality of goods and materials, and the relationship of kinds of material to the type of play, and specifically, to the type of character. He should know that the stiffness and weight of a material determines the way it hangs and the kind of folds it makes. He should be aware of the devices of linking and interlining, which are used to imitate stiff materials at a lower cost.

He should consider the surface of material, not only for color but also for sheen and decoration. He should investigate the various kinds of cloth paint that are available to enrich materials. A knowledge of dyes and the comparative simplicity of their use is also important, for frequently, amateur groups can refurbish their costumes instead of buying new ones for each new play.

When a play is being considered for selection, the whole problem of costs of renting or procuring costumes should be studied. A dramatics group should build up a wardrobe from the donations of members and friends. If costumes are to be rented, application for them should be made as far in advance as possible. Measurement blanks may be obtained when application is made for the costumes. Arrangements should also be made with costuming houses regarding the use of costumes in dress rehearsals. Actors must have time to become accustomed to moving about in their costumes, particularly those that are very different from modern dress.

Care should be taken in the selection and grouping of colors, avoiding clashes not only in costumes but also in settings and in furniture. In order to ensure harmony, permanent settings and furnishings should be neutral in tone.

MAKE-UP. The main use of make-up is to lend characterization to the actor. If his own appearance does not fit the role, make-up may be used as a supplement. It is also designed to counteract lighting effects which may make some members of the cast look almost macabre.

Within limits, the face may be modelled with make-up in very much the same way that clay may be modelled with the fingers. By darkening the portions to be depressed and lightening the portions to be brought out, it is possible to change the contour of the face. Character lines are placed on the eyes or in the furrows in the brow; lines from the base of the nose and corners of the mouth represent age. Wigs and beards can ordinarily be rented from costume houses. The dressing of wigs, which should be of natural hair, should be entrusted only to a person with hairdressing experience.

When there is doubt about the use of make-up, it is preferable to use too little rather than too much. If used unwisely, make-up may ruin a play. Whenever it calls too much attention to itself, make-up, on stage as well as off, is artificial and objectionable.

Some make-up requires a great deal of time for application. Actors are therefore frequently asked to report at least two hours before the time scheduled for the dress rehearsal and the final production.

GROUP PLAY READING

Sometimes amateur groups find it impractical to present plays to the public. Perhaps the necessary equipment is lacking, or there is inadequate time for rehearsal. Frequently, there is not enough money for costumes and sets; and sometimes, the members of such groups are more interested in a group activity than in play production.

For such a group, the reading of a play may be a very rewarding dramatic experience. Reading a play is an excellent exercise for classes in speech and dramatics as well as for various amateur and community groups. Such a reading provides good training in the interpretation of lines and experience in voice range. Group reading may be done in a classroom, on the stage of an auditorium or theater with the curtain as backdrop, or in front of audiences without benefit of a stage.

The Reading Group and Its Organization. The organization of any reading group centers on the director. He is responsible for a careful study of the play or selection, including all the lines and the stage directions. He has to arrange the placing of the performers so that each may be clearly heard and entrances and exits may be made without confusion. He usually chooses the readers for all the roles, makes any adaptations in the script required because of deletion of scenes and dialogue, and takes charge of rehearsals.

Before the play is read to the audience, the director should give an introduction that will help those present to understand and enjoy the play. He should indicate briefly the setting for each act and should introduce each character. The person being introduced should stand and remain standing while the director gives a complete description of the age, appearance, and behavior of the character, as well as his part in the play. This process helps the audience to clarify its notion about each character. If the scene changes throughout the play, the director should give a description of each setting at the beginning of each act.

Selection of a Play. A play should be selected for reading with as much care as if it were to be produced and acted before a first-night audience. The elements of universal appeal found in all great literature should be inherent in the play. Since there are no theatrical costumes or sets, the readers must rely on their oral interpretations to give meaning to the performance. The play, therefore, must have fine literary quality that is well adapted to reading aloud. Plays that are read in groups must depend on the lines, the rhythm, and the dramatic effects of words rather than on action, for there is little action in the reading of a play.

Those plays which depend almost entirely on action for their effects and subsequent success are not suitable for group reading. Some plays, however, may be more effectively read than acted. Ibsen's dramas, especially the thesis plays such as *Enemy of the People* and *Ghosts;* Chekhov's *The Cherry Orchard* and *Uncle Vanya;* Thornton Wilder's *Our Town;* and the Greek tragedies, such as *Electra, Antigone, Trojan Women,* and *The Agamemnon,* offer excellent possibilities for group reading. Sometimes a chorus may be used during group reading to provide appropriate "action" or background in the form of music, sound effects, and responses.

Still another consideration in selecting a play for group reading is the number of readers required. Since this kind of reading is done in an informal room more frequently than on a stage, the characters should not exceed twelve; otherwise, confusion will result. Since the characters will not be wearing distinctive costumes or using stage make-up, the audience is likely to have difficulty in following the characterizations if too many actors are involved.

Preparation of the Text. If a play is too long, it should be cut to an appropriate length. An hour and a half to two hours should be the maximum time for play reading. One-act plays may be successfully used for group reading.

In order to reduce the number of characters in a play to be read, minor characters may be omitted more easily than they can in a stage production. Lines that are not necessary for the development of the plot, or characters that do not deal directly with the movement of the plot, should be deleted.

Selection of the Cast. The selection of readers is similar to the selection of a cast for a play. However, greater emphasis is placed on the age of the prospective reader, who, unlike the actor in a stage play, cannot rely on make-up or costumes to help to convey the age of the character. In both stage productions and group reading of plays, improvisations and deletions in scenes and dialogue may enable an all-male group to act or to read a play without having the female roles actually portrayed. The reverse, of course, is also true.

Analysis of the Play. An analysis of a play for group reading entails a careful study of the deleted sections as well as of the parts to be read. Some clue to a character or his reaction to another character may be found in a deleted passage. In a stage play, actual physical action may help to further the plot, but in a play interpreted orally, the activity is subordinated to the reading. Hence, great care must be taken to show the progression of plot through the use of voice alone.

The Problem of Impersonation. The problem of impersonation in a play that is read differs from the same problem in a stage production in that the director of the former assumes some of the responsibilities of the actor. He sets the stage by introducing the character and telling the audience the character's age, occupation, and other salient facts. The actor must then impersonate the character. In a stage play, the actor has sole responsibility for introducing and maintaining the role.

Rehearsals. The problem of rehearsals is much simpler in group play reading than in stage production. Group actors may read their assigned parts in private and appear for two, three, or perhaps four rehearsals with the group. The task of the director is to rehearse, introducing each act and scene as he will introduce them on the occasion of the final reading.

The Mechanics of Production. Whenever the play is to be read for an audience, a playbill which will enable it to have a better understanding of what is going on should be provided. An outline of the action scenes, with the setting of the play and the time and place of the action, should be included. A brief description of the characters also helps.

In preparing for a stage production, open-mindedness about the director's criticisms of interpretation, acceptance of his changes of mind, promptness at rehearsals, courtesy toward members of the cast, and the avoidance of all distractions when others are speaking are all evidence of good rapport and a mature attitude toward group endeavors. If the play has been conceived as a group project and has been directed and rehearsed with co-operation on the part of the cast, the final performance should show the results of fine teamwork.

Exercises

1. Select five plays that you think would be appropriate for production by some dramatics group to which you belong or which you know. Discuss problems of casting and producing in each play.

2. Assume that the plays named above are to be produced during the same season by the same group. In what order would you produce them? Justify your choices. Which would you replace if the plays were to be done in a series? Why? What replacements would you suggest?

3. Observe several rehearsals of an amateur play in a school or community group. What are the most serious problems that beset the cast?

4. Observe later rehearsals or dress rehearsals of the same group. To what extent have the problems indicated above been solved?

5. Select a play (comedy, tragedy, drama, melodrama, spectacle, farce) that you think would be satisfactory for reading to an audience. Justify your choice. Indicate the ways in which you would adapt this play to a two-hour time limit.

10

Speaking over the Air

To the present-day speaker, broadcasting is commonplace. The chances are that if he has to speak in public at all, he will eventually have to broadcast his remarks to a completely unseen audience. He may be called upon to speak from a radio or television station which may or may not have a studio audience, or he may address an immediate group of persons in a hall or auditorium while his remarks are broadcast to a much larger unseen audience.

THE GROWTH OF RADIO AND TELEVISION

Speaking over the air, though not a difficult technique, is a comparatively new one in the field of communications. The first radio broadcast, which concerned the Harding-Cox Presidential election returns, was made on July 7, 1920, from Station KDKA in Pittsburgh, Pennsylvania. Television was first used at the opening of the New York World's Fair in 1939 and featured an address by the late President Roosevelt. Network programming for television had its beginning on January 12, 1940, when the NBC station in New York and the General Electric station in Schenectady broadcast the first network telecast by use of high frequency radio relay link.

The amazing growth of both media is shown by the fact that as of November 1, 1952, there were 2,988 radio stations and 110 television stations. Moreover, authorization for 2,053 new television stations in 1,291 cities was given in 1952 by the FCC (Federal Communications Commission) when it ended its three-and-one-half-year ban on new television stations.

PROBLEMS IN SPEAKING OVER THE AIR

The rules and suggestions offered in this chapter refer mainly to speech problems encountered in talking over the air. Many of these principles are applicable in part to radio and television dramatics, newswriting, and commercials, but each of these fields of radio and television has additional tenets regarding preparation and presentation of material.

The Problem of Audience Relationship. One of the first tenets of any branch of public speaking is that the speaker should know as much as possible about his audience. Obviously, the speaker cannot know his radio or television listeners as thoroughly as he might understand a specially assembled group.

THE DIFFICULTY OF "KNOWING THE AUDIENCE." To know with any precision the age range, for instance, or the educational background, or sex, or interests of a radio audience is practically impossible. Whereas a "public speaker" addresses a stag party, a women's club, a student assembly, or a union meeting, the speaker who broadcasts may be addressing whole families. In spite of the fact that there are news programs of an adult nature, and children's programs, women's programs, comedy programs, and dramatic or literary programs that are limited in appeal, it is never entirely possible to know who is tuning in at any given time.

To some extent, the time of day of the broadcast determines the type of audience. In the daytime, more women listen than men; in the evenings and on week ends, the number of men listeners increases. The kind of station also helps to determine the audience. A merely local station, for example, provides an audience comprised of listeners in the immediate vicinity; a station connected with a network provides a more heterogeneous audience because it reaches a wider area.

THE DIFFICULTY OF JUDGING AUDIENCE REACTION. An experienced speaker in front of an audience can readily sense boredom, disagreement, or antagonism in his listeners. He can, if necessary, change his material, add a story, clarify a point, or in some other way get control of the group. The radio speaker can neither feel the boredom nor sense the growing hostility of his audience. Even a studio audience may not warn him of the reactions of the larger group of unseen listeners.

Audiences, even when they are bored or hostile, are in general reasonably polite to public speakers. They will frequently suffer through a speech rather than cause a disturbance. Radio and television audiences, however, have no compunction about tuning in another station or turning off the receiver in boredom or exasperation.

The Problem of Competition. The usual public speaker may have little competition for attention. A group has gathered for the specific purpose of hearing him. On the air, however, the speaker is faced with the realization not only that there is continuous competition, depending somewhat on the hour of the broadcast, but also that there are many families who are accustomed to hearing the same program week after week and who do not welcome an interruption in routine. If a speaker is broadcasting at a time when he competes with the program of a famous comedian, or with a popular soap opera, he may have a relatively small audience. Even if he does not compete with any such popular program, he may find that he is scheduled to appear at an hour when few listeners are available.

The Problem of Adhering to a Time Schedule. Ordinarily, public speakers or participants in group discussions in non-broadcast situations take too much time, especially if, in the latter case, the chairman is too polite to interrupt. Many speakers start a new speech every time they attempt to answer a question. This procedure is not possible on the air, since thirty seconds is the maximum leeway at the end of a program. The speaker who does run overtime is simply cut off the air. Such incidents are embarrassing and are usually indicative of the speaker's inexperience.

Since programs start punctually, a radio or television speaker should reach the station ahead of time so that he will not be out of breath when he starts to speak. All material should be rehearsed until it is perfectly timed. Allowance should be made for announcements, introductions, commercials, and applause or laughter from the audience. Rehearsals with an actual recording will help in this respect.

The speaker should also have a story or additional comments available so that, if in spite of his preparation he has spoken more rapidly than he had planned, he will not find himself in front of the microphone with one or two minutes left but with nothing to say. He should also mark material for deletion in the event that he is running overtime. One easy method of marking the manuscript for deletions is to use brackets around sentences and paragraphs that may be omitted without interfering with the continuity of the speech, discussion, or skit, and to place numbers in the margins as indicators to the marked passages. The speaker himself may decide which material to omit; but if more than one speaker or performer is involved in the program, the director or prompter (who should be carefully checking the time) should signal the number of the paragraph to be omitted.

The Problem of "Mike Fright." Inexperienced speakers on the air are sometimes unduly frightened by the microphone. Even some who are experienced still have feelings of "mike fright." Although there is no sure method for curing this condition, the speaker who prepares his material well and who keeps his mind on his topic should not be nervous after he has mastered the technique of using a microphone. The television speaker may find that the use of visual aids such as charts, maps, diagrams, and cartoons helps in decreasing his tension.

A tight voice, extremely rapid speech, the rustling of papers, and a nervous cough all indicate a lack of poise. The well-adjusted speaker will conceal from his audience any sign of tension and discomfort. Although he may prefer speaking to an interested and alert group instead of addressing an unseen audience, he is likely to find that practice will eventually enable him to perform adequately in spite of the microphone.

Many interviewers and masters of ceremonies on the air have developed techniques to minimize the nervousness of guests on radio and television. Some use the device of clowning sufficiently to have the studio audience and the guests join in laughter; some ask questions requiring monosyllabic answers until the guests seem to be at ease; others attract the attention of the audience and the guests to visual aids of one kind or another until the "ice is broken."

Actually, the techniques of voice control mentioned in Chapter 12 will help put the speaker at ease whether on or off the air. Deep breathing will take his mind off the problem of how he sounds and will give him an appearance of poise. As his self-consciousness lessens, he will feel and look better poised.

DIFFERENCES BETWEEN RADIO
AND TELEVISION SPEAKING

Both radio and television depend essentially on the voice and the ability of the speaker to read and to communicate well, but television is also concerned with posture, appearance, facial expressions, costumes, make-up, backdrops, lighting, and the effective use of cameras. Radio permits the voice to enter the listener's living room, but television enables the whole personality of the speaker to invade it.

The Use of Manuscripts. Radio speakers generally read from a manuscript, or at least refer to one during the program. Television broadcasters, however, must use their notes inconspicuously.

Because television has rapidly become the center of home entertainment, the speech used for it must be as informal as possible. To see a speaker read his material or to hear prompting would dispel illusions. Television producers have been hard pressed to find ways of meeting this problem, a serious one in the case of long speeches or difficult cues for actors.

While many devices, ranging from large hand-painted cards to a variety of concealed cues, have been tried, the most practical answer to the problem to date is the *Teleprompter*. This device, set at eye level of the performers, automatically unrolls a script whose inch-high letters, printed by special typewriter, can be read twenty-five feet away. Apart from its obvious use for the inconspicuous reading of lines, the Teleprompter has cut rehearsal time significantly, in some cases as much as twenty-five per cent, with a resultant saving in money.

Posture and Gestures. In an effort to appear informal and conversational, many speakers overlook the importance of good posture before the television camera. The speaker who slouches in his chair or leans forward so that his head is at an awkward angle or who shifts his weight too frequently from one foot to the other will end by distracting his audience and interfering with his communication. The speaker must look as though he were at ease, but not as though he were going to collapse. Practice before a full-length mirror will help to eradicate the most glaring faults of posture.

Another difference between radio and television performance is the factor of gestures and facial expressions. Mannerisms which may be accepted as part of the personality in public speech, and which may be harmless in a radio address, may ruin a television performance. Only those gestures which grow out of the material and help to communicate the idea should be used. Repetition of unnecessary facial and hand mannerisms detracts from the appearance of the speaker and may interfere seriously with his communicative powers.

SIMILARITIES BETWEEN RADIO
AND TELEVISION SPEAKING

Both radio and television require some speech and voice techniques that are essentially different from those for other forms of oral communication. Both also have some similar rules for form and content of material. The major pitfalls that beset the radio or television speaker are likely to be concerned with: (1) the use of voice, (2) familiarity with microphone techniques, (3) problems of articulation, (4) tempo, (5) the conversational approach, (6) the choice of words, and (7) sentence structure.

The Use of Voice. Novice speakers on the air should keep in mind that the loudness of the sound picked up by the microphone varies in geometric ratio to its distance from the source of the sound. In other words, the sounds picked up by the microphone at a distance of one foot will be four times as loud as those picked up at a distance of two feet, assuming that the same degree of force has been used initially. For this reason, the speaker should remain at the same distance from the microphone during his entire speech. Unless he varies the volume as he moves, his voice will be too loud or will fade annoyingly without any relationship to his subject matter.

Familiarity with Microphone Techniques. Familiarity with microphone techniques will help the speaker on the air analyze his own voice problems. If he has talked to large audiences, acted in large theaters, or sung in opera, he may have difficulty at first with the technique of breathing for the microphone. He cannot breathe so vigorously as he would when speaking from a platform in a large hall. He must learn not only to breathe more quietly than he would ordinarily in public address but also to avoid breathing directly into the microphone, so that the sound will not be unduly amplified. Frequency modulation (FM), in particular, picks up involuntary lip noises, swallowing, salivation, and marked inhalation of breath.

Problems of Articulation. Radio speech, like speech for all other occasions, should be clearly articulated, smooth in rhythm, and reasonably free from defects and marked regional dialects.

Slurring of medial consonants, as in *liddle* for *little,* and the omission of syllables, as in *probly* for *probably,* are especially disturbing on the air. The major objective is the communication of ideas. Speech that draws attention to itself detracts from such communication.

Tempo. The tempo of speech on the air should be comparable to that of ordinary conversation. It may help the speaker to visualize a specific group or person whom he wishes to reach in a purely conversational way. As in conversation, rate may vary with changes in subject matter, or, in the reading of lines from a play, with changes in characters.

The Conversational Approach. The speaker on the air must convey the impression that he is talking *with* his listeners, not talking *at* them. Because of the personal nature of radio and television, the speaker must use a conversational tone. He must use contractions and other weak forms. (See page 179.) If he substitutes strong forms, his speech will become stilted, and a barrier will be set up between him and his audience.

The Choice of Words. As in conversation, the words used in radio and television should be casual and not too difficult. The speaker on the air should never lose sight of the heterogeneity of his audience. He should not "talk down" to his listeners, but neither need he use words he would not ordinarily use in conversation. He should avoid abstract words and "glittering generalities," and if he must use technical terms or words, he should explain them clearly, preferably with concrete examples or definitions.

The speaker over the air should also avoid slang because it is usually trite and weakens his material. He should avoid blasphemy as a matter of good taste. He should not use foreign words and phrases that might be unknown to most of his listeners. Tongue twisters, that is, phrases and sentences that contain too many similar sounds, should be deleted or rewritten; the recurrence of sibilant sounds is especially distracting.

Sentence Structure. In speech on the air more than in other forms of address, simple sentences are essential. A long, complicated sentence is difficult for listeners to follow, while a short sentence is more conversational and, hence, easier to understand. There should, of course, be some variety in sentence structure because too many short sentences may give a staccato effect.

Special attention should be given to the opening sentence. This sentence serves as the bait to reach other minds and should therefore capture the attention of the radio audience. Moreover, because some members of the radio or television audience may tune in late, the major ideas should be restated occasionally during the speech, but not necessarily in the same words. The repetition of the central theme in the same words would obviously alienate many listeners who had heard the beginning of the speech. Restatement with variations and new meaning will hold interest.

PRACTICAL HINTS FOR SPEAKING OVER THE AIR

If a speaker on the air is to be effective, he must make each listener feel the impact of a personal message. In order to inspire this feeling, his voice should be conversational in tone and carefully modulated. He must also prepare the organization of his speech as well as rehearse the actual presentation. After the introductory remarks (which should have captured the listeners' attention), he should proceed according to a definite plan of development toward proof of his contentions.

Organization of the Speech. The ideas in a speech on the air should be limited to a few clearly worded ones that can be easily repeated and developed. The speaker should have a simply stated thesis with arguments and examples to substantiate it. He must forego introducing secondary topics or ideas because the limitations of time will prevent their full development and the chance of repeating them, and the speaker is likely to defeat his own purpose.

Perhaps the best check on the organization and development of a topic is the preparation of an outline with the main contentions and arguments clearly and concisely stated. Adherence to the outline will help to prevent rambling and digression by the speaker. The outline will also help in his use of transitions, which should be clear and informal. Outlining will also ensure a logical development, subordinating less important material.

Dramatic examples, stories containing a great deal of action, and incidents full of human interest are valuable assets to the radio speaker. He should avoid statistics and use word pictures in preference because the latter are more effective and less tiring to an audience. Figures have the same disadvantage that abstractions have; they are not sufficiently vivid for the casual listener. The speaker should also avoid a numerical order to stress his points. This device, which may be effective in writing and sometimes in public speaking, is likely to sound pompous or unfriendly or overly didactic on the air. Good transitions are especially necessary for clarity and continuity.

Preparations for Making the Speech. The radio speaker who wishes to be effective will take advantage of studio time for rehearsals at the broadcasting station. In addition, he will rehearse his material sufficiently so that it sounds as though it were being discussed casually with a group of friends rather than being read. Rehearsing radio material with friends can be very helpful. The reactions may disclose abstractions, rambling sentences, defects of structure, or too difficult a vocabulary. Three or four listeners provide a helpful group, but even one listener is better than no audience at all.

Recordings are extremely useful in order that the speaker may study the total effect of his presentation. He may be able to correct defects and then record again. Not only will he be able to judge his timing accurately, but he will also be able to note sentence structure, transitions from one idea to another, word choice, general informality, and the dull pauses that need to be improved for the final rendition.

The television speaker will do well to have recordings made of his material and, if possible, to have motion pictures made of his presentation. Many speakers are completely unaware of the fact that they are using gestures which are not related to content. Objective viewing of gestures and facial expressions in a motion picture may have the same effect as hearing one's voice objectively. Such a viewing may lead to the eventual eradication of distracting mannerisms.

Expensive equipment for recording is not necessary for the purpose of getting an overall effect of a speech. There are available a large number of tape or wire recorders that are inexpensive to operate and maintain.

In addition to organizing his speech and preparing for its delivery, the speaker should listen to other radio programs, especially on national networks. An analysis of the speakers who are popular will be rewarding, as will a study of the streamlining of material and the direct journalistic style employed by good radio speakers.

Exercises

1. Listen to three radio and three television broadcasts of a serious nature. Indicate the objectives of these programs, and evaluate the extent to which these objectives have been met.

2. Organize a discussion group for the appraisal of some controversial problems. Approximate the conditions of a broadcasting station in your final discussion.

3. Visit a local radio or television studio. Be prepared to discuss the actual problems involved in the production of a radio or television program.

4. Investigate the activities in radio and television for adult education groups in your community. Find out to what extent they are making use of radio and television programs.

5. List three radio programs and three television programs that you would be willing to recommend. State your reasons for recommendation in each case.

PART TWO

Speech Sciences

11

The Mechanisms of Speech and Hearing

Since the ability to *speak* correctly is closely allied with the ability to *hear* speech sounds correctly, students of speech should have a knowledge of the mechanisms of both speech and hearing. An understanding of the physiological processes involved in speaking and hearing requires a study of data from the specialized fields of neurology, anatomy, and physics.

This chapter provides a minimum knowledge and explains the necessary technical terms of this phase of speech. Students majoring in speech should also consult one or several of the comprehensive texts listed in the Tabulated Bibliography.

THE NERVOUS SYSTEM

A stimulus to speak may come from any environmental factor affecting the sense organs or from any thought processes of the speaker. Hearing is frequently the sensory activity which stimulates speech; an individual hears the question of another person and is stimulated to answer. Other sensations, such as those of sight, smell, and touch, may also constitute a speech stimulus.

These stimuli are received by the *sensory* branches of the nervous system and are conducted to the brain. The brain then interprets the stimuli, determines the ideas to be communicated by speech, and initiates the nerve impulses which control the speech mechanism. For example, the auditory nerve conducts the sensory nerve impulses from the ear to the brain, where recognition of the sound occurs.

The sensory branches which receive these various stimuli belong to the *peripheral* nervous system, which consists of the nerves extending from the brain and the spinal cord to the outlying parts of the body. The brain and the spinal cord belong to the *central* nervous system.

143

The Peripheral Nervous System. The peripheral nervous system is composed of *cranial nerves* and *spinal nerves*. The cranial nerves conduct sensory impulses from parts of the head and internal organs to the brain. The spinal nerves conduct sensory impulses from the arms, legs, and trunk of the body to the spinal

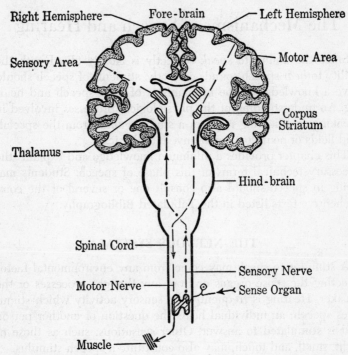

FIG. 1—Sectional view of the spinal cord and brain. The line of dots and dashes (− . − .) shows the pathway of a sensory impulse from a sense organ to the sensory area of one side of the brain. The broken-dash line (− − −) shows the pathway of a motor impulse from the motor area of one side of the brain to a group of muscles. These pathways exist on both sides of the brain and spinal cord, but are shown on one side here to simplify the diagram.

cord; *nerve fibers* in the spinal cord conduct those spinal nerve impulses to the brain.

The Central Nervous System. In the central nervous system, the brain receives and interprets the stimuli for speech. All stimuli are conducted over sensory nerve fibers to the *thalamus*, a junction point for sensory nerves located in the interior of the brain. Nerve impulses are then conducted to the various brain areas.

Each type of stimulus is received by a specialized area of the brain. Separate sensory areas exist for sight (visual area), sound (auditory area), smell (olfactory area), and touch (tactual and

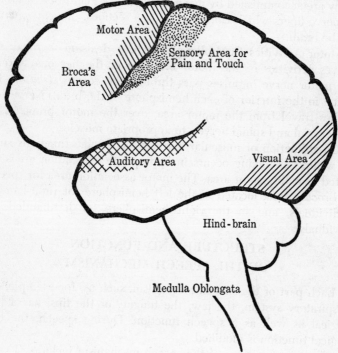

FIG. 2—Side view of the left hemisphere of the brain showing the location of sensory and motor areas.

kinesthetic area). Adjacent to these areas are *association areas*, where recognition and interpretation of the stimuli occur. For example, the sound of a person's voice is experienced as a sensation in the auditory area, but the recognition of the person's voice and the understanding of the meaning of the words occur in the auditory association area. After the recognition of the significance of any stimulus, the thought processes start in the frontal area, where the decision to speak takes place.

Sensations are produced in the brain on the side opposite the one where the stimulus originated. For example, sensations of sound affecting the left ear are produced in the right auditory area. Nerve impulses cross from one side of the body to the other in the spinal cord or lower parts of the brain before passing through the thalamus to the sensory areas of the brain. Co-ordination and integration of activities involving both sides of the body are accomplished by means of the *corpus callosum,* a group of nerve fibers which connects the two sections, or *hemispheres,* of the brain.

Motor Activities Controlling Speech. A decision to speak involves activities of the motor branches of the nervous system. All motor nerve impulses pass through the *corpus striatum,* located in the interior of each hemisphere of the brain. Nerve impulses travel from the motor area, over the motor branches of the cranial and spinal nerves, to appropriate muscles.

Co-ordination of muscular activity for specific functions such as writing or talking occurs in appropriate association areas located near the motor area. The motor association area for speech is *Broca's Area,* located in the left hemisphere for right-handed individuals, and in the right hemisphere for left-handed individuals.

STRUCTURE AND FUNCTION
OF THE SPEECH MECHANISM

Each part of the speech mechanism, such as, for example, the respiratory system, the jaw, the tongue, or the lips, has a biological as well as a speech function. During speech, the biological function is modified.

The main functions of the speech mechanism include (1) respiration, (2) phonation, (3) resonance, and (4) articulation.

Respiration. During respiration, air is inhaled or drawn into the lungs (*inhalation*) and is exhaled or forced out under pressure (*exhalation*). Biologically, the lungs are the chief organs of respiration and provide the necessary oxygen for the body. The release or interruption of the flow of air by the vocal cords in the larynx, lips, tongue, or parts of the throat during exhalation produces the speech sounds.

INHALATION. During inhalation the chest cavity is enlarged by the contraction of the chest muscles and the *diaphragm,* a large, dome-shaped muscle which separates the chest from the abdominal cavities. When the diaphragm contracts, it moves downward. Its downward movement compresses the visceral organs (stomach, liver, kidneys, etc.) and causes the abdominal walls to move outward. The rib arches move upward and outward. The capacity of the chest is increased in three directions: top to bottom, front to back, and side to side.

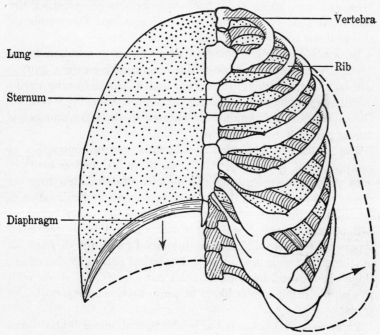

Fig. 3—Exposed view of the ribs, lungs, and diaphragm in resting (expiratory) positions. Broken-dash lines show the expansion of the ribs and diaphragm during inspiration and the increased capacity of the chest.*

The enlargement of the chest cavity decreases the air pressure in the lungs so that air rushes in to equalize the pressure. This process is controlled automatically by a nerve center in the brain —the *medulla oblongata* (see Fig. 2). When the blood passing through the medulla oblongata contains an excess of carbon dioxide, nerve impulses are sent to the muscles of inhalation. The muscles contract, and the lungs take in more oxygen.

EXHALATION. During normal quiet breathing, the process of exhalation is passive, involving only a relaxation of the dia-

* Reprinted with adaptations with permission of the publisher from *Fundamentals of Physiology* by Elbert Tokay, published by Garden City Books, 1944, page 90.

phragm and the chest muscles of inhalation. Relaxation permits the diaphragm to move upward and the ribs to move downward and inward. This movement decreases the size of the chest cavity, compresses the lungs, and forces the air out.

During speech, however, there is active muscular contraction. Muscles surrounding the abdomen contract, compressing the visceral organs and forcing the diaphragm up. These muscles also pull the ribs downward and inward.

BREATH CONTROL FOR SPEECH. The process of respiration differs during speech from the process during normal breathing. During normal quiet breathing, inhalation and exhalation occur rhythmically, approximately fourteen to sixteen times per minute. During speech, inhalations are shorter in duration and occur during pauses between phrases.

The muscles of inhalation remain in a state of contraction to prevent rapid exhalation. The muscles of exhalation contract with greater force, causing the muscles of inhalation to relax slowly and to compress the lungs. Proper control of exhalation is essential for the most effective production of the voice.

Experiments have shown that it makes little difference whether a person's type of inhalation is abdominal (with the diaphragm) or thoracic (with the chest). However, clavicular breathing (high chest breathing with shoulder movements) interferes with the supply of air and is likely to cause tension in the neck and throat.

Phonation. Phonation is the production of sound by the *vocal cords*, which are folds of muscle tissue located in the larynx. The *larynx*, the organ of voice, is the modified upper part of the *trachea*, the main trunk of the system of tubes by which air passes to and from the lungs. During phonation the vocal cords are moved together, and the pressure of air from the lungs sets them vibrating.

STRUCTURE OF THE VOCAL CORDS. The vocal cords, then, are the vibrators which produce speech sounds. Biologically, the vocal cords, which are completely relaxed during quiet breathing, are used as a valve to prevent foreign particles from entering the trachea and the lungs.

The vocal cords project into the larynx from each side. The larynx is composed of cartilages, muscles, and other body tissues. The cartilages form the structure to which the vocal cords and muscles are attached. The *thyroid cartilage,* the *cricoid cartilage,* and the *epiglottis* form the supporting structures of the larynx. The *arytenoid cartilages* are situated on top of the cricoid cartilage at the back of the larynx.

ACTION OF THE VOCAL CORDS. The *glottis,* the space between the vocal cords, is open during silence and closed during phona-

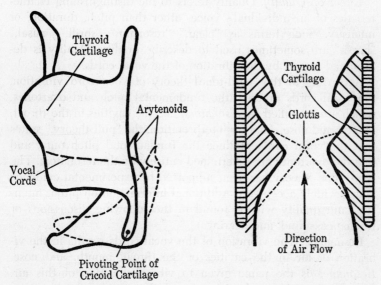

FIGS. 4, 5—At the left is a side view of the larynx. The dotted lines indicate the tilted position of the cricoid cartilage when the vocal cords are tensed. At the right is a sectional view of the larynx, showing the position of the vocal cords. Heavy lines describe the position of the cords when the glottis is open; dotted lines show their position during phonation.

tion. Muscles within the larynx move the vocal cords together so that the inner edges touch each other. The elastic nature of the vocal cords permits them to vibrate as the air is exhaled under pressure. Muscular action also controls the position and tension of the cords, which, in turn, influence the pitch, intensity, and quality of the voice.

Effect on Pitch. The pitch of the voice is determined primarily by the length, mass, and tension of the vocal cords. The relatively longer and thicker cords of the adult male produce a pitch level almost an octave lower than that of the adult female. Changes in muscular tension produce vocal inflection and pitch variation. Increased tension raises the pitch; muscular relaxation lowers it.

Effect on Intensity. The intensity (volume) of the voice is determined in part by the amplitude of vocal-cord vibration. In producing louder tones, the vocal cords vibrate with greater amplitude of movement than they do for softer tones.

Effect on Quality. Quality refers to the distinguishing characteristics of an individual's voice, other than pitch, duration, or intensity. Such terms as "clear," "resonant," "shrill," "nasal," "harsh" are sometimes used to describe quality. Quality is determined in part by the vibration of the vocal cords.

According to the "cord-tone" theory of vocal-cord vibration, the vocal cords produce the fundamental pitch and overtones, which are amplified by *resonators,* i.e., the cavities in the throat, mouth, and nose. Another interpretation, the "puff theory," states that the vocal cords produce the fundamental pitch only, and that the overtones are determined entirely by the resonators. The "cord-tone" theory has been supported by experimental evidence and is widely accepted. (Additional information on pitch, intensity, and quality will be found in the following discussions of resonance, sound, and hearing.)

Resonance. The vibration of the vocal cords results in the vibration of air in the cavities of the throat, mouth, and nose. *Resonance* is the name given to vibratory action of this air. Resonance increases the intensity of the voice and is a major factor in determining voice quality.

THE PRIMARY RESONATORS. The primary resonators are the *pharynx,* the *oral cavity,* and the *nasal cavity.* Other so-called "resonators" have little effect on voice quality.

The Pharynx. The pharynx, the cavity of the throat, is considered the most important resonator of the human voice. Its resonance characteristics are controlled primarily by the *constrictor muscles,* which form the sides of the pharyngeal cavity. Effective use of the pharynx as a resonator depends upon a reasonable amount of relaxation in the pharyngeal muscles, with changes in vowel and voice quality determined by minor changes in muscular tension.

The Oral Cavity. The oral cavity reinforces the overtones, which are primarily responsible for the distinguishing characteristics of each vowel and consonant sound. The *palate* forms the roof of the oral cavity. It is composed of a hard anterior or *hard palate,* and a soft posterior or *soft palate.* The hard palate consists of projections of the upper jaw fused at the center. The gum ridge portion of the hard palate is known as the *alveolar ridge.* The soft palate, or *velum,* is composed of muscles which

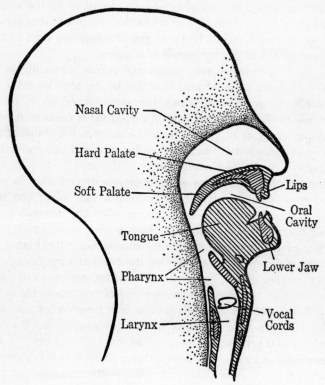

Fig. 6—A sectional view of the head and neck.

extend the palate into the back of the mouth. The small projection of tissue in the lower center portion of the soft palate is known as the *uvula.*

The Nasal Cavity. The nasal cavity is almost entirely enclosed by the bones of the head. The *septum,* composed of bone and cartilage, divides the nasal cavity in the center. Biologically, the nose serves to admit air to the lungs.

Nasal resonance is controlled primarily by the activity of the soft palate, which opens and closes the entrance from the pharynx.

Also, constrictor muscles in the upper part of the pharynx exert a "squeezing" action on the muscular walls around the soft palate so that the entrance to the nasal cavity is closed firmly. The soft palate is raised for the production of all sounds except *m, n,* and *ng.* Because of the sympathetic vibrations of the hard and soft palates, some nasal resonance may exist in the normal voice for all vowel sounds even when the soft palate is raised.

KINDS OF RESONANCE. The two types of resonance are (1) *cavity resonance,* and (2) *sympathetic resonance.*

Cavity Resonance. Cavity resonance occurs when air in the cavities of the head is set into vibration by the tone from the vocal cords. Resonance increases the intensity of some of the overtones in the vocal cord tone. An overtone is reinforced when its frequency (rate of vibration) is the same as the resonant frequency of the cavity. The resonant frequency is determined by the cavity's physical characteristics.

The size of the resonator is one factor in determining its resonance frequency: the larger the resonator, the lower the resonance frequency (low pitch); the smaller the resonator, the higher the resonance frequency (high pitch). Another factor is the size of the opening: the larger the opening, the higher the frequency; the smaller the opening, the lower the frequency.

The "surface-effect" theory holds that the tension in the muscular walls of the vocal resonators affects resonance characteristics. Soft-walled cavities accentuate low frequencies and tend to "muffle" the tone, whereas hard walls accentuate the high overtones and produce a "metallic" effect.

Sympathetic Resonance. Sympathetic resonance is believed to occur in the vocal resonators from the sounding-board effect of the bones and muscles of the head, neck, and chest. Although vocal cord vibrations are impressed upon the bones and muscles, most authorities believe that these vibrations have little effect upon the quality of the sound which reaches the ear of a listener.

Articulation. Articulation refers to the modification of the vocal tone by the tongue, lips, jaw, and soft palate in order to produce speech sounds. The flow of air is interrupted or modified by these organs in making vowel or consonant sounds. For some consonant sounds, the vocal cords do not vibrate. (The production of speech sounds is described in Chapters 15 through 17.)

CONTROL OF THE SPEECH MECHANISM

For some aspects of speech, conscious control of the speech muscles is possible. An individual can develop an awareness of his effort to control the abdominal muscles for breath support. He can become aware of the relative amount of tension or relaxation of the throat muscles. He can also deliberately move the lower jaw, lips, and tongue into the proper positions for making the speech sounds.

He cannot, however, develop conscious control of all aspects of speech production. It is difficult to develop conscious control of the movements of the soft palate, and it is almost impossible to concentrate deliberately on changing the tension of the vocal cords to produce a change in pitch.

During most speaking activities, control of the speech muscles is accomplished by the nervous system without the speaker's paying any deliberate attention to specific speech muscles. Most people learn to listen to their own voices and to adjust their voices when they are not satisfied with what they hear. For most persons, concentration on the meaning of the words spoken is the primary means by which the nervous system automatically controls the speech mechanism.

SOUND

Vocal sounds are transmitted through the air as sound waves. Sound waves in air move outward in all directions from a vibrating source, and travel at the rate of 1,080 feet per second.

Characteristics of Sound. The pitch of a sound is determined by its frequency: the higher the frequency, the higher the pitch. *Frequency* is the rate of vibration of the source producing the sound; it is the number of complete vibrations (cycles) occurring in one second.

Intensity, the primary factor in determining the loudness of a sound, is the amount of sound energy which flows through a unit area of a sound wave. *Time* refers to the duration of the sound and is usually measured in seconds or in fractions of a second. *Wave composition* refers to the form of the sound wave, which is determined by the frequency and intensity of the components

154 *Speech*

of the wave. The quality of a sound is determined by its wave composition, which may be simple or complex and may produce either tones or noises.

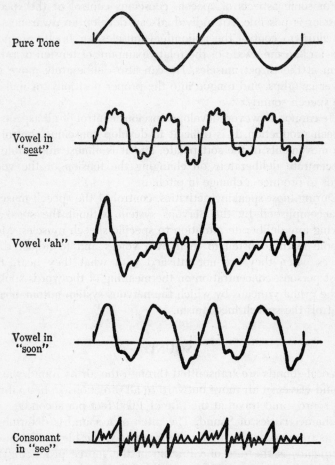

Pure Tone

Vowel in "s<u>ea</u>t"

Vowel "ah"

Vowel in "s<u>oo</u>n"

Consonant in "<u>s</u>ee"

Fig. 7—Sound wave patterns for representative sounds.

A *tone* is a sound to which a definite pitch can be assigned. A *pure tone* is produced by vibrations occurring at only one frequency. A *complex tone* consists of two or more component pure tones produced simultaneously and "blended" into one sound. The components of a complex tone are the fundamental and the overtones. The *fundamental* is the component of lowest frequency; the *overtones* are the components whose frequencies are higher than the frequency of the fundamental.

Noise is a complex sound of such rapidly changing frequency that no definite pitch can be assigned. Vowels and voiced consonants are tones, while unvoiced consonants are noises.

Acoustics. *Acoustics* may be defined as the sum of the qualities—for example, the absence of echo or reverberation—that determine the value of a room with respect to distinct hearing. The acoustics of the room may alter the sound by reflection and absorption. A sound wave striking a surface is partially reflected and partially absorbed. A hard surface reflects a large portion of the sound energy, producing a "live" effect. A soft surface absorbs a large percentage of the sound energy and tends to "muffle" or "deaden" the sound.

An *echo* is the result of a single reflection of a sound wave. *Reverberation* occurs when there are repeated reflections of a sound wave from the walls of a room. Some reverberation is advisable for speech, although excessive reverberations may interfere with a listener's ability to discern what has been said.

HEARING

Hearing refers to the reception of sound by the ear, its analysis, and its transmission to the brain. The ear consists of three parts—the outer, the middle, and the inner. The sense organ for hearing is the *organ of Corti,* located in the inner ear. Sound is conducted to the inner ear through the outer and middle ears.

The Hearing Mechanism. The *pinna,* or external part of the outer ear, directs the sound waves to the *auditory meatus,* a canal which conducts the sound to the *eardrum.* The *eardrum* is stretched across the opening of the auditory meatus between the outer and middle ears and vibrates from the pressure variations of the sound waves. The *Eustachian tube* connects the middle ear with the outside air through the nasal cavity to equalize the air pressure on both sides of the eardrum.

In the cavity of the *middle ear,* the vibrations of the eardrum are transmitted to the oval window and the inner ear by means of the ossicles. The *oval window* consists of a membrane covering the opening between the middle and inner ears. The *ossicles* (*hammer, anvil,* and *stirrup*) are three small bones which connect the eardrum with the oval window and cause the oval window to vibrate in a pattern similar to the sound wave which vibrates the eardrum.

The *inner ear* consists of three bony and membranous structures: the *vestibule,* the *semicircular canals,* and the *cochlea,* the

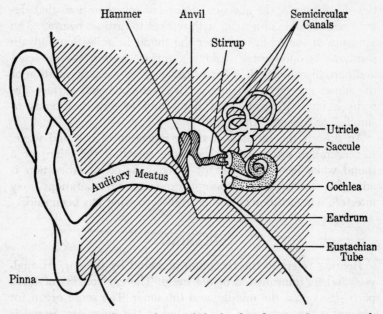

Fig. 8—A sectional view of part of the head, indicating the outer, middle, and inner ear.*

part concerned with hearing. The *vestibule* is the oval cavity forming the entrance to the cochlea and consists of two small sacs, the *utricle* and *the saccule;* the *semicircular canals* (the superior, the posterior, and the inferior) furnish nervous impulses associated with equilibrium; the *cochlea* is a spiral-shaped cavity filled with fluid and is divided into three canals.

The *vestibular* and *tympanic canals* of the cochlea are filled with *perilymph* fluid. These canals are connected with each other at the apex of the cochlea. The *cochlear canal* is separated from the vestibular canal by *Reissner's membrane* and from the

* Reprinted with adaptations with permission of the publisher from *Fundamentals of Physiology* by Elbert Tokay, published by Garden City Books, 1944, page 215.

tympanic canal by the *basilar membrane*. The cochlear canal is
filled with *endolymph* fluid.

Vibrations of the oval window set up vibrations in the perilymph of the vestibular and tympanic canals. These vibrations
are transmitted to the endolymph by Reissner's membrane and

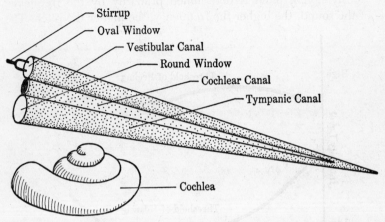

Fig. 9—A diagram of the cochlea uncoiled, revealing its canals.*

the basilar membrane. Vibrations of the endolymph stimulate
the hair cells of the organ of Corti, located on the basilar membrane. The hair cells touch the *tectorial membrane*, which

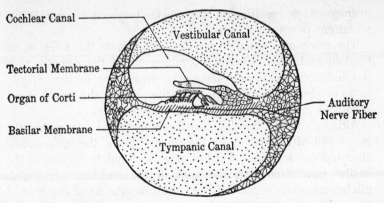

Fig. 10—A cross-section view of the cochlea.*

* Reprinted with adaptations with permission of the publisher from *Fundamentals of Physiology*
by Elbert Tokay, published by Garden City Books, 1944, page 216.

covers the organ of Corti. Associated with the hair cells are the end organs of the auditory nerve which conducts the auditory nerve impulses to the brain, resulting in the sensation of hearing.

Pitch. Pitch is that attribute of auditory sensation which locates sounds at different positions along a musical scale. As previously noted, pitch is determined primarily by the frequency of the sound; the higher the frequency, the higher the pitch. The

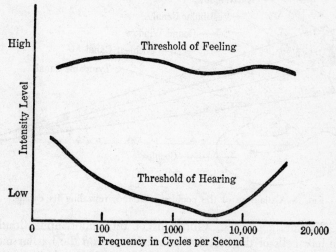

Fig. 11—Frequency and intensity ranges of the ear.

average ear is sensitive to frequencies between 16 and 16,000 vibrations per second.

The pitch of a complex tone corresponds to the pitch of its fundamental. Even when the fundamental of the complex tone is eliminated, as in telephone transmission or in low fidelity radio or phonograph reproduction, the pitch of the sound corresponds to the pitch of the "missing" fundamental.

Although many theories have been proposed concerning the manner of pitch analysis by the ear and brain, the most widely accepted one indicates that low pitches stimulate regions of the basilar membrane near the apex of the cochlea, while high pitches stimulate regions of the basilar membrane at the base of the cochlea.

Loudness. Loudness is the magnitude of the auditory sensation. It is determined primarily by the intensity of the sound, but it also is dependent upon the frequency. If the frequency is held constant, the loudness will increase as the intensity is increased. If the intensity is held constant, however, the loudness will vary as the frequency is varied, since the ear is not equally sensitive to all frequencies.

Loudness is believed to be related to the number of auditory nerve fibers which conduct the impulses to the brain; the stronger the stimulus, the greater the number of conducting fibers, and the greater the loudness. The ear is capable of hearing sounds over a wide range of intensities. Sounds whose intensities give a minimum perceptible sensation are said to be at the *threshold of hearing*. Sounds which are so loud as to produce sensations of pain are said to be at the *threshold of feeling*.

Quality. Quality is that attribute of auditory sensation whereby two different sounds may be distinguished even when the pitch, duration, and loudness are the same. For example, two persons may say "ah" at the same pitch, duration, and loudness, but the differences in voice quality will still be discernible. Although few data exist on the perception of quality, it appears to depend primarily upon the frequency and intensity of the overtones in the sound. The quality will change if either the frequency or the intensity of one or more overtones is changed.

Articulation. Articulation in relation to hearing refers to the ability of an individual to recognize vowels and consonants and to understand the meaning of speech. Experiments show that vowels and consonants may be recognized when many frequency components are eliminated or their intensities greatly reduced.

Vowels depend for their recognition upon the presence of frequencies from 200 to 3,000 cycles per second. Consonants require frequencies between 300 and 8,000 cycles per second. Even when many individual speech sounds cannot be recognized, however, the context may sometimes be understood if these same sounds are used in meaningful phrases or sentences.

Exercises

1. To observe muscular action for breath control, stand erect, but at ease. Place your hand on your abdomen near your lower ribs. Take a deep breath and sustain the sound *ah* as long as you can. Notice that the ribs and abdomen move inward slowly as

you sustain *ah*. Force yourself to hold *ah* as long as possible; feel the strain in your abdominal muscles as you strive to force out all the air from your lungs. Take another deep breath and say "Hey!" abruptly and loudly. Notice the quick inward movement of the abdominal wall which forces the air out.

2. To feel the vibration of the vocal folds, place your index finger at one side of your "Adam's apple." As you say *ah* loudly, feel the vibration with your finger tip. Whisper *ah* and note that you do not feel any vibration. Say the sound of *z*—not the letter name—and feel the vibration. Say the sound of *s*—not the letter name—and notice that you do not feel any vibration.

3. To determine the effect of the size of a resonator on pitch and quality, take a quart size "soda-pop" bottle. Blow over the mouth of the bottle and note that a low-pitched sound is made. Fill the bottle about two-thirds full of water. Blow over the mouth of the bottle and note that the smaller air cavity produces a higher-pitched sound. Next, yawn three times to relax your throat muscles. Then, as you maintain a yawning sensation in your throat, say *ah* in a low pitch of medium volume. Now say a harsh, shrill *ah* sound and feel the constriction in your throat muscles.

4. To observe how the size of the mouth cavity and the size of the mouth opening affect vowel quality, sustain the sound *uh*. As you sustain it, shift to saying *ah*. Note that you have opened your mouth wider to say the *ah* sound. Repeat *uh* but this time shift to the long *e* sound. Note that your lips are in a smiling position and that your tongue is arched in the front of your mouth. Say *uh* again and shift to the $\overline{oo}$ sound. Note that your lips are rounded and that your tongue is arched toward the back of your mouth.

5. To observe the relationship between hearing and articulation of consonant sounds, listen to a newscast with the radio tone control set at *treble*. Quickly turn the tone control to *bass* and note how the sounds of *s*, *f*, *th*, *p*, and *sh* are difficult to identify.

12

Basic Drills for Speech and Voice[1]

In view of the complexity of the voice mechanism and the wide difference in the structure of mouths, lips, tongues, palates, and other organs of speech, it is amazing that sounds are produced that are readily understood—that are, in fact, intelligible to the listener. Any injury or damage to the vocal mechanism may result in faulty voice reproduction. If there is no physical barrier, the production of speech sounds may usually be improved and the quality of voice enhanced provided that sufficient time is spent in correct practice.

PHYSICAL AND MENTAL REQUISITES
FOR EFFECTIVE SPEECH

Vigorous and correct voice production requires a great deal of energy. If a speaker is ill or tired, he may not be able to provide the necessary force for rich, melodious tones. Many persons who realize the validity of this statement for singing disregard its importance for speaking. Consequently, sufficient rest, a well-balanced diet, good posture, relaxation, and a modicum of exercise are all factors to be considered in a program of voice improvement.

The voice reveals not only the speaker's physical condition but also his mental state. Irritability, worry, and general depression are all reflected in the quality of voice as clearly as facial expressions are reflected in a mirror. A positive attitude toward life, self-confidence, and buoyancy are needed if the voice is to be used with maximum efficiency.

[1] The exercises in this chapter are based largely upon those in Chapters III and IV of Dorothy Mulgrave's *Speech for the Classroom Teacher* (rev. ed.; New York: Prentice-Hall, Inc., 1946). Used by permission of the publisher.

Relaxation. The artist or musician who has a tense arm or taut fingers cannot perform creditably. Nor can the speaker who is suffering from undue tension expect to have a clear, vibrant voice. General nervousness, poor breathing habits, interrupted rhythm, or too great rapidity may indicate the speaker's lack of ease. A speaker whose entire body is functioning in a co-ordinated manner will show this integration in his general vitality and in the quality of his voice.

Voice cannot be divorced from the total personality. Persons who are tense vocally are usually tense in other ways. Undue tension leads to fatigue and may affect health. Causes of tension should be analyzed as carefully as general health habits. Once the underlying causes have been established, they should be removed, if possible, or at least subordinated. The task of honestly facing unfounded worries and negative attitudes which set up tensions is a difficult one. It may require a reorganization of thinking and the establishment of new methods of meeting problems. Certainly, it requires courage and an affirmative approach to life. The problem is not insurmountable, however, since relaxation is dependent in part on the mind. Without relaxation, the body cannot be well co-ordinated, nor the voice free and vibrant.

The exercises which follow have been planned as aids for relaxation. They should be practiced slowly, systematically, and thoroughly.

Exercises for Relaxation

1. Stand erect with your feet apart. Lower your head forward on your chest. Let it hang until it seems to pull your body down with its weight. Let your arms dangle. Do not bend your knees, but let your head descend toward the floor. Let your fingers touch the floor. Slowly resume an erect position. Repeat this exercise five times in the beginning. As you increase your facility, increase the number of times. Avoid fatigue. If you yawn your throat will be relaxed.

2. Lie on a flat surface. Listen to a recording of soft music. Relax the muscles of your face, neck, shoulders, arms, torso, legs, and feet. If necessary, begin by tensing muscles and then relaxing them in order to get the feeling of repose.

3. Select a poem containing restful, pastoral descriptions. Read

it aloud slowly. Is this practice as relaxing as hearing soft music? Or less relaxing?

Posture. Posture is a basic factor in relaxation. Poor posture not only results in incorrect body alignment but also interferes with breathing. The resulting voice quality will be tense or perhaps inaudible.

Good posture is a requisite for health as well as for effective voice. The person who is round-shouldered or who habitually slouches or holds on to a chair or table when he speaks seldom impresses his audience favorably. The speaker must be at ease himself if he is to put his audience at ease.

Many persons are unaware of their bad posture. The old exercise of walking around a room with a book on one's head is still a good test of posture. If the book falls, posture is poor.

Check your posture in front of a full-length mirror. If the feet are too far apart, the stance is awkward; if they are too close together, the speaker looks uncomfortable. An easy stance is one in which the heel of one foot approximates the arch of the other. Weight may be easily shifted from the ball of the forward foot to the heel of the back foot. In this way unnecessary motion may be avoided. If his knees are very slightly relaxed, the speaker will feel more comfortable than if they are tense. A feeling of ease communicates itself to an audience.

Breath Control. Ordinarily, breathing is an involuntary process, but disciplined or "acquired" breathing must be used for activities such as swimming, running, singing, or speaking. (The processes involved in breathing for speech have been described in Chapter 11.)

Daily exercises for controlled breathing are listed below. They should be performed systematically either outdoors or in a well-ventilated room.

Exercises for Breathing

1. With the tip of your finger, close one nostril, inhaling a slow, deep breath through the other. Place one hand on your diaphragm and feel the expansion that takes place. Exhale slowly, dividing the outgoing breath into three parts. Put your hand to your lips to feel the outgoing air. Repeat this exercise several times. Do not be alarmed by dizziness; with repeated practice this tendency will disappear.

2. Repeat Exercise 1, closing your other nostril. Say *ah* softly on the exhalation.

3. Repeat Exercise 1 without holding either nostril. Say *ah*, using more volume than in Exercise 1.

4. Inhale slowly; feel your diaphragm expand. Exhale slowly, counting 1, 2, 3, 4.

5. Practice breathing exercises lying on a flat surface. If you have difficulty in establishing correct breathing habits, do not vocalize until you are sure you are using your diaphragm rather than your upper chest.

6. Practice breathing exercises standing in a well-ventilated room. Inhale slowly; exhale slowly, saying short phrases, such as: (*a*) high noon, (*b*) low tone, (*c*) warm day, (*d*) far away, and (*e*) fine time.

7. Increase the number of words you can say in one breath. Try phrases with three words, then four, and so on until you can say a sentence of several words on one breath.

BASIC SPEECH DRILLS

It is not within the scope of this volume to provide extensive drill material for speech and voice. A few carefully selected exercises have been included which may be considered minimum essentials for increasing the flexibility of the speech organs.

Many students believe that reading aloud daily will improve their speech. Unless the speech organs are trained correctly, however, such a procedure may be highly undesirable. Incorrect practice does more harm than good.

To obtain maximum benefit from the exercises that follow, systematic daily work is essential. These exercises may be compared to finger exercises for piano playing. Small muscles are harder to control than large ones. Hence, a great deal of practice with the lips, tongue, and palate may be required before these speech organs are sufficiently controlled for some of the difficult sound combinations of English.

Exercises for Increasing the Flexibility of the Tongue

1. Open your mouth; hold your jaw down firmly. Be sure that your tongue, rather than your jaw or lips, does the work. Use a mirror to be sure you are right.

2. Raise the tip of your tongue to the ridge of your upper front teeth. Move it slowly backward along the hard palate. Then ad-

vance the tongue over the palate until it reaches the teeth ridge again. Repeat forward and backward movement eight times. Relax. Be sure that your tongue does not leave your palate during this exercise and that your jaw and larynx remain still.

3. Groove your tongue; advance it slowly as far out of your mouth as possible. Draw it back into your mouth. Repeat eight times. Relax. (If you cannot groove your tongue, use a tongue depressor or a stick of hard candy. Try to curl your tongue around the depressor or candy.)

4. Rotate your tongue around your lips, beginning at the right side. Repeat four times. Relax. Repeat, beginning at the left side. Repeat four times. Relax.

Exercises for Increasing the Flexibility of the Lips

1. Pout your lips. Relax. Pout. Relax. Do this exercise eight times.

2. Practice the following words, exaggerating the *p, b,* and *m: pop, pip, pipe, pope, pomp, pump, bib, imbibe, bubble, bauble, babble, bumble, mumble, murmur, mumbling.*

3. Spread your lips for the sound of the vowel in *eat*. Round them for the vowel sound in *ooze*. Repeat eight times.

Exercises for the Soft Palate

1. Raise the tip of your tongue to your upper gum ridge. Say *n*. Drop the tip of your tongue and raise the back of your tongue to your soft palate. Say the final sound in *sing*. Practice these two consonants to the count of eight. Relax. Repeat. Relax.

2. Open your mouth; look in a mirror and observe the action of your uvula when you breathe in. Pant. Relax. Pant. Relax.

3. Yawn or simulate a yawn. Analyze what happens to your palate.

BASIC VOICE DRILLS

In the voice, as in any other musical instrument, there are three inherent tone characteristics: *pitch, volume,* and *quality*. Because these characteristics are highly individualized, it is possible at times to identify a speaker, even if he is not visible to the listener, after hearing only one or two words.

Pitch. The pitch of a tone is its place in a musical scale. Just as the pitch of stringed instruments is determined mainly by the length and tautness of the strings, so, too, is the pitch of voice determined in part by the length, tension, and thickness of the vocal cords.

A good pitch level is one a little below the middle of the entire pitch range of the voice. A high pitch usually indicates emotion, while a low one is likely to be used for serious or impressive occasions. Lack of variation in pitch results in a monotonous tone.

One method of ascertaining the best pitch level is that of testing on a piano the limits of tone that can be comfortably attained. After the range has been determined, the tone that is a third below the middle pitch of the range may be selected as the best one for use in ordinary conversation.

Exercises for Pitch

Read aloud the following selections, paying special attention to the pitch of your voice for each. Which selections require a high pitch? Why? Which ones require a low pitch? Why?

a.

There is sweet music here that softer falls
Than petals from blown roses on the grass,
Or night-dews on still waters between walls
Of shadowy granite, in a gleaming pass;
Music that gentlier on the spirit lies,
Than tired eyelids upon tired eyes;
Music that brings sweet sleep down from the blissful skies.
Here are cool mosses deep,
And through the moss the ivies creep,
And in the stream the long-leaved flowers weep,
And from the craggy ledge the poppy hangs in sleep.

—TENNYSON

b.

The more my wrong, the more his spite appears:
What, did he marry me to famish me?
Beggars, that come unto my father's door,
Upon entreaty have a present alms;
If not, elsewhere they meet with charity:
But I,—who never knew how to entreat,
Nor never needed that I should entreat,—
Am starv'd for meat, giddy for lack of sleep;
With oaths kept waking, and with brawling fed:

—SHAKESPEARE

c.

Send but a song oversea for us,
    Heart of their hearts who are free,
Heart of their singer, to be for us
    More than our singing can be;
Ours, in the tempest at error,
    With no light but the twilight of terror;
      Send us a song oversea!

                    —SWINBURNE

d.

The gray sea and the long black land;
And the yellow half-moon large and low;
And the startled little waves that leap
In fiery ringlets from their sleep,
As I gain the cove with pushing prow,
And quench its speed i' the slushy sand.

                    —BROWNING

e.

Bury the Great Duke
    With an empire's lamentation;
Let us bury the Great Duke
    To the noise of the mourning of a mighty nation;
Mourning when their leaders fall,
Warriors carry the warrior's pall,
And sorrow darkens hamlet and hall.

                    —TENNYSON

Volume. Volume refers to the power, that is, the general or average loudness of the voice, and depends upon controlling the outgoing breath. The throat should be relaxed and should be regarded as a channel for air to reach the resonating chambers so that the tone may be reinforced.

Ordinary conversation requires little energy unless there is some inescapable background noise. In a large room, especially if the acoustics are poor, more energy and, hence, more breath are required to reach the entire audience. Not only should the volume be adequate at the beginning of a phrase, but also it should be sustained to the end of a phrase.

Many speakers assume they are using their voices correctly simply because they can be heard. Audibility is not the only criterion for effective use of the voice. Volume may vary from a whisper to a loud and forceful tone during a single speech before the same audience. The speaker should think of the last row as the place his voice must reach, and he should endeavor to learn something of the acoustics of the room.

Exercises for Volume

1. Prepare a selection for oral reading. Increase your volume according to the following situations:

   a. Read to a very small group in a small room.
   b. Read from a platform in a medium-sized room.
   c. Read from a platform in a large room.
   d. Read from a platform in an auditorium where there is a balcony.

2. Practice each vowel sound in the following sentence softly, first with medium, then with maximum, volume: He will tax their land last.

3. Read the following in a conversational tone:

   Speak the speech, I pray you, as I pronounced it to you, trippingly on the tongue: but if you mouth it, as many of your players do, I had as lief the town-crier spoke my lines. Nor do not saw the air too much with your hand, thus; but use all gently: for in the very torrent, tempest, and, as I may say, the whirlwind of passion, you must acquire and beget a temperance that may give it smoothness.

   —SHAKESPEARE

4. Read the following explosively:

                                        Awake! awake!—
   Ring the alarum bell:—murder and treason!—
   Banquo and Donalbain! Malcolm! awake!
   Shake off this downy sleep, death's counterfeit,
   And look on death itself! up, up, and see
   The great doom's image! Malcolm! Banquo!
   As from your graves rise up, and walk like sprites,
   To countenance this horror!

                                        —SHAKESPEARE

5. Select an oration. Read it as though you were speaking to a large audience out-of-doors. Control your use of volume according to the meaning.

Quality. Of the physical properties distinguishing voice quality, the most important is the reinforcement of vibrations. Vibration of the vocal cords might be described as the beginning of voice, since in order for the voice to be heard, the vibration must be reinforced in the pharynx and the oral and nasal cavities. (This reinforcement of vibration, called "resonance," has been described in detail in Chapter 11.)

It is true that voice quality is to some extent predetermined by the size and shape of the resonators. It is also true that the quality of the voice may be improved and its resonance increased by a knowledge of both the breathing technique for speaking or singing and the accurate articulation of sounds. Systematic work and the application of the principles of correct breathing to all speech situations will eventually result in improvement in voice quality.

Exercises for Quality and Resonance

1. Select a prose passage in which you think a conversational tone should be used.

2. Choose a short poem for oral reading. Find one in which the nasal continuants, *m, n,* and *ng,* are used frequently.

3. Hum *m* before all the vowel sounds.

4. Hum *m* after all the vowel sounds.

5. Hum *n* before all the vowel sounds.

6. Hum *n* after all the vowel sounds.

7. Read the following excerpts aloud, noting changes in voice quality that accompany each mood.

a.

God of our fathers, known of old,
    Lord of our far-flung battle-line,
Beneath whose awful Hand we hold
    Dominion over palm and pine—
Lord God of Hosts, be with us yet
Lest we forget—lest we forget!
                                    —KIPLING

b.

We are the music makers,
    And we are the dreamers of dreams,
Wandering by lone sea-breakers,
    And sitting by desolate streams—
World-losers and world-forsakers,
    On whom the pale moon gleams—
Yet we are the movers and shakers
    Of the world for ever, it seems.
                            —ARTHUR O'SHAUGHNESSY

Exercises for Supporting Tone

1. Yawn or simulate a yawn. Note the feeling of freedom in your throat and the upward movement of your soft palate.

2. Say the vowels in the following words, holding each vowel to a count of four: *be, cool, calm, all, fur.* Repeat, saying each of these vowels as though it were the final sound in a sentence.

3. Practice the following phrases, sustaining the tone and imagining you are talking outdoors to several hundred persons:

    a. Ring the alarm bell!

    b. Boomlay, boomlay, boomlay, boom!

    c. Rejoice, you men of Angiers, ring your bells.

    d. Wherefore rejoice? What conquest brings he home?

    e. Out of the north, the wild news came.

4. Give the following directions as though you were speaking in a large gymnasium:

    a. One, two, three, four!

    b. Halt!

    c. Forward march!

    d. Right about face!

    e. Left about face!

5. Select a patriotic speech. Read it as though you were delivering it for the first time to an audience of five hundred.

13

The Sounds of English

There are languages in which the spelling indicates the sounds of the letters. Such languages, including Spanish, Italian, Russian, Greek, and Hungarian, are said to be spelled phonetically. In others, notably Gaelic, French, and English, it is not always possible to determine the sound from the spelling. These languages are said to be spelled unphonetically.

PHONETIC INCONSISTENCIES
OF ENGLISH SPELLING

Examples of phonetic inconsistencies abound. What has happened is that twenty-six letters in the written alphabet have had to be adjusted to approximately forty sounds in the spoken language. The following discussion will indicate some of the problems that arise because of variations in spelling and sound.

Vowel Sounds. In English, for example, it is commonly said that there are five vowels. An examination of a few simple words will show that there are more than five. The *a* of *ate;* the *a* of *at;* the *a* of *calm;* the *a* of *care;* the *a* of *walk,* and the *a* of *alone* all represent separate and distinct sounds, only one of which contains the sound *a* that was represented by the letter in the alphabet. To add to the confusion, there are many words, such as *they* and *eight,* in which no letter *a* appears, but in which the sound may be heard.

An analysis of the sound of *e* presents similar problems. The single *e* in *be;* the double *ee* in *bee;* the *eo* in *people;* the *oe* in *phoenix;* the *ae* in *Caesar;* the *ea* in *lease;* the *ua* of *quay;* the *i* of *fatigue;* the *ie* of *believe,* and the *ei* of *receive* represent one sound. These same spellings, however, may also represent a great many other sounds.

A single *e* in *met* is different from a single *e* in *be* or *they; ea* in

171

leather differs in sound from *ea* in *lease, ear,* and *earth; ei* in *reign,* from *ei* in *either* and *reiterate; eo* in *George,* from *eo* in *people; ua* in *quay,* from *ua* in *quarrel* and *quart; i* of *machine,* from *i* in *light* and *lit;* and *ie* in *believe,* from *ie* in *sieve.*

The same kind of inconsistency may be found in the spellings and sound values of *i, o,* and *u.*

Consonant Sounds. Consonants, like vowels, frequently represent more than one sound. The *n* and *g* in *sing,* for example, join to form a sound quite different from *n* or *g* in a word like *congratulate.* The *s* at the beginning of *sees* looks like the final *s,* but sounds quite different. The *ti* of *tire* differs from the *ti* of *notion.* Likewise, the *ci* of *circus* differs from the *ci* of *facial.* Such illustrations might be given for almost all consonants in the language.

The Use of Silent Letters. Another problem that adds to the complexity of English is the prevalence of silent letters, many of which were pronounced at some time in the history of the language. Letters such as *k* in *knee; b* in *debt; p* and *l* in *psalm; w* and *c* in *wreck; gh* in *night; g* in *gnaw,* and *b* in *numb* are examples of common words containing one or more silent letters.

The Use of Two Letters for One Sound. A sound may not only have more than one value, but it may also be represented by more than one letter as in the case of *th* in *thin* and *th* in *then.* Conversely, one letter frequently represents two sounds, as in the case of *i* in *side, o* in *go,* and *a* in *ale.* Those who think of *i, o,* and *a* as vowels may find it difficult to think of them as diphthongs. In the words indicated, there are two vowels, said very quickly, constituting a diphthong.

Letters with Different Sound Values. To heighten the difficulties, not all the twenty-six letters have sound values. The letter *c,* for example, has no value of its own, but becomes *s* in *city* or *k* in *could; q,* which must be followed by *u* in spelling, may have a value of *kw* in *quick,* or *k* in *bouquet;* and *x* assumes the value of *ks* in *exit, gs* in *exist, z* in *xylophone,* and *ksh* in *luxury.* The twenty-six letters have thus been reduced to twenty-three, but the fact remains that there are approximately forty sounds.

METHODS OF INDICATING SOUNDS

With a language as unphonetically spelled as English, it is difficult to represent sounds so that they may be accurately pro-

ā	āle	b	ba´by, be
ȧ	chȧ·ot´ic	ch	chair, much
â	câre	d	day, den
ă	ădd	du̇	ver´dure (-du̇r)
ȧ	ăc·count´	f	fill, feel
ä	ärm	g	go, be·gin´
ȧ	ȧsk	gz	ex·ist´ (ĕg·zĭst´)
á	so´fá	h	hat, hen
ē	ēve	hw	what (hwŏt)
ē̦	hē̦re	j	joke, jol´ly
ē̦	ē̦·vent´	k	keep, kick
ĕ	ĕnd	ks	tax (tăks)
ẽ	si´lẽnt	kw	queen (kwēn)
ē	mak´ẽr	l	late, leg
ī	īce	m	man, me
ĭ	ĭll	n	no, none
i̯	char´i̯·ty	ng	sing, long
ō	ōld	p	pa´pa, pin
ȯ	ȯ·bey´	r	rap, red
ô	ôrb	s	so, this
ŏ	ŏdd	sh	she, ship
ŏ	sŏft	t	time, talk
ŏ	cŏn·nect´	th	thin, through
oi	oil	t̶h̶	then (t̶h̶ĕn)
o͞o	fo͞od	tu̇	na´ture (-tu̇r)
o͝o	fo͝ot	v	van, re·vive´
ou	out	w	want, win
ū	cūbe	y	yet
u̇	u̇·nite´	z	zone, haze
û	ûrn	zh	az´ure (āzh´ẽr)
ŭ	ŭp		
u̇	cir´cŭs		

nounced. Many methods have been tried but have been discarded because they were inaccurate, cumbersome, or impractical. The three major ways of indicating sounds at the present time are through diacritical marks, simplified spelling, and the International Phonetic Alphabet.

Diacritical marks. Most dictionaries use a system of marks or signs over letters to indicate sounds and also to provide a key word for each sound. To be used accurately, this system depends upon a thorough knowledge of English sounds and a precise adaptation of the marks involved. The circumflex ô, shown diacritically in the word ôrb, may be consistently mispronounced in other words containing the same sound, if the key word is not properly pronounced.

In diacritically marked dictionaries,

italics are sometimes used to supplement the marks over letters. Thus italicized "*ŏ*" indicates a different sound from unitalicized "ŏ." Unless the user notices and properly interprets the italics, his pronunciation of unstressed syllables will be stilted and unnatural. He must observe that the "*ŏ*" of *connect* has no relation to the "ŏ" of *odd* and that the "*ă*" of *account* has no relation to the "ă" of *add*.

Another disadvantage of diacritical marks is that no system has been universally agreed upon. Each dictionary may adopt its own method of indicating sound. (Because *Webster's New International Dictionary* is very widely used, the key to pronunciation from this dictionary is given in chart on page 173.)

Simplified Spelling. The ordinary twenty-six-letter alphabet is utilized in simplified spelling. Because English spelling is too misleading to be used consistently, arbitrary combinations are devised to represent sounds. For example, the single vowel sound in *first* is represented as "uhr," and the vowel in *rate* as "ay." Thus, the word *first-rate* would be indicated as FUHRST RAYT. Unstressed vowels are shown as *uh,* as in WIZ duhm, or *uhr* in FUHR thuhr. This method is obviously not a very satisfactory one because it is based on an unscientific premise, namely, English spelling. The addition of extraneous letters can hardly be said to have a simplifying effect.

The International Phonetic Alphabet. The most accurate method of representing sounds is through the International Phonetic Alphabet, commonly called the IPA, designed by philologists in 1888 as a key to all languages. A special letter was assigned to each sound, regardless of the language in which the sound appeared.

Such a system is universal and may be compared to a musical scale which can be recognized by musicians all over the world or to a number concept which can be readily understood by mathematicians. It contains approximately 105 letters, each of which symbolizes a single sound which may occur in one or more languages. Since about forty of these sounds occur in English, only these phonetic letters need be learned by students of English speech. (This list is given later in this chapter.)

Because the same sound may not be made in exactly the same way in all languages, various signs or modifiers are used to show subtle differences. The sound of *t,* for example, which is made in English with the tip of the tongue on the upper gum ridge, is made with the tongue against the upper teeth in some languages and against the lower teeth in others. In English, this sound is produced with a slight breath before a vowel or a pause as in *tie;* it is then said to be an aspirated sound. Before a consonant, as in *try,* there is no aspiration or audible breath. In many languages, the sound of *t* is never aspirated.

These and other variations may be demonstrated by what is called "narrow transcription." This type of transcription shows all that is known about a sound and is obviously more accurate than the usual method of "broad transcription," which merely indicates the letters of the phonetic alphabet. For practical purposes, broad transcription may be quite adequate. The use of narrow transcription depends on the linguistic background of the student and his desire to speak as a native whichever language he is studying. For foreigners in any languages it is invaluable.

PROCESSES OF PHONETIC TRAINING

Ability to use phonetics involves four major processes: (1) the *ear* must be trained to hear sounds accurately; (2) the *speech organs* must be trained to make speech sounds accurately; (3) the *eye* must be trained to recognize the letters of the phonetic alphabet; and (4) the *hand* must be trained to write the phonetic letters legibly and quickly.[1]

The material on sounds in Chapters 15, 16, and 17 has been organized phonetically. Vowels have been grouped according to their position in the mouth; diphthongs have been arranged according to their second elements; and consonants have been placed according to the speech organs producing them, beginning with lip sounds.

[1] Cf. Margaret P. McLean, *Good American Speech* (rev. ed. New York: E. P. Dutton & Co., Inc., 1952), pp. 41–42.

PHONETIC ALPHABET

English Vowels

Printed Form	*Key Word*	*Printed Form*	*Key Word*
[i:][2]	he	[o]	omit
[ɪ]	it	[ɔ:]	all
[e]	end	[ɒ][5]	not
[ɛ:][3]	wear	[ɑ:]	alms
[æ]	at	[ɜ:]	earn
[ə][4]	ask	[ə]	alone
[u:]	noon	[ʌ]	up
[ʊ]	wood		

[2] Two dots (:) following a sound mean that the sound is long.

[3] In some American speech ɛ: is a pure vowel; generally, however, it is the first element of the diphthong in *wear*.

[4] In British speech, the sound of ə becomes the *a* of *alms*; in American speech, it is frequently pronounced as the *a* of *at*.

[5] In American speech, the sound in *not* varies from one very much like the vowel in *all*, though a little shorter, to a relaxed vowel as in *alms*.

English Diphthongs [6]

Printed Form	*Key Word*	*Printed Form*	*Key Word*
[eɪ][7]	day	[ɪə]	ear
[əɪ]	time	[ɛə]	air
[ɔɪ]	oil	[ʊə]	sure
[oʊ]	go	[ɔə][8]	ore
[aʊ]	now		

[6] When two vowels occur in close proximity, they are not necessarily elements of a diphthong. Note the similarity in sound between the diphthong in the first syllable of *serious* and the pure vowels in the second and third syllables. *Material, cafeteria, thawing,* and *clawing* provide other examples.

[7] A curved line (˘) placed above a letter indicates the unstressed element of a diphthong. While it is not entirely necessary to use this mark, in the interests of accuracy it is included as an aid in differentiating between two pure vowels and a diphthong.

[8] The diphthong in *ore* is frequently used as a pure vowel, depending on its place in a sentence and the rate of speech.

English Consonants

Printed Form	Key Word	Printed Form	Key Word
[p]	*p*ie	[s]	*s*ee
[b]	*b*oy	[z]	*z*oo
[m]	*m*e	[ʃ]	*sh*oe
[ʍ]	*wh*oa	[ʒ]	gara*g*e
[w]	*w*e	[ɹ] [9]	*r*ay
[f]	*f*oe	[j]	*y*ou
[v]	*v*ie	[k]	oa*k*
[θ]	*th*in	[g]	*g*o
[ð]	smoo*th*	[ŋ]	ki*ng*
[t]	*t*ie	[h]	*h*oe
[d]	*d*ie	[tʃ]	*ch*ew
[n]	*n*o	[dʒ]	*j*oy
[l]	*l*ie		

[9] There are three letters used in the International Phonetic Alphabet to indicate the sound of *r*. Uvula *r* of French and German is shown with a capital (*R*); trilled *r* of Spanish and other languages is shown with an upright *r* phonetically (*r*); the English sound, especially when preceding a vowel, is shown with an inverted form (ɹ). An upright *r* is not wrong; it is not quite so accurate as an inverted one.

Exercises

1. Compare the vowel sounds of any foreign language with those of English.

2. Find ten examples of words with silent letters. Trace the history of these words in an etymological dictionary or elsewhere to determine when the letters became silent.

3. Pronunciation does not change suddenly. Can you find evidence of this statement in changing pronunciation in your community? Indicate ten words for which there are varied pronunciations.

4. There are only nine consonants that require new letters in the International Phonetic Alphabet. Using the IPA chart in this chapter, indicate these nine.

5. Compare the ways in which *Webster's Dictionary* and the IPA deal with the nine consonants referred to in (4) above.

14

Sounds in Connected Speech

Change is the underlying principle of all living languages. Nowhere is this principle more clearly to be seen than in English words where the quality of the vowel depends upon whether or not it is in a stressed syllable. The letter *a*, for example, may look the same in the words *add* and *senate*. An attempt to pronounce both *a's* in the same way would show a lack of knowledge of the language. The principle involved in words such as these is one of weakening vowels in unstressed syllables. Similar changes also take place in words that are customarily unstressed.

ASSIMILATION

The attraction of one sound for another results in the phonetic process known as *assimilation*. Usually, assimilation tends to make sounds and sound combinations easier to pronounce because the motions of the vocal organs have been simplified.

When a sound influences the sound that follows it, the process is called *progressive assimilation*. The influence of *b* on *s* in *observe* is an example.

When a sound influences the sound or sounds that precede it, the process is called *regressive assimilation*. Words such as *raspberry* and *comptroller* are interesting examples of this very common type of assimilation. In *raspberry*, the *b* has influenced the *s* and the *p* has become silent, as is often the case with clusters of consonants. In *comptroller*, the tongue-gum sounds *t* and *r* influence the labials *m* and *p*, which change into a tongue-gum consonant *n*.

Sometimes sounds affect each other mutually and disappear, leaving in their place a third sound that may be quite unlike the original sounds. This process is called *progressive-regressive-*

reciprocal assimilation. Words such as *nature, feature, picture,* and *future,* in which *tu* becomes *ch* in sound, are excellent examples of this type of assimilation. When *n* and *g* assimilate in words such as *sing, ring, bringing,* the resulting sound differs from those which are customarily associated with the letters *n* and *g.*

While assimilation is a necessary concomitant of a language stressed as strongly as English, it is possible to overassimilate, producing speech that is almost unintelligible. The sentence "How do you do?" in quick, overassimilated speech may sound something like "Howjudo?" or "Where did you eat?" may become "Wheredjeat?" Obviously, assimilation that obscures meaning should be avoided.

WORD EMPHASIS

In order to avoid word-wise speaking and reading and to convey ideas accurately, it is necessary to stress words properly. It is equally important to know which words *not* to stress. Just as the musical phrase subordinates some notes and stresses others, so, too, the linguistic phrase subordinates some words and stresses others. Because nouns, main verbs, adjectives, and adverbs are normally stressed, the weakening of less vital words provides variety and helps clarify the meaning of a sentence.

The term *strong form* applies to the form of the word when it is stressed. The term *weak form* applies to the usual pronunciation of subordinate words in connected speech. The vowel becomes weak or obscure, and sometimes a consonant sound may drop out completely. In a phrase such as *bread and butter* in quick speech, the word *and* loses its *d* before a consonant and may also lose its vowel. The remaining sound *n* is called a *syllabic sound.*

Strong or Stressed Forms. Words that are usually subordinated include articles, prepositions, pronouns, conjunctions, and auxiliary verbs. Such words have a stressed or strong form which is used when they are mentioned alone, that is, not as part of a context, or when they are stressed in context to alter the meaning. When a speaker stresses *am* in a sentence such as "I am going," he implies that nothing can stop him. Under normal circumstances in conversation, he would weaken the auxiliary verb by using the form *I'm,* thus making it an unstressed or weak form.

Weak or Unstressed Forms. Some words have more than one weak form. Words such as *should* and *would*, for example, may have a weak vowel, or merely the consonant *d*, as in *I'd*, *he'd*, *they'd*. The weak form of *the* differs before a consonant and before a vowel, being stronger in the latter case. When prepositions are in a strong position, as at the beginning or end of a phrase, they may have a stronger vowel than in the middle of a phrase. Thus, in the phrases "of the two" and "all you thought of," the *of* would be a strong form, whereas in the phrase "a pair of gloves," the preposition would be weak.

In conversation, weak forms are used freely and without hesitancy. In reading, however, many persons make the error of giving every word equal emphasis under the mistaken notion that they are reading distinctly. The use of weak forms is as important in reading as in speaking. If the sentence "John is planning to read the book at the first opportunity" were read with equal emphasis on each word, the result would be a meaningless word list. In reading, as in speaking, important words should be stressed and unimportant ones subordinated.

The use of a strong form may change the meaning of a sentence. The meaning of the phrase "I *was* going" is different from the meaning of "I was *going*."

A normally weak word may be stressed for contrast. When the cat speaks to the fox in the Aesop fable, she uses strong forms to show contrast: "This is *my* plan; what are *you* going to do?"

On this page, a paragraph has been reproduced in diacritical marks. It includes many instances of weak forms. Their pronunciation is indicated by means of italics. In phonetic transcription, (ə) is used predominantly to show weakening. This sound is known as the *schwa,* the *neutral vowel,* or the *obscure vowel.*

1 Jŏn Kär′vēr hăd klīmd Môn′ Blän′, hăd sēn ᵗh̶ē̶ mōōn rīz
2 ō′vēr ᵗh̶ē̶ Täj Ma·häl′ mô′sŏ·lē′ŭm, ăn ᵗh̶ē̶ sŭn rīz ō′vēr ᵗh̶ē̶
3 Hĭ·mä′la·yaz ăt Där·jē′lĭng; hē ăd shŏt tī′gērz ĭn ᵗh̶ē̶ kŭn′trĭ
4 nôrth ŏv Dĕl′ĭ, ăn lī′ŭnz ĭn Rŏ·dē′zhĭ·a; hē ăd wĭn′tērd ăt Nēs
5 ăn spĕnt a sŭm′ēr a·mŭng′ ᵗh̶ē̶ nôr·wē′jăn fyôrdz. Hĭz făm′ĭ·lĭ
6 hăd bĭn A·mĕr′ĭ·kăn fēr tĕn jĕn′ēr·ā′shŭnz, bŭt hē ăd nĕv′ēr
7 bĭn wĕst ŏv Dē Moin′, Ī′ŏ·wa. Sō ŏn ᵗh̶ĭ̶s̶ Jōōn môr′nĭng ăz
8 ᵗh̶ē̶ trān dē ̣lŏŏks′ pŏŏld out ŏv Kăn′zas Sĭt′ĭ, hē wŭz ĭn ŭn·nŏn′
9 kŭn′trĭ. Ŭp ᵗh̶ē̶ văl′ĭ ŏv ᵗh̶ē̶ Kăn′zas ᵗh̶ē̶ grāt mŏ·gŭl′ hŏld
10 ᵗh̶ē̶m̶, hwīl Kär′vēr ĭn ᵗh̶ē̶ bŏŏ·fā′ kär wŭz ēt′ĭng ăn ä·lä·kärt′
11 brĕk′fast. Frŭm tīm tu tīm ᵗh̶ē̶ chän′jĭng păn′ŏ·rä′ma ŏv

12 kôrn'fēld' ăn rĭv'ẽr ĭn·vē'g'ld ĭm frŭm hĭz dā'zhû'nā', bŭt fẽr ~~the~~
13 mōst pärt hē gāv strĭkt ă·tĕn'shŭn tŭ ~~the~~ pŏm'ĕ·lō, kŏf'ĭ, rōlz,
14 ăn bēf ä lä mōd' hwĭch hē ăd ôr'dĕrd frŭm ~~the~~ mĕn'ū. Åf'tẽr
15 brĕk'făst hē rĕd ĕk'sûrpts frŭm à Dår'tá'nyäɴ' rŏ·măns', ăn
16 mūzd ~~that the~~ plānz sēmd nŏt vẽr'ĭ dĭf'ẽr·ĕnt frŭm ~~the~~ stĕps ŏv
17 Rŭsh'à ēr ~~the~~ lä'nōz ŏv är'jĕn·tē'ná. Ĭn ~~the~~ åf'tẽr·nōōn' ~~the~~
18 bū'tŭ·fōōl sēn'ẽr·ĭ à·lŏng' ~~the~~ Är'kăn·sô Rĭv'ẽr à·rouzd' ĭm
19 sŭm'hwŏt' frŭm ~~the~~ hà·bĭt'ū·ăl än'wē ŏv à ràth'ẽr blä·zā'
20 glōb'trŏt'ẽr. Thē jĕn't'l, rĭth'mĭk ŏs'ĭ·lā'shŭn ŏv ~~the~~ trän wŭz
21 sō sōōth'ĭng ~~that~~ hwĕn ĭz bûrth wŭz rĕd'ĭ åf'tẽr sŭp'ẽr hē
22 nēd'ĕd nŏ sŏ'pŏ·rĭf'ĭk, bŭt drŏpt ŏf ēz'ĭ·lĭ tŭ slēp.*

REGIONAL DIALECTS

The three major regional dialects in the United States are roughly classified as Eastern, Southern, and Northern, although some phoneticians refine this classification still further. Because of constant shifts in population, the wide influence of radio and television, and education, it is impossible to say exactly where the linguistic borderlines are. In general, educated and cultured speakers in all areas use less conspicuous dialects than those who are uneducated. Hence, dialects may represent either slight variations or such marked deviations that speech may be almost unintelligible outside the boundaries of a limited area.

Consonants. The pronunciation of consonants varies little in different linguistic areas. Differences in the pronunciation of *r* present the most troublesome problem in regional differences. (Rules governing the use of this consonant will be found in Chapter 17.)

The use of *n* for *ng* as in *goin'* and *comin'* is more noticeable in Southern speech than in Eastern or Northern, though it may, of course, be heard in all areas. The misuse of *ngg* for *ng* is especially common to the foreign language sections of metropolitan areas.

Vowels. While almost every state may present slight deviations in the production of vowel sounds, in Southern speech, as distinct from Eastern or Northern, the most commonly altered sounds include: substitution of *i* for *e* as in *tin* for *ten;* a so-called "flat *a*" in such words as *sand* and *land;* and the tendency to make all pure vowels into diphthongs and most diphthongs into triphthongs or combinations of three vowels. In some Eastern

---

* From *The Americanization of Carver,* published by G. & C. Merriam Co.

and Northern speech, vowels are nasalized, especially before such consonants as *m, n,* and *ng.*

MELODY IN CONNECTED SPEECH

The tune or melody of a language is called its *intonation.* Each language has its own melody or intonation pattern, which is one of its most subtle characteristics. A German linguistic scholar, Hermann Klinghardt, after studying the intonation patterns of ancient languages, evolved a method that has materially simplified the study of English intonation. In this system, which attempts to picture intonation, a horizontal line, known as the measuring line, is used to indicate the normal pitch of the voice. A dot is used for every syllable. A heavy dot ● indicates a stressed syllable; a light dot ˑ shows an unstressed syllable. The last stressed syllable in a breath group has the symbol ↗ (known as a down-glide).

English intonation is characterized by two main tendencies:

1. A complete thought ends with a falling inflection, or downglide.

Examples

a. She is coming. ˑ ˑ ˑ ↗ ˑ

b. The students have arrived. ˑ ● ● ˑ ● ↗

c. The class starts promptly. ˑ ● ● ↗ ˑ

d. The play has a tragic ending. ˑ ● ˑ ˑ ● ● ↗ ˑ

e. The instructor read the article to the group.
ˑ ˑ ● ˑ ● ● ˑ ● ˑ ˑ ↗

When a question begins with a question word, such as those indicated below, the same principle of falling inflection obtains.

Examples

a. When is his plane due? ● ˑ ˑ ● ↗

b. Where are the new books? ● ˑ ˑ ● ↗

c. What route does he plan to take? ● ● ˑ ˑ ● ˑ ● ↗

d. How long is the book? ● ● ˑ ˑ ↗

e. Why have the plans been changed? ● ˑ ˑ ● ˑ ↗

2. An incomplete thought or a question that does not begin with a question word ends with a rising inflection, or an up-glide, as indicated by the examples below.

Examples

a. Despite the bad weather ﹒ ● ﹒ ● ᴣ ﹒

b. Having admitted the facts ● ﹒ ﹒ ● ﹒ ﹒ ᴣ

c. Is he coming? ﹒ ﹒ ᴣ ﹒

d. Has he read the review? ﹒ ﹒ ● ﹒ ﹒ ᴣ

e. Is the evidence conclusive? ﹒ ﹒ ● ﹒ ﹒ ﹒ ᴣ ﹒

Exercises

1. List ten examples of assimilation that are commonly used by good speakers.

2. Give ten examples of assimilation that are considered poor.

3. Indicate ten words that you constantly use in their weak forms.

4. Read a paragraph or two aloud. On the first reading, use only strong forms. Note the word-wise, stilted quality of the reading. Reread, using weak forms. Note the difference in intelligibility.

5. Compose five short declarative sentences; five questions; and five questions beginning with question words such as *when, where, how, why,* and *who.* Indicate the intonation pattern for each.

15

English Vowels

A vowel is a speech sound produced by an uninterrupted flow of vocalized breath. The distinguishing characteristic of each vowel is produced by the size and shape of the resonators and by the modifications of the lips, tongue, and jaw.

Vowels are classified as *front-*, *back-*, and *mid-*vowels, depending upon whether they are made with the front, back, or middle of the tongue. In other words, the front of the tongue is high at the beginning of the front-vowel scale; the back of the tongue is high at the beginning of the back-vowel scale; and the middle of the tongue is slightly raised in the production of the mid-vowels. (An examination of the Chart of English Vowels on page 185 and of the sentences in this chapter containing these sounds will indicate the order in which the vowel sounds should be studied for greatest progress.)

FRONT VOWELS

The front vowels are made with the tip of the tongue against the lower front teeth. The front of the tongue is high at the beginning of the front-vowel scale and relaxed slightly for each succeeding vowel.

Vowel Sound in *He*. (Other spellings: *ea*t, b*ee*t, fat*i*gue, re*cei*pt, gr*ie*f, p*eo*ple, ph*oe*nix, C*ae*sar, qu*ay*, su*i*te.) To produce the vowel sound in *he*, the highest front vowel in English, brace the tip of your tongue against your lower teeth. Raise the front of your tongue toward your hard palate. Be sure that your lips are spread and that your teeth almost meet. This is the only vowel in the English language made with spread lips.

184

CHART OF ENGLISH VOWELS

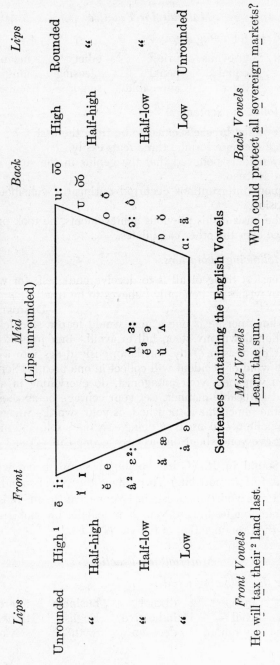

	Front	Mid (Lips unrounded)	Back		
Lips Unrounded	High ¹ ē i:		u: ōō	High	Rounded
"	Half-high ĭ ɪ		ʊ o͝o	Half-high	"
	ĕ e		o ŏ		
"	Half-low â² ɛ²:	ʊ̈ ɜ:	ɔ: ŏ	Half-low	"
		ĕ⁸ e	ɒ ŏ		
	ă æ	ŭ ʌ			
"	Low ȧ ɵ		α: ä	Low	Unrounded

Sentences Containing the English Vowels

Front Vowels
He will tax their ² land last.

Mid-Vowels
Learn the sum.

Back Vowels
Who could protect all sovereign markets?

¹ "High" refers to tongue placement, not to pitch.
² Note that ɛ: (â) is almost universally used in English as a blend of vowels, or a diphthong, rather than as a pure vowel.
³ In addition to ē, the following symbols are used to show the weak or obscure vowel in Webster's New International Dictionary: ă, ·., ĕ, ŏ, ŭ, ä, ɪ, ô.

Material for Practice

Pronounce the following words:

stream	grievous	priest	edict	mean
mien	equal	penal	pleasing	unique
league	brief	agreeable	senior	senile

Read the following sentences:

1. The evening breeze seemed to be from the east.
2. Each athlete performed three feats easily.
3. Many readers believed that the genius in the story would not succeed.
4. Frequent interruptions occurred during the vehement discussion.
5. On the basis of his previous achievements, he took precedence over the other candidates.

Read the following quotations:

1. The easiest thing of all is to deceive one's self; for what a man wishes he generally believes to be true.
   —DEMOSTHENES
2. A tedious person is one a man would leap a steeple from, gallop down any steep hill to avoid.—BEN JONSON
3. What the reason of the ant laboriously drags into a heap, the wind of accident will collect in one breath.—SCHILLER
4. When you meet your antagonist, do everything in a mild and agreeable manner. Let your courage be as keen, but at the same time as polished, as your sword.—SHERIDAN
5. True politeness consists in being easy one's self, and in making everyone about one as easy as one can.—POPE

Vowel Sound in *It*. (Other spellings: s*y*rup, b*ee*n, w*o*men, g*ui*lt, s*ie*ve, forf*ei*t, portr*ai*t.) To produce the vowel sound in *it*, brace the tip of your tongue against your lower teeth. Raise the front of your tongue toward your hard palate, but not quite so high as in the pronunciation of the vowel in *he*.

Material for Practice

Pronounce the following words:

gift	inch	dismal	business	interest
friction	civil	indicative	English	thinking
vanilla	sycamore	decision	myth	scissors

Read the following sentences:

1. Skill and precision require considerable discipline.
2. The invalid gossiped maliciously.
3. His fiction abounded in vivid descriptions.
4. A militant spirit existed beneath the judicial manner.
5. The political index was unfamiliar and difficult to interpret.

Read the following quotations:

1. If a man will begin with certainties, he will end with doubts; but if he will be content to begin with doubts, he shall end in certainties.—BACON
2. The principal office of history I take to be this: to prevent virtuous actions from being forgotten, and that evil words and deeds should fear an infamous reputation with posterity.—TACITUS
3. True education makes for inequality; the inequality of individuality, the inequality of success; the glorious inequality of talent, of genius; for inequality, not mediocrity, individual superiority, not standardization, is the measure of the progress of the world.—FELIX E. SCHELLING
4. In the country of the blind, the one-eyed man is king.
   —MICHAEL APOSTOLIUS
5. In our country and in our times no man is worthy the honored name of statesman who does not include the highest practicable education of the people in all his plans of administration.—HORACE MANN

Vowel Sound in *End.* (Other spellings: weather, many, Maryland, leopard, heifer, bury, friend, said, aesthetic, guest.) To produce the vowel sound in *end,* brace the tip of your tongue against your lower teeth. Raise the front of your tongue very slightly toward your hard palate.

Material for Practice

Pronounce the following words:

mental	twenty	direct	meant	steady
settled	send	Wednesday	guest	tread
seven	question	incredible	kerosene	pleasure

Read the following sentences:

1. Ten lecturers suggested recognized methods.
2. The enemy presented a credible impression.

3. Sympathetic friends read the confession without censure.
4. Several eccentric inventors resented the use of metal weapons.
5. Ten members protested the adoption of such desperate and selfish measures.

Read the following quotations:

1. I assure you that I had rather excel others in the knowledge of what is excellent, than in the extent of my power and dominion.—ALEXANDER THE GREAT
2. Advice is seldom welcome; and those who want it the most always like it the least.—LORD CHESTERFIELD
3. They defend their errors as if they were defending an inheritance.—EDMUND BURKE
4. Enmity is anger watching the opportunity for revenge.
   —CICERO
5. Integrity of life is fame's best friend,
   Which nobly, beyond death, shall crown the end.
   —JOHN WEBSTER

Vowel Sound in *Wear*. This sound will be included among the diphthongs on page 205.

Vowel Sound in *At*. (Other spellings: pl*ai*d, g*ua*rantee.) To produce the vowel sound in *at*, rest the tip of your tongue against your lower teeth. Relax your jaw; open your mouth more widely than for preceding vowels.

Material for Practice

Read the following words:

atom	manager	grandstand	campus	carried
active	garrulous	sandwich	handkerchief	rational
scatter	January	attractive	automatic	azure

Read the following sentences:

1. The naturalist had an admirable attitude.
2. Plans were made to print adequate financial analyses nationally.
3. Her family imagined the change in plans would be calamitous.
4. The narrative told of the fanatical attacks of the savages.
5. Stories told at random added to the lamentable lack of facts in the case.

Read the following quotations:

1. Let us then stand by the constitution as it is, and by our country as it is, one, united, and entire; let it be borne on the flag under which we rally in every exigency, that we have one country, one constitution, one destiny.
   —DANIEL WEBSTER

2. I would not anticipate the relish of any happiness, nor feel the weight of any misery, before it actually arrives.
   —ADDISON

3. An anvil to receive the hammer's blows and to forge the red-hot ore, he, without a groan, endured in silence.
   —AESCHYLUS

4. Man's capacities have never been measured; nor are we to judge of what he can do by any precedents, so little has been tried.—THOREAU

5. Man is not the creature of circumstances, circumstances are the creatures of men. We are free agents, and man is more powerful than matter.—DISRAELI

Vowel Sound in *Ask*. (Other spelling: *aunt*.) The vowel in *ask* is the lowest and most relaxed of the front vowels. To produce this sound, relax your tongue against your lower teeth. Your mouth should be more open than for preceding vowels and your jaw more relaxed.

Use of this sound varies throughout the English-speaking world. In British speech it is never used as a pure vowel, but as part of the diphthong in *my*. (See page 201.) In American speech it is an acceptable pure vowel, before the following syllable endings: *st* as in la*st; sk* as in ta*sk; f* as in hal*f; ss* as in cla*ss; th* as in pa*th*. This sound is also used in pronouncing some words from the French with the spelling *an*, as in dem*a*nd or ch*a*nce. The use of this vowel or the one in *at* in the above words depends on the part of the country from which the speaker comes.

Material for Practice

Pronounce the following words:

dance	advance	branches	tasks	moustache
passed	chant	calf	answer	fasten
crafty	laughing	craftsman	mask	caste

Read the following sentences:

1. The grant to the university had not only many advantages but also a few disadvantages.
2. Headmasters talked to the boys after class.
3. The cask became unfastened.
4. Orders from the command post came in the afternoon.
5. Lunch baskets were scattered on the grass near the path.

Read the following quotations:

1. The fireflies dance thro' the myrtle boughs.
   —FELICIA DOROTHEA HEMANS
2. The path of precept is long, that of example short and effectual.—SENECA
3. Let nothing pass that will advantage you.—DIONYSIUS CATO
4. Dawn, meanwhile, had restored her gentle light to weary men, recalling them to task and toil.—VIRGIL
5. What is chance but the rude stone which receives its life from the sculptor's hand? Providence gives us chance—and man must mould it to his own designs.—SCHILLER

BACK VOWELS

The back vowels are made with the back of the tongue high at the beginning of the scale. For the last three vowels on the back-vowel scale, the tip of the tongue hits the lower front teeth.

Vowel Sound in *Noon*. (Other spellings: fr*ui*t, gr*ou*p, tr*ue*, pr*o*ve, sh*oe*, tw*o*, dr*ew*, rh*eu*m, man*oeu*ver.) To produce the vowel in *noon,* the highest in tongue placement of the back vowels, round your lips or pout. Your tongue should not touch your teeth, but should be arched toward your soft palate.

Material for Practice

Pronounce the following words:

include	ruler	issue	loom	spoons
booth	shoot	rouge	balloon	zoo
choose	tools	June	chewed	blooming

Read the following sentences:

1. Groups gathered around the pool in the afternoon.
2. The soup was too cool.

3. All the recruits wanted to know the destination of the cruise.
4. Two shades of blue were included in the chart.
5. Some tools were left in the canoe by mistake.

Read the following quotations:

1. The prudent man may direct a state; but it is the enthusiast who regenerates it, or ruins.—BULWER-LYTTON
2. The roots of education are bitter, but the fruit is sweet.

—ARISTOTLE

3. It is saying less than the truth to affirm that an excellent book (and the remark holds almost equally good of a Raphael as of a Milton) is like a well-chosen and well-attended fruit tree. Its fruits are not of one season only.

—COLERIDGE

4. We are, in truth, more than half what we are by imitation. The great point is, to choose good models and to study them with care.—LORD CHESTERFIELD
5. Doing easily what others find difficult is talent; doing what is impossible *for talent* is genius.—AMIEL

Vowel Sound in *Wood*. (Other spellings: p*u*ll, w*ou*ld, w*o*man, W*o*rcestershire.) To produce the vowel sound in *wood*, round your lips and raise the back of your tongue toward your soft palate. Note that both your lips and tongue are slightly more relaxed than for the vowel in *noon*.

Material for Practice

Pronounce the following words:

stood	good	bush	should	brook
pulley	crooked	hood	could	cookies
pudding	cushion	push	pull	soot

Read the following sentences:

1. Balls of wool were put into a nook under the counter.
2. The butcher overlooked the message.
3. The good wood was easily separated from the damp wood.
4. A coach undertook to look for the book on football.
5. The cook mistook the sugar for the salt.

Read the following quotations:

1. Doing a favour for a bad man is quite as dangerous as doing an injury to a good one.—PLAUTUS

2. Fortune hath somewhat the nature of a woman; if she be too much wooed, she is the farther off.

—Emperor Charles V

3. There is often as much good sense required in knowing how to profit from good advice as there is to give it.

—La Rochefoucauld

4. Books are the compasses and telescopes and sextants and charts which other men have prepared to help us navigate the dangerous seas of human life.—Jesse Lee Bennett

5. That is a good book which is opened with expectation and closed with profit.—Amos Bronson Alcott

Initial Vowel Sound in *Omit*. To produce the initial sound in *omit*, round your lips. Raise the back of your tongue slightly toward your soft palate. This sound is usually a pure vowel in an unstressed syllable, as in *obey*, or *polite*, or in a stressed syllable followed immediately by an unstressed vowel, as in *knowing* or *Noah*.

Material for Practice [4]

Pronounce the following words:

obedient	cocaine	mosaic	sowing	police
opine	phonetic	foment	growing	notation
oblige	protest (*v.*)	tomorrow	Ohio	rotating

Read the following sentences:

1. Yellow curtains framed the window.
2. Many speakers omitted the motto.
3. The widow wished to borrow the music which was on top of the piano.
4. A rotunda protected the procession from the storm.
5. A protracted illness accounted for the athlete's absence from the Olympic Games.

Vowel Sound in *All*. (Other spellings: *awl*, c*au*ght, c*ou*rt, br*oa*d, extra*o*rdinary, Ge*o*rge, dw*ar*f.) To produce the vowel sound in *all*, round your lips and project them. Note that whereas the vowel in *noon* is pouted, the one in *all* is projected in lip position.

---

[4] Additional material for practice will be found in the chapter on the diphthong, page 202.

Material for Practice

Pronounce the following words:

Georgia	audible	yawning	because	warning
sword	thawed	vault	warm	aural
falling	fault	warp	sought	formidable

Read the following sentences:

1. The audience thought it fortunate that the story was reported orally.
2. The author had exhausted all normal sources in an attempt to find the portrait.
3. According to all present, the subject was extraordinarily important.
4. The water in the cauldron was scalding.
5. All nautical activity was fraught with danger because of the storm.

Read the following quotations:

1. He who is false to present duty breaks a thread in the loom, and will find the flaw when he may have forgotten its cause.—HENRY WARD BEECHER
2. Fortune can give no greater advantage than discord among the enemy.—TACITUS
3. Of all our faults, that which we excuse the most easily is idleness.—LA ROCHEFOUCAULD
4. There is this difference between renown and glory—the latter depends upon the judgments of the many, the former on the judgments of good men.—SENECA
5. Of all villainy, there is none more base than that of the hypocrite, who, at the moment he is most false, takes care to appear most virtuous.—CICERO

Vowel Sound in *Not*. (Other spellings: w*a*tt, tr*ou*gh, ackn*ow*ledge.) To produce the vowel sound in *not,* round your lips slightly. Relax your tongue against your lower teeth.

Throughout the country there is a great deal of variation in the use of this sound. A sound as relaxed as the vowel in *calm* or as tense as the vowel sound in *caught* is sometimes used. Since the use of this sound is determined regionally, try to be consistent in whatever variation you use.

Material for Practice

Pronounce the following words:

authority	cloth	chocolate	monotonous	foreign
coral	knowledge	officer	scholar	forehead
logic	bonds	historical	constant	obligated

Read the following sentences:

1. The scholar's occupations were sketched chronologically in his biography.
2. Volume one of the novel was too involved in plot.
3. Both the doctors and the office staff of the hospital enjoyed the hot coffee.
4. A stenographer, who spoke in a soft voice, acknowledged the loss of the watch.
5. The cost of building a modern college on the lot was impossibly high.

Read the following quotations:

1. The best plan is, as the common proverb has it, to profit by the folly of others.—PLINY THE ELDER
2. Intolerance itself is a form of egoism, and to condemn egoism intolerantly is to share it.—GEORGE SANTAYANA
3. Inasmuch as ill deeds spring up as a spontaneous crop, they are easy to learn.—CERVANTES
4. Debt is a grievous bondage to an honorable man.
   —PUBLILIUS SYRUS
5. Even so, when the framework of the world is dissolved, and the final hour, closing so many ages, reverts to pristine chaos, then the fiery stars will drop into the sea, and earth will shake off the ocean,—and the whole distracted fabric of the shattered firmament will overthrow its laws.—LUCAN

Vowel Sound in *Alms*. (Other spellings, h*ea*rth, s*e*rgeant, mem*oi*r, gu*a*rd.) To produce the vowel in *alms*, relax your tongue against your lower teeth; open your mouth and relax your lower jaw. This sound is the *most open vowel* in the English language because the mouth is open to its widest position. Also concentrate on relaxing your tongue so that there is no depression in it as you practice this sound.

Material for Practice

Pronounce the following words:

balm	harp	almond	hearth	guard
father	artifice	barn	stars	alarm
heart	guitar	arms	garden	particle

Read the following sentences:

1. A partisan group gathered around the hearth.
2. The architect calmly smoked a cigar.
3. Harp music provided the background for the drama.
4. The artist had a suave manner.
5. The farmer started off tardily in his cart.

Read the following quotations:

1. Architecture is pre-eminently the art of significant forms in space—that is, forms significant of their functions.

—CLAUDE BRAGDON

2. There is no such thing as a dumb poet or a handless painter. The essence of an artist is that he should be articulate.

—SWINBURNE

3. Architecture is frozen music.—GOETHE
4. The heart has such an influence over the understanding, that it is worth while to engage it in our interest.

—LORD CHESTERFIELD

5. Harmony makes small things grow; lack of it makes great things decay.—SALLUST

MID–VOWELS

The mid-vowels are made with the middle of the tongue slightly raised toward the hard palate.

Vowel Sound in *Earn*. (Other spellings: *urn*, *fir*, *work*, *guerdon*, *journal*, *term*, *myrrh*, *colonel*, *amateur*.) To produce the vowel sound in *earn*, rest the tip of your tongue against your lower teeth; arch the middle of your tongue slightly. Note that your lips should be in a neutral position, not rounded nor spread.

Material for Practice

Pronounce the following words:

defer	ferns	research	urgent	journey
birds	firm	discern	adjourn	worthy
turned	curb	pertinent	murmur	emerge

Read the following sentences:

1. The clerk erred in her personal interpretation of the sermon.
2. An early volume of the journal irked the earnest amateurs.
3. The colonel heard that the plans for the merger were absurd.
4. Although he was disturbed by the unseemly mirth, the interpreter terminated the interview with a few courteous words.
5. The architect preferred not to incur the wrath of the church wardens.

Read the following quotations:

1. He who errs quickly, is quick in correcting the error.—BACON
2. Adversity makes a man wise, though not rich.

—THOMAS FULLER

3. The greatest object in the universe, says a certain philosopher, is a good man struggling with adversity; yet there is a still greater, which is the good man that comes to relieve it.—GOLDSMITH
4. The globe we inhabit is divisible into two worlds: the common geographical world, and the world of books.

—LEIGH HUNT

5. Nothing is so galling to a people, not broken in from the birth, as a paternal or, in other words, a meddling government, a government which tells them what to read and say and eat and drink and wear.—MACAULAY

Initial Vowel Sound in *Alone*. (Other spellings: rec*e*nt, circ*u*s, c*o*nnect, pi*ou*s, porp*oi*se, n*a*tion, mak*e*r, profess*o*r, sulph*u*r, elix*i*r, medioc*re*, sat*yr*, barg*ai*n.) This sound, which is the weakest vowel in English, is described in a variety of ways. Some phoneticians call it the *neutral* or *obscure vowel;* others, the *indeterminate* or *indefinite vowel;* still others, the *voiced murmur* or *schwa.* This vowel never occurs in a stressed syllable.

To produce this sound, your lips should be in a neutral position and your tongue relaxed.

Material for Practice

Pronounce the following words:

arrive	consumer	pattern	attain	zephyr
about	forget	contend	comfortable	member
sofa	modern	appear	surface	actor

Read the following sentences:

1. Originally, the collection of jewels was imported from Asia at the turn of the century.
2. The conspirators agreed that the problem would be difficult to avoid.
3. Conflicting opinions confused the jurors.
4. A small faction of interested persons contested the appointment.
5. The defendant gathered his friends around him.

Read the following quotations:

1. Men acquire a particular quality by constantly acting in a particular way.—ARISTOTLE
2. Paradoxes are useful to attract attention to ideas.
   —MANDELL CREIGHTON
3. To be idle and to be poor have always been reproaches, and therefore every man endeavors with his utmost care to hide his poverty from others, and his idleness from himself.—SAMUEL JOHNSON
4. Ignorance is a voluntary misfortune.—UNKNOWN
5. Guilt is present in the very hesitation, even though the deed be not committed.—CICERO

Vowel Sound in *Up*. (Other spellings: t*ou*ch, s*o*me, bl*oo*d, d*oe*s.) There is some disagreement among phoneticians as to the exact placement of the tongue for the production of the vowel sound in *up*. It is generally agreed, however, that you should raise the middle of your tongue very slightly and keep your lips in a neutral position in producing this sound.

Material for Practice

Pronounce the following words:

mumble	nourish	brush	tongue	buffalo
company	wonder	shutter	bluffing	plucking
courage	trouble	covered	rough	lucky

Read the following sentences:

1. Because of the large sums of money involved, the blunder was doubly serious.
2. The judge hurried to meet his son.
3. Only one of the firemen was overcome while smothering the flames.

4. Many publishers struggle to obtain manuscripts of high cultural value.
5. The younger man suffered from the abrupt withdrawal of public trust.

Read the following quotations:

1. Everyone excels in something in which another fails.
   —PUBLILIUS SYRUS
2. Let our object be, our country, our whole country, and nothing but our country. And by the blessing of God, may that country itself become a vast and splendid monument, not of oppression and terror, but of wisdom, of peace, and of liberty, upon which the world may gaze with admiration forever.—DANIEL WEBSTER
3. Our enemies come nearer the truth in the judgments they form of us than we do in our judgment of ourselves.
   —LA ROCHEFOUCAULD
4. Who can be called noble who is unworthy of his race, and distinguished in nothing but his name?—JUVENAL
5. Hereditary nobility is due to the presumption that we shall do well because our fathers have done well.—JOUBERT

16

English Diphthongs

A diphthong is produced when two vowel sounds are pronounced in the same syllable. Each diphthong begins with one vowel sound and ends with another, but the sounds are enunciated so quickly that is impossible to tell where one ends and the other begins.

ELEMENTS OF DIPHTHONGS

The two component parts of a diphthong are called its elements. The first element in an English diphthong is always stronger than the second; the second is never stressed. In phonetics, the mark (˘) over the second element of a diphthong shows that it is short and weak.

PRONUNCIATION OF DIPHTHONGS

There are nine diphthongs in English. Some authorities include the *ū* of *ūse* as a diphthong, but the manner of making this sound varies. Since many speakers produce it with the *y* of *yes*, which is a vowel-like consonant, and the vowel in *fo͞od*, rather than with two vowels, it is not treated as a diphthong in this book.

Diphthongs may be grouped according to their second elements. For example, three diphthongs end in the vowel sound in *it*, as shown in the following sentence: *Play my choice:* [eĭ] (ā); [âĭ] (ī); [ɔĭ] (oi).

Two diphthongs end in the vowel sound in *wood*, as shown by: *Slow down:* [oŭ] (ō); [aŭ] (ou).

Four diphthongs end with the weak vowel used initially in *alone*, as shown by: *Clear their poor shore:* [iə̆] (ē); [ɛə̆] (â); [uə̆] (o͞or); [ɔə̆] (ōr).

Diphthong in *Day*. (Other spellings: p*ai*n, r*eig*n, th*ey*, br*ea*k, cr*oque*t, g*au*ge.) To produce this diphthong, rest the tip of your

199

tongue against your lower teeth, as in the vowel in *end*. In completing the diphthong, raise the tip of your tongue very slightly to the position for the vowel in *it*.

Material for Practice

Pronounce the following words:

blame	painted	praise	places	fate
bouquet	radio	ancient	eight	plaintiff
prevail	patriot	claim	planes	situation

Read the following sentences:

1. The complaint stated that the apparatus should have been saved.
2. Miscellaneous data pertaining to related occupations were mailed on the same day.
3. Ancient fables were enacted on the stage.
4. In the face of grave danger, the aviator gave an amazing display of bravery.
5. The famous painter was dismayed at the failure of his protégé's painting.

Read the following quotations:

1. In great straits and when hope is small, the boldest counsels are the safest.—LIVY
2. Those who compare the age in which their lot has fallen with a golden age which exists only in imagination, may talk of degeneracy and decay; but no man who is correctly informed as to the past, will be disposed to take a morose or desponding view of the present.—MACAULAY
3. Nature contains the elements, in colour and form, of all pictures, as the keyboard contains the notes of all music.
—J. McNEILL WHISTLER
4. The primary indication, to my thinking, of a well-ordered mind is a man's ability to remain in one place and linger in his own company.—SENECA
5. While an author is yet living, we estimate his powers by his worst performance; and when he is dead, we rate them by his best.—SAMUEL JOHNSON

Diphthong in *Time*. (Other spellings: l*ie*, l*ye*, def*y*, h*eigh*t, g*ey*ser, rh*y*me, gu*i*de, b*uy*, ch*oir*, qu*ire*.) To produce the first element of this diphthong, relax your tongue against your lower teeth as for the vowel in *ask;* for the second element, raise the tip of your tongue to the position for the vowel in *it.*

Material for Practice

Pronounce the following words:

mild	decline	define	knife	lightning
ivory	tricycle	combine	arthritis	preside
vitamin	pilot	reply	night	primarily

Read the following sentences:

1. Winding roads led to an aisle of pine trees.
2. Every ninth child in the line was assigned a part.
3. The site for the new high school is five miles from the island.
4. The tyrant was deposed by foes who had been conspiring against him for a long time.
5. Before he became acclimated to the island, the blind man resigned his post.

Read the following quotations:

1. Eternity is not an everlasting flux of time, but time is as a short parenthesis in a long period.—JOHN DONNE
2. Anybody can become angry—that is easy; but to be angry with the right person, and to the right degree, and at the right time, and for the right purpose, and in the right way—that is not within everybody's power and is not easy.—ARISTOTLE
3. We require from buildings, as from men, two kinds of goodness; first, the doing their practical duty well; then that they be graceful and pleasing in doing it; which last is itself another form of duty.—RUSKIN
4. I desire to see the time when education, and by its means, morality, sobriety, enterprise and industry, shall become much more general than at present.—ABRAHAM LINCOLN
5. In the highest civilization, the book is still the highest delight. He who has once known its satisfactions is provided with a resource against calamity.—EMERSON

Diphthong in *Oil.* (Other spellings: roy*al,* bu*oy.*) To produce the first element of this diphthong, project your lips as for the vowel in *all;* for the second element, raise the tip of your tongue to the position for the vowel in *it.*

Material for Practice

Pronounce the following words:

coins	poisonous	destroy	rejoicing	avoiding
oysters	rejoinder	disappointment	moisture	annoyed
ointment	adjoining	joyous	appointment	choice

Read the following sentences:

1. Joy over the new toy made the boy boisterous.
2. Employers should check carefully the records of their employees.
3. Noisy voices spoiled a poignant scene.
4. Choices for the appointment were limited.
5. The speaker had poise and a buoyant manner.

Read the following quotations:

1. No man who is in fear, or sorrow, or turmoil is free, but whoever is rid of sorrows and fears and turmoils, that man is by the self-same course rid of slavery.—EPICTETUS
2. Give yourself time and room; what reason could not avoid, delay has often cured.—SENECA
3. His voice was thin, as voices from the grave.—TENNYSON
4. Troilus had rather Troy were borne to Greece than Cressid borne from Troy.—SHAKESPEARE
5. Genius? It is the power to be a boy again at will.

—J. M. BARRIE

Diphthong in Go. (Other spellings: road, foe, sew, yeoman, mauve, beau, brooch.) To produce the first element of this diphthong, round your lips and raise the back of your tongue to the half-high position of the first vowel in *omit;* for the second element, raise the back of your tongue slightly to the position of the vowel sound in *wood*.

Material for Practice

Pronounce the following words:

remote	locomotives	oval	spoken	suppose
depose	pony	disclose	sewed	alone
postpone	fold	local	loaves	oppose

Read the following sentences:

1. Old outmoded photographs were sold at the auction.
2. The rower was alone on the ocean in an open boat.

3. He wrote a note for the amount he owed.
4. Long cloaks, trimmed with precious stones, were in vogue then.
5. The tones of the organ rose slowly and seemed to fill the old church.

Read the following quotations:

1. Now sloth triumphs over energy, indolence over exertion, vice over virtue, arrogance over courage, and theory over practice in arms, which flourished and shone only in the golden ages.—CERVANTES
2. For just as I approve of a young man in whom there is a touch of age, so I approve of the old man in whom there is some of the flavor of youth. He who strives thus to mingle youthfulness and age may grow old in body, but old in spirit he will never be.—CICERO
3. Alone of the gods, Death loves not gifts; no, not by sacrifice, nor by libation, canst thou aught avail with him; he hath no altar nor hath he hymn of praise; from him, alone of gods, Persuasion stands aloof.—AESCHYLUS
4. To know what you prefer, instead of humbly saying Amen to what the world tells you you ought to prefer, is to have kept your soul alive.—R. L. STEVENSON
5.   To fear the foe, since fear oppresseth strength,
     Gives in your weakness strength unto your foe,
     And so your follies fight against yourself.
                                        —SHAKESPEARE

Diphthong in *Now*. (Other spellings: f*ou*nd, s*au*erkraut.) To produce the first element of this diphthong, relax your tongue against your lower teeth as for the vowel in *alms*. Then raise the back of your tongue to the position for the vowel sound in *wood*.

Material for Practice

Pronounce the following words:

rebound	powerful	tower	without	doubtful
shower	aloud	devout	ground	proud
brown	hour	boughs	crown	astounded

Read the following sentences:

1. An ounce of prevention is worth a pound of cure.
2. Many townspeople were aroused by the announcement.

3. The clown frowned as he bounded around the stage.
4. Crowds of people prowled around the flower beds for hours.
5. There is often doubt about the way to pronounce proper nouns.

Read the following quotations:

1. Of all the inanimate objects, of all men's creations, books are the nearest to us, for they contain our very thoughts, our ambitions, our indignations, our illusions, our fidelity to truth, and our persistent leaning toward error. But most of all they resemble us in their precarious hold on life.—JOSEPH CONRAD

2.   Our purses shall be proud, our garments poor;
     For 'tis the mind that makes the body rich;
     And as the sun breaks through the darkest clouds,
     So honour peereth in the meanest habit.

                                        —SHAKESPEARE

3. I have seen the glories of art and architecture, and mountain and river; I have seen the sunset on the Jungfrau, and the full moon rise over Mont Blanc; but the fairest vision on which these eyes ever looked was the flag of my country in a foreign land. Beautiful as a flower to those who love it, terrible as a meteor to those who hate it, it is the symbol of the power and glory, and in honor, of fifty millions of Americans.—GEORGE FRISBIE HOAR

4. The book is doubly gifted: it moves to laughter, and by its counsel teaches a wise man how to live.—PHAEDRUS

5.   So clouds replenish'd from some bog below,
     Mount in dark volumes, and descend in snow.

                                             —POPE

Diphthong in *Ear*. (Other spellings: h*ere*, p*ier*ce, ven*eer*, w*eir*d.) To produce the first element of this diphthong, brace the tip of your tongue against your lower teeth as for the vowel in *it*. For the second element, relax your tongue for the weak mid-vowel used initially in *alone*.

Material for Practice

Pronounce the following words:

austere	series	sheers	theater	theorum
queer	steering	sincere	query	realize
gear	yearly	dear	serious	superior

Read the following sentences:

1. Unfortunately, the material appeared to be inferior.
2. Many directors failed to realize that the theater in that era was really dreary.
3. The rent was nearly a year in arrears.
4. Both speakers answered the query clearly.
5. Vera feared that the earrings had been lost for a long period.

Read the following quotations:

1. Appearances to the mind are of four kinds: things either are what they appear to be; or they neither are, nor appear to be; or they are, and do not appear to be; or they are not, and yet appear to be. Rightly to aim in all these cases is the wise man's task.—EPICTETUS
2. Of Forests, and Enchantments drear,
   Where more is meant than meets the ear.
   —MILTON
3. Yet still we hug the dear deceit.—NATHANIEL COTTON
4. By experience we find out a shorter way by a long wandering. Learning teacheth more in one year than experience in twenty.—ROGER ASCHAM
5. The man who fears nothing is not less powerful than he who is feared by every one.—SCHILLER

Diphthong in *Air.* (Other spellings: w*ear*, wh*ere*, p*are*, h*eir*, pr*ayer*, e'*er*, th*ey're.*) This diphthong has as its first element a sound rarely used as a pure vowel in English. To produce the first element, rest the tip of your tongue against your lower teeth for a sound between the vowel in *end* and the vowel in *at.* For the second element, relax your tongue for the weak mid-vowel used initially in *alone.*

Material for Practice

Pronounce the following words:

chary	wearing	prairie	fares	careful
compare	caring	snare	flare	hairpin
chairs	airplane	heiress	staircase	precarious

Read the following sentences:

1. Mary and Sarah found the glare unbearable.
2. All the beach chairs were repaired promptly after the storm.

3. The heir to the fortune was scarcely aware of the number of shares of stock he had.
4. Various sketches were fairly hilarious.
5. From the landing at the top of the stairs, they had an unimpaired view of the lake.

Read the following quotations:

1. What cannot be repaired is not to be regretted.

—SAMUEL JOHNSON

2. Know Nature's children all divide her care;
   The fur that warms a monarch warm'd a bear.

—ALEXANDER POPE

3. What they dare to dream of, dare to do.—J. R. LOWELL
4. It is uncertain where death may await thee, therefore expect it everywhere.—SENECA
5. Wherever the Fates, in their ebb and flow, lead, let us follow.—VIRGIL

Diphthong in *Sure*. (Other spellings: p*oor*, *Eu*rope, *you're*.) To produce the first element of this diphthong, raise the back of your tongue to the position of the vowel sound in *wood*. For the second element, relax your tongue for the weak mid-vowel used initially in *alone*.

Material for Practice

Pronounce the following words:

bureau	securing	fury	insured	cure
mature	surely	injurious	poor	furiously
endure	curious	detour	brochure	during

Read the following sentences:

1. The tourists were sure that their insurance covered all airplane flights.
2. Members of the jury were furious at the length of time required to secure a decision.
3. The artist was assured that the mural would be hung in the European wing.
4. Her maturity was somewhat obscured by her demure manner.
5. Pure water was difficult to procure on the moor.

Read the following quotations:

1. Words but direct, example must allure.
   —Sir William Alexander

2. Better it were little to feign,
   And cleanly cover that cannot be cured:
   Such ill as is forced must needs be endured.
   —Spenser

3. Nothing befalls any man which he is not fitted to endure.
   —Marcus Aurelius

4. That action is best which procures the greatest happiness for the greatest numbers.—Francis Hutcheson

5. How to gain, how to keep, how to recover happiness is in fact for most men at all times the secret motive of all they do, and of all they are willing to endure.—William James

Diphthong in *Ore*. (Other spellings: d*oor*, tow*ard*, *o'er*, b*oard*, p*our*.) To produce the first element of this diphthong, project your lips as for the vowel sound in *all*. For the second element, relax your tongue for the weak mid-vowel used initially in *alone*.

Note that a pure vowel is sometimes substituted for this diphthong, especially in the middle of a phrase, as in: *Close the door, please.*

Material for Practice

Pronounce the following words:

shore	pores	implore	deplorable	chores
bore	stores	ignore	pouring	roaring
adoring	evermore	exploring	oars	soars

Read the following sentences:

1. The clerks in the store wore uniforms.
2. The speaker deplored the fact that the core of the matter had not been reached.
3. It was impossible to ignore the lore of the country.
4. The oars were left near the seashore.
5. Four floors were restored in the building.

Read the following quotations:

1. Avarice, mother of crimes, greedy for more the more she possesses, ever searching open-mouthed for gold.
   —Claudian

2. The bore is usually considered a harmless creature, or of that class of irrational bipeds who hurt only themselves.
   —Maria Edgeworth

3. The south wind searches for the flowers whose fragrance
   late he bore,
   And sighs to find them in the wood and by the stream no
   more.

—BRYANT

4.   Once more the liberal year laughs out
                     O'er richer stores than gems of gold;
                  Once more with harvest song and shout
                     Is nature's boldest triumph told.

—WHITTIER

5. I am not the flag; not at all. . . . I am no more than you
   believe me to be and I am all that you believe I can be. I
   am whatever you make me, nothing more.

—FRANKLIN K. LANE

Exercises

1. Pronounce the letters *a, e, i, o,* and *u.* Listen carefully to the
sounds for each letter. How many pure vowels are there in this
group of letters?

2. Group the following words into two categories. In one,
place all the words containing diphthongs; in the other, all the
words with pure vowels in their stressed syllables (note how frequently two letters in the spelling stand for only one sound): *fear,
head, great, flare, are, hear, heard, gear, gate, greed, poor, school,
door, seed, sheathe, autumn.*

3. Pronounce the following words in groups, noting the length
of the diphthongs:

| rate | voice | out | ride | code |
| right | coat | raid | noise | crowd |

Can you deduce a rule about the length of diphthongs from the
above examples?

4. Do you hear more vowels made into diphthongs than are
included in this chapter? If so, which vowels are they? Is this
tendency to fracture vowels a characteristic of the regional
speech in your area?

5. Pronounce the following words, listening carefully to the final
sound: *more, pour, soar, roar, ignore.* Does the final sound vary
when the word is used in the middle of a short phrase, as in:
*more time; pour the water; to soar above the clouds; ignore the
principle?* Is the final sound of *more, pour, soar, roar,* and *ignore*
the same in the phrase as it is when the word is alone?

17

English Consonants

Unlike vowel sounds, which are produced by a free flow of breath, consonant sounds are caused by an interruption to the flow of breath by the organs of articulation. In other words, the lips, tongue, teeth, or velum may sufficiently interfere with the flow of air to cause audible friction, thus producing consonant sounds as in the words, *fee, tea, three,* and *key,* respectively.

CLASSIFICATION OF CONSONANT SOUNDS

Consonants may be classified according to: (1) voiceless or voiced sounds; (2) the manner of articulation; and (3) the place of articulation.

Classification According to Voiceless or Voiced Sounds; Cognates. Unlike vowels, all of which are voiced, consonants fall into two groups, voiceless and voiced. If there is no vibration of the vocal cords when a sound is produced, as in the case of *f* or *t,* it is a *voiceless* sound. If there is a vibration, it is a *voiced* sound, as in the case of *v* or *d.* Most of the voiceless sounds have voiced counterparts known as *cognates.* (Thus, *b, d, v,* and *g* are the cognates of *p, t, f,* and *k.*)

Classification According to the Manner of Articulation. Consonants in English are commonly classified according to the way in which they are produced.

STOP-PLOSIVES. These consonants, also called plosives, stops, and explosives, are produced by a stopping and then a sudden releasing of the flow of air. The stop-plosives are *p, b, t, k,* and *g.*

CONTINUANTS. Continuants, unlike stop-plosives, may be continued or prolonged during a breath. They are classified into *nasals, laterals,* and *fricatives.*

Nasals. Nasal continuants are *m, n,* and *ng* (ŋ). These sounds are produced by stopping the air in the mouth and emitting it through the nostrils.

Lateral. The only lateral sound in English is *l*, made by placing the tip of the tongue on the upper gum ridge and emitting air over the sides of the tongue.

Fricatives. Fricatives are produced by forcing the breath through a very narrow opening formed by the organs of articulation. Fricative sounds are *f*, *v*, *th* in *thin*, *th* in *then*, *r*, *h*, *s*, *z*, *sh*, and *zh*. Of these, the last four, *s*, *z*, *sh*, and *zh*, are also called sibilant, or hissing, sounds.

GLIDES. Glides are characterized by continuous movement of a speech organ or organs while the sound is being produced. The glides include *w* in *we*, *wh* in *when*, and the initial sound in *yes*.

VOWEL-LIKE CONSONANTS. The vowel-like consonants are so called because they have some of the characteristics of vowels. There is, for example, very little interruption of air in their production. They include: *w*, *r*, *l*, *m*, *n*, *ng* (ŋ), and the *y* of *yes*.

GLOTTAL SOUNDS. Glottal sounds are those produced in the glottis, which is the name given to the opening between the vocal cords. The only acceptable glottal sound in English is *h*, as in *here*.

AFFRICATE SOUNDS. Affricate sounds are stops or plosives followed immediately by fricatives. The affricates include *ch* in *chair* and *j* in *jam*. These two sounds may also be classified as sibilant, since they end with sibilant sounds.

SYLLABIC SOUNDS. Syllabic sounds are those which take the place of a vowel in forming a syllable. They occur, therefore, only in weak syllables, as in *able, chasm,* and *eaten.* In diacritically marked dictionaries, they are usually designated in the following way: '*l*, '*m*, and '*n*. In phonetic transcription, a small vertical line is placed under the syllabic sound, as in *l̩*, *m̩*, and *n̩*.

Classification According to the Place of Articulation. Consonants may be classified according to the organs of articulation that produce them. Lip sounds are produced by the lips; tongue-teeth sounds by the tongue and teeth; tongue-gum sounds by the tongue on the upper gum ridge; the palatal sound by the action of the front of the tongue on the hard or bony portion of the palate; soft-palate sounds by the action of the back of the tongue against the soft palate or velum; and the glottal sound by the action of the glottis. In English the glottal sound is *h*.

In the present chapter, the consonants are classified according to place of articulation.

LABIAL (OR LIP) SOUNDS

Labial sounds are divided into two classes: (1) Bilabial consonants, so called because they are made by the action of the lips. Bilabial consonants include *p, b, m, w,* and *wh* in *whoa.* (2) Labiodental consonants are produced by the pressure of the upper teeth on the lower lip. These are *f* and *v.*

Consonant Sound in *Pie.* (Other spellings: pe*pp*er, hiccou*gh.*) This consonant is a bilabial, stop-plosive, voiceless sound. To produce it, close your lips and quickly separate them.

Material for Practice

Pronounce the following words:

pry	supper	people	pauper	cape
pirate	peppermint	corpse	pomp	wrap
preparation	pump	helped	proper	proprietor

Read the following sentences:

1. The plot was based on an adaptation of an old Spanish play.
2. Competent and experienced Shakespearean actors put on the production.
3. A popular landscape architect landscaped the municipal building.
4. Rapid progress was apparent in many aspects of the sculptor's work.
5. Some of the apple and peach trees on the property belonged to a prosperous planter.

Read the following quotations:

1. He was wont to speak plain, and to the purpose, like an honest man and a soldier.—SHAKESPEARE
2. Flowers have an expression of countenance as much as men or animals. Some seem to smile; some have a sad expression; some are pensive and diffident; others again are plain, honest and upright, like the broadfaced sunflower and the hollyhock.—HENRY WARD BEECHER
3. To complain of the age we live in, to murmur at the pres-

ent possessors of power, to lament the past, to conceive
extravagant hopes of the future, are the common dispo-
sitions of the greatest part of mankind.—EDMUND BURKE

4.   Four things come not back:

The spoken word; The sped arrow;
Time past; The neglected opportunity.
—OMAR IBN AL-KHATTAB

5. To talk nonsense, or poetry, or to dash between the two, in
a tone of profound sincerity, and to enunciate solemn
discordances with received opinion so seriously as to convey the impression of a spiritual insight, is the peculiar
gift by which monomaniacs, having first persuaded themselves, contrive to influence their neighbors, and through
them to make conquest of a good half of the world, for
good or for ill.—GEORGE MEREDITH

Consonant Sound in *Boy*. (Other spelling: e*bb*.) This consonant is the voiced cognate of *p*. To produce it, press your lips
together; voice the sound as you release your lips.

Material for Practice

Pronounce the following words:

bubble	grumble	rebellion	laborer	responsible
imbibe	neighbor	stumble	Barbara	capable
bauble	humble	rebate	baseball	amber

Read the following sentences:

1. Combat scenes were described in the beginning of the book.
2. Publishers objected to the observations made on the broadcast.
3. The artist was not responsible for the publicity about his
exhibit.
4. A barely noticeable resemblance existed between the
brothers.
5. Even against a battalion of formidable combatants, the
rebels were brave.

Read the following quotations:

1. The probability that we may fail in the struggle ought not
to deter us from the support of a cause we believe to be
just.—ABRAHAM LINCOLN

2. Unblest is he who thinks himself unblest.—SENECA
3. A dear bargain is always disagreeable, because it is a reflection upon the judgment of the buyer.

—PLINY THE YOUNGER

4. Wisdom is the abstract of the past, but beauty is the prom-
ise of the future.—O. W. HOLMES
5.   But, should you lure
From his dark haunt beneath the tangled roots
Of pendent trees the monarch of the brook,
Behoves you then to ply your finest art.

—THOMSON

Consonant Sound in *Me*. (Other spellings: ha*mm*er, hy*mn*.)
This consonant is a bilabial, voiced, nasal, continuant sound. To
produce it, keep your lips closed rather than separated as you did
to produce *p* and *b*. As your soft palate is lowered, air is forced
through your nose.

This sound may take the place of a vowel in a weak syllable.
It is then called a *syllabic consonant,* as in *chasm.*

Material for Practice

Pronounce the following words:

murmuring	million	mine	chasm	animal
fumed	elms	warm	humming	forum
summon	music	crumb	main	memorable

Read the following sentences:

1. The compiler accomplished a monumental task in preparing
the volume.
2. Many men, famous in the field of mass communication,
conducted the symposium.
3. A man of medium height mended the umbrella.
4. The pamphlet described new methods of dealing with films.
5. Timely reminders were written on the margins of the manuscript.

Read the following quotations:

1. There is no mood to which a man may not administer the
appropriate medicine at the cost of reaching down a volume from his bookshelf.—ARTHUR BALFOUR

2. It is the common wonder of all men how, among so many million of faces, there should be none alike.

—SIR THOMAS BROWNE

3. What holy cities are to nomadic tribes—a symbol of race and a bond of union—great books are to the wandering souls of men: they are the Meccas of the mind.

—G. E. WOODBERRY

4. It is a most mortifying reflection for a man to consider what he has done, compared with what he might have done.

—SAMUEL JOHNSON

5.   O purblind race of miserable men,
         How many among us at this very hour
         Do forge a lifelong trouble for ourselves
         By taking true for false, or false for true!

—TENNYSON

Consonant Sound in *Whoa*. To produce this voiceless consonant, raise the back of your tongue. Round your lips; separate them quickly. Actually the sound *h* precedes *w*, an approximation to the Old English spelling of *hw*.

Material for Practice

Pronounce the following words:

wheel	whip	overwhelm	whine	where
when	whirl	everywhere	whet	whistle
why	whisper	wheat	whether	whippoorwill

Read the following sentences:

1. White flowers were placed where they could be seen easily.
2. Whirling wheels disturbed the whining dog.
3. Which of Whittier's poems are on the list?
4. What quantity of wheat is to be sold?
5. The train whistle seemed overwhelmingly loud to the passengers.

Read the following quotations:

1. What a man does, not what he feels, thinks, or believes, is the universal yardstick of behavior.

—BENJAMIN C. LEEMING

2. Why does the rose her grateful fragrance yield?—JOHN GRAY
3. What is a great life? It is the dream of youth realized in old age.—ALFRED DE VIGNY

4. What is more melancholy than the old apple trees that linger about the spot where once stood a homestead, but where there is now only a ruined chimney rising out of a grassy and weed-grown cellar?—HAWTHORNE

5. When I read rules of criticism, I immediately inquire after the works of the author who has written them, and by that means discover what it is he likes in a composition.
—ADDISON

Consonant Sound in We. (Other spellings: *qu*een, per*su*ade, *o*nce, mem*oir*.) This consonant is a voiced, bilabial glide. To produce it, round your lips, raise the back of your tongue. Separate your lips quickly.

Material for Practice

Pronounce the following words:

weary	witness	querulous	twice	persuasion
wisdom	warrior	queer	twirl	wonder
suave	quick	quaint	swear	anyone

Read the following sentences:

1. Members of the choir could not be dissuaded easily.
2. The weather cleared quickly.
3. A quorum was required for the meeting to begin.
4. One of the men was quite old and quarrelsome.
5. A quick switch in plans was made because of the wintry wind.

Read the following quotations:

1. Of the things which man can do or make here below, by far the most momentous, wonderful, and worthy are the things we call Books!—CARLYLE
2. The only faith that wears well and holds its color in all weathers, is that which is woven of conviction and set with the sharp mordant of experience.—J. R. LOWELL
3. Love of fame is the last weakness which even the wise resign.—TACITUS
4. To sing well and dance well are accomplishments which advance one very little in the world.—ROUSSEAU
5. One is never so ridiculous for the qualities he has as for those he pretends to have.—LA ROCHEFOUCAULD

Consonant Sound in Foe. (Other spellings: *ph*antom, lau*gh*, o*ff*.) This consonant is a voiceless, fricative, labiodental sound.

To produce it, place your lower lip lightly against the edges of your upper teeth; blow the air out through the narrow channel thus formed.

Material for Practice

Pronounce the following words:

fountain	faith	defect	cough	rough
freedom	friends	coffee	conform	half
physician	emphasis	suffice	enough	epitaph

Read the following sentences:

1. His course in ethics was the famous "Philosophy Four."
2. If sufficient effort had been made, the plan might have been effective.
3. Phials of camphor were found in the office.
4. The physician noticed that Francis coughed frequently.
5. Deafening confusion emphasized the effect of the statement.

Read the following quotations:

1. Even from a foe a man may wisdom learn.—ARISTOPHANES
2. Surfeit has killed many more men than famine.—THEOGNIS
3. Fragrant the fertile earth after soft showers.—MILTON
4. The fatal tendency of mankind to leave off thinking about a thing, when it is no longer doubtful, is the cause of half their errors.—J. S. MILL
5. It is futile to assign the place an artist is likely to take in the future. There are fashions in immortality as there are trivial fashions.—WILLIAM ROTHENSTEIN

Consonant Sound in *Vie.* (Other spellings: o*f*, Step*he*n.) This sound is the voiced cognate of *f*, and is made in the same way, with the lower lip lightly held against the edges of the upper teeth.

Material for Practice

Pronounce the following words:

vain	verse	envy	inveigle	native
view	velvet	invigorate	vowels	votive
vice	shovel	investigate	nominative	revolve

Read the following sentences:

1. The poet conveyed his ideas by means of narrative verse.
2. No motive could be found for the vicious plan.

3. After their victory the victors were in a jovial mood.
4. The vicar voted to have the meeting in November.
5. Very few liked the vivid color on the otherwise conservative volume.

Read the following quotations:

1. Every evil in the bud is easily crushed; as it grows older, it becomes stronger.—CICERO
2. The counsels of pusillanimity very rarely put off, whilst they are always sure to aggravate, the evils from which they would fly.—EDMUND BURKE
3. Envy, among other ingredients, has a mixture of the love of justice in it. We are more angry at undeserved than at deserved good fortune.—WILLIAM HAZLITT
4. I would rather that my enemies envy me than I should envy my enemies.—PLAUTUS
5. He who writes couplets wishes, I suppose, to please by brevity. But what is the use of brevity, tell me, when there is a whole book of it?—MARTIAL

LINGUADENTAL (OR TONGUE–TEETH) SOUNDS

The *th* of *thin* and the *th* of *then* are the only two consonants in English made with the tip of the tongue against the edge of the upper teeth. These sounds are sometimes called *linguadental*.

Initial Consonant Sound in *Thin*. (Other spelling: *phth*isis.) This consonant is a voiceless, fricative sound. To produce it, press the tip of your tongue lightly against the edges of the upper teeth (or slightly between the upper and lower teeth), blowing breath through the narrow channel thus formed.

Material for Practice

Pronounce the following words:

thorn	throat	strengthen	nothing	beneath
thesis	thrill	ether	breadth	dearth
thousand	lengthen	zither	moth	forth

Read the following sentences:

1. Youthful enthusiasts left the theater cheering.
2. The theatrical director thought the length of the stage too great for its width.

3. In spite of the fact that he was thin, the theological student had great strength.
4. Clyde Griffiths is the name of the leading character in *An American Tragedy* by Theodore Dreiser.
5. The author felt thwarted when he learned that the story was not authentic.

Read the following quotations:

1. Enthusiasm as the genius of sincerity, and truth accomplishes no victories without it.—BULWER-LYTTON
2. The Gothic cathedral is a blossoming in stone subdued by the insatiable demand of harmony in man.—EMERSON
3. Unceasingly contemplate the generation of all things through change and accustom thyself to the thought that the nature of the Universe delights above all in changing the things that exist and making new ones of the same pattern. For everything that exists is the seed of that which shall come out of it.—MARCUS AURELIUS
4. Mankind was never so happily inspired as when it made a cathedral: a thing as single and specious as a statue to the first glance, and yet on examination, as lively and interesting as a forest in detail.—R. L. STEVENSON
5. If I were called upon to choose between beauty and truth, I should not hesitate; I should hold to beauty, being confident that it bears within it a truth both higher and deeper than truth itself.—ANATOLE FRANCE

Final Consonant Sound in *Smooth*. (Other spelling: soo*the*.) This sound is the voiced cognate of the consonant in *oath*. To produce it, press the tip of your tongue lightly against the edge of your upper teeth. (Like its voiceless cognate, it may be made with the tip of the tongue slightly between the teeth.)

Material for Practice

Pronounce the following words:

though	than	heathen	either	without
this	these	neither	clothe	writhe
that	seething	rhythm	seethe	loathe

Read the following sentences:

1. The rhythm of the Northern tunes bothered the musicians.
2. Many speakers mouth their words.

3. The clothes were rather heavy for a Southern cruise.
4. Neither of the leather covers was attractive.
5. The brothers soothed the dog who was breathing with difficulty and writhing in pain.

Read the following quotations:

1. The countenance is the portrait of the mind, the eyes are its informers.—CICERO
2. A physician can sometimes parry the scythe of death, but has no power over the sand in the hourglass.

—HESTER LYNCH PIOZZI

3. To retire is not to flee, and there is no wisdom in waiting when danger outweighs hope, and it is the part of wise men to preserve themselves today for tomorrow, and not risk all in one day.—CERVANTES
4. Slavery is but half abolished, emancipation is but half completed, while millions of free-men with votes in their hands are left without education. Justice to them, the welfare of the States in which they live, the safety of the whole Republic, the dignity of the elective franchise,— all alike demand that the still remaining bonds of ignorance shall be unloosed and broken, and the minds as well as the bodies of the emancipated go free.

—ROBERT C. WINTHROP

5. Men, by their constitutions, are naturally divided into two parties: 1. Those who fear and distrust the people, and wish to draw all powers from them into the hands of the higher classes. 2. Those who identify themselves with the people, have confidence in them, cherish and consider them as the most honest and safe, although not the most wise, depository of the public interests.

—THOMAS JEFFERSON

ALVEOLAR (OR TONGUE–GUM–RIDGE) SOUNDS

Consonants such as *t, d, n,* and *l* that are produced with the tip of the tongue touching the upper gum ridge; or *r, s, z, sh,* and *zh* that are produced with the tip of the tongue near the gum ridge, but not touching it, are known as *alveolar* or tongue-gum-ridge sounds. They are also called *lingua-alveolar* sounds.

Consonant Sound in *Tie.* (Other spellings: *th*yme, ask*ed*.) This consonant is a voiceless stop-plosive. To produce it, press the tip of your tongue lightly against your upper gum ridge. Release breath by lowering your tongue quickly.

Material for Practice

Pronounce the following words:

team	taught	stopped	detected	dental
twenty	tight	tenant	little	title
trill	asked	practiced	bottle	cattle

Read the following sentences:

1. The president of the university wrote a caustic letter.
2. Twenty candidates passed the written test.
3. Students were frequently late because of inefficient elevator service.
4. Forty-eight states ratified the amendment.
5. Ten students with excellent personalities were selected for the task.

Read the following quotations:

1. Subtlety may deceive you; integrity never will.
   —OLIVER CROMWELL
2. Ask counsel of both times: of the ancient time what is best; and of the latter time what is fittest.—FRANCIS BACON
3. A day differs not a whit from eternity.—SENECA
4. Curiosity is one of the most permanent and certain characteristics of a vigorous intellect.—SAMUEL JOHNSON
5. Yesterday the greatest question was decided which ever was debated in America; and a greater perhaps never was, nor will be, decided among men. A resolution was passed without one dissenting colony, that those United Colonies are, and of a right ought to be, free and independent States.—JOHN ADAMS

Consonant Sound in *Die*. (Other spelling: sa*dd*le.) This consonant is the voiced cognate of *t*. To produce it, press the tip of your tongue lightly against your upper gum ridge. As in the production of *t*, release breath by lowering your tongue quickly.

Material for Practice

Pronounce the following words:

diamond	humid	banded	couldn't	hadn't
doubled	hundred	provident	wouldn't	intended
dread	candidate	didn't	shouldn't	drowned

Read the following sentences:

1. As the day drew to a close, the driver found the road unendurably dreary.
2. Their discoveries, accidental and incidental, laid the foundations of modern medicine.
3. Seldom has greater diplomacy been evident.
4. The diamonds disappeared suddenly, and their disappearance was shrouded in mystery.
5. The wisdom of reducing the debt rapidly was apparent to the creditor.

Read the following quotations:

1. The poorest day that passes over us is the conflux of two eternities; it is made up of currents that issue from the remotest Past and flow upwards to the remotest Future.
   —CARLYLE
2. To my mind, the best and most faultless character is his who is ready to pardon the rest of mankind, as though he daily transgressed himself; and at the same time is as cautious to avoid a fault as if he never forgave one.
   —PLINY THE YOUNGER
3. Only that day dawns to which we are awake. There is more day to dawn. The sun is but a morning star.—THOREAU
4. Pericles separated his whole force into eight divisions, had them draw lots, and allowed the division which got the white bean to feast and take their ease, while the others did the fighting.—PLUTARCH
5. Olympus, the abode of the gods, that stands fast forever. Neither is it shaken by winds nor ever wet with rain, nor does snow fall upon it, but the air is outspread clear and cloudless, and over it hovers a radiant whiteness.—HOMER

Consonant Sound in *No.* (Other spellings: i*nn*er, *comp*troller.) To produce this continuant sound, press the tip of your tongue lightly on your upper gum ridge as you did for *t* and *d*. Instead of releasing your tongue as you did for these sounds, keep your tongue on your gum ridge until *n* is completed. Your soft palate should be lowered so that air will pass out through your nose.

This sound may take the place of a vowel in a weak syllable. It is then called a *syllabic consonant,* as in *written.*

Material for Practice

Pronounce the following words:

pneumatic	undertaken	occasion	nonsense	notion
suspense	candor	incision	continue	intensive
unanimous	sunshine	ancient	content	erroneous

Read the following sentences:

1. A business analyst never had an opportunity to analyze the information.
2. An excellent account of an enormous and unexplored country may be found in this novel.
3. Fundamentally unimportant, but extensive, changes undermined the financial status of the firm.
4. One can understand the confusion on the part of enemies of the plan.
5. It was encouraging to learn that the funds would be replenished in the winter.

Read the following quotations:

1. Next in importance to freedom and justice is popular education, without which neither freedom nor justice can be permanently maintained.—JAMES A. GARFIELD
2. You cannot possibly have a broader basis for any government than that which includes all the people, with all their rights in their hands, and with an equal power to maintain their rights.—WILLIAM LLOYD GARRISON
3. A consistent man believes in destiny, a capricious man in chance.—BENJAMIN DISRAELI
4. Nothing is so easy but it becomes difficult when done with reluctance.—TERENCE
5. Events will take their course, it is no good our being angry at them; he is happiest who wisely turns them to the best account.—EURIPIDES

Consonant Sound in *Lie*. (Other spelling: *ll*ama.) This consonant is a voiced, lateral glide. To produce it, press the tip of your tongue against your upper gum ridge; widen the front of your tongue. Note that air passes over the sides of your tongue.

This sound may take the place of a vowel in a weak syllable. It is then called a *syllabic consonant*, as in *little*.

Material for Practice

Pronounce the following words:

loan	aloud	pleasure	bubble	eclipse
flame	goldenrod	rule	needle	double
clash	whirl	blot	illuminate	globule

Read the following sentences:

1. Sea gulls flew swiftly overhead.
2. Reflected sunlight lighted the room brilliantly.
3. Although the revival was short-lived, the actor played the leading role magnificently.
4. As the novel was too long, the author might easily have left out at least a couple of subplots.
5. Yellow lanterns were strung along the lake.

Read the following quotations:

1. Glory in excess is fraught with peril; 'tis the lofty peak which is smitten by heaven's thunderbolt.—AESCHYLUS
2. Let us do nothing abjectly, nothing timidly, nothing sluggishly.—CICERO
3. We are never so virtuous as when we are ill. . . . It is then a man recollects that there are gods, and that he himself is mortal; . . . and he resolves that if he has the luck to recover, his life shall be passed in harmless happiness.
   —PLINY THE YOUNGER
4. Corrupt influence, which is in itself the perennial spring of all prodigality, and of all disorder; which loads us, more than millions of debt; which takes away vigour from our arms, wisdom from our councils.—EDMUND BURKE
5. Not till earth be sunless, not till death strike blind the skies, May the deathless love that waits on deathless deeds be dead.
   —SWINBURNE

Consonant Sound in *See.* (Other spellings: *sch*ism, gla*ss*, ri*ce*, quart*z*.) This consonant is a voiceless, sibilant fricative. To produce it, anchor the sides of your tongue lightly to the sides of your upper teeth, leaving the tip of your tongue free, not touching your gums or teeth. Be sure that your upper and lower teeth are close together.

Material for Practice

Pronounce the following words:

see	sign	adversary	historical	mists
circle	suggestion	statistics	coax	tasks
Saturday	whistle	listen	race	grasps

Read the following sentences:

1. Interest in the famous case waned as time elapsed.
2. The psychology of persuasion is a fascinating subject.
3. Some of the incidents that preceded the festival added extensively to the costs.
4. Studies of the sixteenth century sought to trace the history of various institutions.
5. A scientist of high scholastic standing published the chemistry and physics sections of the reports.

Read the following quotations:

1. Greatness of mind is not shown by admitting small things, but by making small things great under its influence. He who can take no interest in what is small will take false interest in what is great.—RUSKIN
2. We should strip the mask not only from men, but from things, and restore to each object its own aspect.
   —SENECA
3. To one who knows, it is superfluous to give advice; to one who does not know, it is insufficient.—SENECA
4. How is it possible to expect that mankind will take advice, when they will not so much as take warning?—SWIFT
5. The preservation of the sacred fire of liberty, and the destiny of the republican model of government, are justly considered as deeply, perhaps as finally staked, on the experiment entrusted to the hands of the American people.
   —GEORGE WASHINGTON

Consonant Sound in Zoo. (Other spellings: bu*s*y, di*sc*ern, *cz*ar, bu*zz*, po*ss*ess, *X*enophon, vi*s*it.) This consonant is the voiced cognate of *s*. To produce it, raise the blade of your tongue toward your gum ridge, but do not touch your teeth or gums. Be sure that your upper and lower teeth are close together.

Material for Practice

Pronounce the following words:

zero	zest	dazzled	quizzical	buzzes
Xerxes	zone	prison	deeds	Chinese
zinc	visitors	exhibit	roads	diseases

Read the following sentences:

1. Opposition to the magazine added to the editors' anxieties.
2. A dozen examiners, all representative in their respective fields, carried on the examinations.
3. Exotic music emphasized the bizarre atmosphere.
4. Writers in the symposium criticized the results of a mechanized civilization.
5. The designs became increasingly confused and puzzling.

Read the following quotations:

1. Every man who observes vigilantly and resolves steadfastly, grows unconsciously into genius.—BULWER-LYTTON
2. Customs may not be as wise as laws, but they are always more popular.—BENJAMIN D'ISRAELI
3. Accusing the times is but excusing ourselves.
   —THOMAS FULLER
4. He who wins a thousand common hearts is therefore entitled to some renown, but he who keeps undisputed sway over the heart of a coquette, is indeed a hero.
   —WASHINGTON IRVING
5. Reason, which ought always to direct mankind, seldom does; but passions and weaknesses commonly usurp its seat, and rule in its stead.—LORD CHESTERFIELD

Consonant Sound in *Shoe*. (Other spellings: na*t*ion, ten*s*ion, mi*ss*ion, cru*c*ial, *ch*agrin, o*ce*an, con*s*cious, *sch*ist.) This consonant is a voiceless, sibilant sound. To produce it, raise your tongue toward your upper gum ridge in a position slightly farther back than that for the production of *s*. Be sure that your upper and lower teeth are close together.

Material for Practice

Pronounce the following words:

shaft	shake	issue	rational	famish
shopworn	chauffeur	cashier	caution	varnish
shield	crashing	motion	finish	furnish

Read the following sentences:

1. The bishop had a national reputation for being a patient and compassionate man.
2. Publication of the hitherto unpublished letters ensured financial success to the publisher.
3. Some of the machines were partially sheltered.
4. Expansion obviously had a commercial value.
5. Ancient traditional rites were shrouded in mystery.

Read the following quotations:

1. Every generation laughs at the old fashions, but follows religiously the new.—H. D. THOREAU
2. Testimony is like the shot of a long-bow which owes its efficacy to the force of the shooter; argument is like the shot of the cross-bow, equally forcible whether discharged by a giant or a dwarf.—FRANCIS BACON
3. The very substance of the ambition is merely the shadow of a dream. . . . I hold ambition of so airy and light a quality that it is but a shadow's shadow.—SHAKESPEARE
4. It is not the shrines of the gods, nor the powers of the air, that send the dreams which mock the mind with flitting shadows: each man makes his own dreams.—PETRONIUS
5. Behavior seemeth to me as a garment of the mind, and to have the conditions of a garment. For it ought to be made in fashion; it ought not to be too curious, it ought to be shaped so as to set forth any good making of the mind, and hide any deformity; and above all, it ought not to be too strait, or restrained for exercise or motion.

—FRANCIS BACON

Final Consonant Sound in *Garage*. (Other spellings: plea*s*ure, vi*s*ion, absci*ss*ion, gla*z*ier.) This consonant is the voiced cognate of the consonant in *shoe*. To produce it, raise the tip of your tongue toward your upper gum ridge in a position slightly farther back that than for the production of the consonant in *zoo*. Be sure that your upper and lower teeth are close together.

Material for Practice

Pronounce the following words:

mirage	measured	explosion	beige	casually
seizure	usurer	intrusion	sabotage	massage
visionary	lesion	precision	usually	artesian

Read the following sentences:

1. Occasionally, the garage door slammed.
2. His usual precision was interrupted by a casual remark.
3. Such an unusual decision affected his prestige.
4. The author, who had poor vision, worked in a leisurely manner.
5. During the entire regime the treasury was at low ebb.

Read the following quotations:

1. To frown at pleasure, and to smile in pain.
   —YOUNG

2. Pleasure admitted in undue degree
   Enslaves the will, nor leaves the judgment free.
   —COWPER

3. A man's greatness can be measured by his enemy.
   —DONN PIATT

4. Thou shalt not lack
   The flower that's like thy face, pale primrose, nor
   The azur'd harebell, like thy veins.
   —SHAKESPEARE

5. But pleasures are like poppies spread.
   —ROBERT BURNS

Consonant Sound in *Ray*. (Other spellings: hu*rr*y.) This consonant is classified as a fricative, voiced, alveolar glide. To produce it, open your mouth slightly; curl the tip of your tongue toward your upper gum ridge. Your tongue should be cupped in shape as you produce this sound.

Pronunciation of this sound is largely a regional matter. It is *usually* pronounced before a vowel, as in *red* or *glorious*. Before a consonant or before a pause, this sound may or may not be produced, depending on regional variations.

When a word ends with the letter *r* and the following word begins with a vowel, the *r* should be pronounced, as in *hear it*. In this case the sound is called a *linking r*. For smoothness and fluency in reading or speaking, linking is essential.

Inserted where it does not occur in the spelling, this sound is called an *intrusive r,* as in *idear of*. This use is provincial and should be avoided. The material for practice on the following page includes exercises for the inclusion of *linking r* and for the exclusion of *r* as an intrusive sound.

Material for Practice

Pronounce the following words:

real	rival	hungry	glory	hundred
wrong	run	break	terrorized	frequent
write	arrival	dreary	horrified	larynx

Read the following phrases, avoiding intrusive r:

law office	saw him	idea of	Virginia or	idea is
saw it	thawing ice	California is	sofa in	drawing a

Read the following phrases, using a linking r:

either of	nature of	primer of	picture is	better able
over it	literature is	character of	over and	finger exercise

Read the following sentences:

1. Over and over again the merry crowd sang the refrain.
2. Although the merits of the deed were controversial, everyone agreed it was very daring.
3. A great variety of trimmed shrubs surrounded the pool.
4. The atmosphere of the camp was tranquil.
5. An angry jury heard the prisoner corroborate the story.

Read the following quotations:

1.   Extreme fear can neither fight nor fly,
       But coward-like with trembling terror die.
       —SHAKESPEARE
2. Every person is responsible for all the good within the range of his abilities, and for no more, and none can tell whose sphere is the largest.—GAIL HAMILTON
3. The care of human life and happiness, and not their destruction, is the first and only legitimate object of good government.—THOMAS JEFFERSON
4. Art is the desire of a man to express himself, to record the reactions of his personality to the world he lives in.
       —AMY LOWELL
5. Flattery corrupts both the receiver and giver.
       —EDMUND BURKE

PALATAL SOUNDS

The sound in the beginning of the word *you* is the only palatal consonant that exists in modern English.

In the middle of a word, as in *fume,* this sound may become almost imperceptibly a vowel in some speech.

Consonant Sound in *You.* (Other spellings: *ewe, union, feud, vignette, value, lieutenant, beauty.*) This consonant may be classified as a voiced, fricative, front-palate glide. To produce it, raise the front of your tongue until it almost reaches your hard palate.

Material for Practice

Pronounce the following words:

yacht	year	new	beautiful	valiant
yawn	unite	neuter	civilian	million
use	billiard	fumes	Italian	onion

Read the following sentences:

1. Annual dues were collected from the lawyers after the reunion.
2. Unanimous and enthusiastic applause greeted the play in spite of its familiar plot.
3. College seniors from California used to visit the canyon regularly.
4. A yellow cover decorated the yearbook.
5. Such congenial behavior was usual at the bureau.

Read the following quotations:

1. A man that is young in years may be old in hours, if he has lost no time.—FRANCIS BACON
2. Youth beholds happiness gleaming in the prospect. Age looks back on the happiness of youth, and, instead of hopes, seeks its enjoyment in the recollections of hope.

    —COLERIDGE

3. Genius, that power which dazzles mortal eyes,
   Is oft but perseverance in disguise.

    —HENRY AUSTIN

4. Humor is the only test of gravity, and gravity of humor, for a subject which will not bear raillery is suspicious, and a jest which will not bear serious examination is false wit.

    —GORGIAS LEONTINUS

5. Philosophy becomes poetry, and science imagination, in the enthusiasm of genius.—ISAAC D'ISRAELI

VELAR (OR SOFT–PALATE) SOUNDS

The sounds of *k*, *g*, and *ng* (ŋ) are the only English consonants made with the back of the tongue against the velum, or soft palate.

Consonant Sound in *Oak*. (Other spellings: *c*ome, *ch*aos, bou*qu*et.) This consonant is a voiceless, stop-plosive, back-tongue, soft-palate sound. To produce it, raise the back of your tongue to your soft palate; release your tongue quickly as you say the sound.

Material for Practice

Pronounce the following words:

call	courteous	extreme	mechanical	recognize
orchid	campaign	excel	wax	tobacco
cause	caught	Arctic	walks	locket

Read the following sentences:

1. The curious document was recorded by the classical scholar.
2. Economic and political questions occurred frequently.
3. While carrying the baskets of food to the picnic, he could not protect himself from the mosquitoes.
4. The target accident took place inexplicably.
5. Careful scrutiny of the lock provided no practical clue.

Read the following quotations:

1. Let every man be *occupied*, and occupied in the highest employment of which his nature is capable, and die with the consciousness that he has done his best.

    —Sydney Smith

2. There is nothing more universally commended than a fine day; the reason is, that people can commend it without envy.—William Shenstone

3. Custom has made dancing sometimes necessary for a young man; therefore mind it while you learn it that you may learn to do it well, and not be ridiculous, though in a ridiculous act.—Lord Chesterfield

4. A character is like an acrostic—read it forward, backward, or across, it still spells the same thing.—Emerson

5. Corporations cannot commit treason, nor be outlawed, nor excommunicated, for they have no souls.

    —Sir Edward Coke

Consonant Sound in Go. (Other spellings: dru*gg*ist, *gh*astly, e*x*ample.) This consonant is the voiced cognate of the consonant in *oak*. It is a stop-plosive, soft-palate consonant. To produce it, raise the back of your tongue to your soft palate; release your tongue quickly as you say the sound.

Material for Practice

Pronounce the following words:

guard	grip	exhaust	example	eggs
govern	forget	exist	brag	vogue
grammar	tiger	exert	log	vague

Read the following sentences:

1. Existing evidence exonerated the gardener.
2. The argument exhibited the ignorance of the group.
3. Gloves and bags were scattered around the grounds.
4. Our graduation exercises were carried out in a dignified manner.
5. The shaggy dog begged to go to his master.

Read the following quotations:

1.   Moreover, something is or seems,
            That touches me with mystic gleams,
            Like glimpses of forgotten dreams.
                                              —TENNYSON

2. Great acts grow out of great occasions and great occasions spring from great principles, working changes in society, and tearing it up by the roots.—WILLIAM HAZLITT

3. I don't know who my grandfather was; I am much more concerned to know what his grandson will be.
                                              —ABRAHAM LINCOLN

4. He has one gift most dangerous to a speculator, a vast command of a kind of language, grave and majestic, but of vague and uncertain import.—MACAULAY

5. Facts, when combined with ideas, constitute the greatest force in the world. They are greater than armaments, greater than finance, greater than science, business and law because they are the common denominator of all of them.—CARL W. ACKERMAN

Final Consonant Sound in King. (Other spellings: i*nk*, to*ngue*, ha*ndk*erchief, co*nqu*er, bro*nchi*al.) In the production of this nasal continuant sound, raise the back of your tongue toward your soft palate, keeping the tip of your tongue low.

DIFFICULTY OF PROPER PRONUNCIATION. This sound is one of the most troublesome in English. Many Americans make the mistake of saying *goin'* and *comin'*, and many foreigners are not clear as to the correct production of the sound, which obviously differs from the *n* and *g* of the alphabet.

Because this is such a troublesome sound, the phonetic letter (ŋ) may be helpful in identifying it. The change from the tip-of-tongue *n* to the back-of-tongue, soft-palate nasal sound is known as *assimilation*. In other words, two sounds, *n* and *g*, have merged and produced an entirely new sound, ŋ.

Sometimes this assimilation takes place even when the *k* or *g* is in the following syllable. For example, in the word *handkerchief*, the *d* has become silent and the *n* has been influenced by the *k*, although the *k* occurs in the following syllable. This phenomenon is likely to take place when the *n* is in a stressed syllable. Compare: *bronchial* with *bronchitis; congress* with *congressional.*

RULES GOVERNING THE USE OF ŋ. It is well to know the rules which govern the assimilation of *n* and *g* in English. What has happened is that *n* has lost its identity before the back consonants *k* and *g*, especially when these sounds occur in the same syllable. For example, in a word such as *rank* or *sink*, the *n* is no longer the *n* of *ran* or *sin*. Assimilation has taken place, and the sound is ŋ.

The following rules should serve as guides for the pronunciation of this sound:

1. When a word ends in the spelling *ng*, the sound is always ŋ. Examples: *sing, bring, bang, ring, hang.* Even such words as *tongue, meringue,* and *harangue* end with the sound of ŋ, in spite of their spelling.

2. If a suffix is added to a word ending in ŋ, the sound remains ŋ, with a few exceptions. Examples: *ringing, singer, hanging, banging, ringer.* Exceptions to the rule include the comparative and superlative of the adjectives *long, strong,* and *young,* and words such as *diphthongal, elongate,* and *prolongate.* In these words, the assimilated nasal sound ŋ and the *g* are both pronounced.

3. When the spelling *ng* is part of the root of the word, the

assimilated nasal sounds ŋ and *g* are pronounced. Examples: *anger, hunger, finger, English.* Among the exceptions are: *gingham, hangar, clangor, Bingham,* and other proper names, such as *Washington, Worthington, Nottingham.*

4. When a word ends in the spelling *nge,* the sound is *n* plus the consonant sound in *joy.* Examples: *plunge, lunge, hinge.*

Material for Practice

Pronounce the following words:

swing	language	flinging	stronger	English
tongue	beginning	banging	finger	languish
length	singer	hangar	linger	banquet

Use the following phrases in sentences:

having an idea	a stronger man
reading a book	a younger child
being informed	a longer string
having occasional	mingled emotions
growing accustomed to	a singular idea
hearing about	a shingled roof
being energetic	a lounging room
looking into	a strange sound
hanging a picture	lunging through
singing a song	a harbinger of spring
banging a door	a lengthy speech
flinging a coin	a strengthened argument
ringing a bell	lengthiness of the speech
bringing in dinner	a strengthener of muscles
clinging to an idea	lengthening shadows

Read the following sentences:

1. The clanging of the bell continued for a long time.
2. Some of the debators strengthened their arguments after a lengthy discussion.
3. Hundreds of commuters were stepping into the Long Island train as the gong rang.
4. A few of the younger children were stronger than their English cousins.
5. The aviator was starting off on a dangerous mission.

Read the following quotations:

1. The wise man does no wrong in changing his habits with the times.—Dionysius Cato

2. In every object there is inexhaustible meaning; the eye sees in it what the eye brings means of seeing.—CARLYLE

3. As long as the evil deed does not bear fruit, the fool thinks it like honey; but when it ripens, then the fool suffers grief.—SUBHADRA BHIKSHU

4. Acting without design, occupying oneself without making a business of it, finding the great in what is small and the many in the few, repaying injury with kindness, affecting difficult things while they are easy, and managing great things in their beginnings: this is the method of Tao.

—LAO-TSE

5. Whenever you are angry, be assured that it is not only a present evil, but that you have increased a habit, and added fuel to a fire. . . . If you would not be of an angry temper, then, do not feed the habit. Give it nothing to help its increase. Be quiet at first, and reckon the days in which you have not been angry. 'I used to be angry every day; now every other day; then every third and fourth day.' And if you miss it so long as thirty days, offer a sacrifice of thanksgiving to God.—EPICTETUS

GLOTTAL SOUND

The only acceptable glottal sound in English is the *h* of *hoe.*

Consonant Sound in *Hoe.* This sound is an aspirate, or puff of breath, uninterrupted by the tongue, lips, or teeth. The air is forced out between the partially closed vocal cords in producing this sound with a resulting friction-like noise. It is generally considered a voiceless sound, but when it occurs between voiced sounds it is frequently voiced as in a word such as *Ohio,* or a phrase such as *a house on the high hill.*

Material for Practice

Pronounce the following words:

humble	horror	hospitable	coherent	inhere
habit	hunger	human	inhibit	cohesive
hone	home	inherent	vehicular	beheaded

Read the following sentences:

1. A house in New Hampshire was included in the inheritance.
2. The hospital harbored the hostages who were in poor health.
3. Humid weather seemed to affect his sense of humor.

4. High up in the hills, away from the highway, was the artist's home.
5. Customary hazards of the trip left the hero undaunted.

Read the following quotations:

1. Hope knows not if fear speak truth, nor fear whether hope be not blind as she:
   But the sun is in heaven that beholds her immortal, and girdled with life by the sea.

   —SWINBURNE

2. That man is happy whom nothing makes less strong than he is; he keeps to the heights, leaning upon none but himself; for one who sustains himself by any prop may fall.

   —SENECA

3. Human felicity is produced not so much by great pieces of good fortune that seldom happen, as by little advantages that occur every day.—BENJAMIN FRANKLIN

4. Whosoever does not regard that he has as most ample wealth is unhappy, though he be master of the world.

   —EPICURUS

5. A man's dignity may be enhanced by the house he lives in, but not wholly secured by it; the owner should bring honor to the house, not the house to its owner.—CICERO

AFFRICATE SOUNDS

Affricates are produced by the blending of two sounds which lose their identity in forming a new consonant. The initial sounds in *chew* and *joy* represent such a blend.

Consonant Sound in *Chew*. (Other spellings: wa*tch,* na*t*ure, righ*t*eous, celes*t*ial, *c*ello, Pu*cc*ini.) This consonant is a combination of two voiceless sounds. To produce this combination, press the tip of your tongue lightly against your upper gum ridge, as for the consonant *t;* then draw it back slightly for the position of the initial sound in *shoe.*

Material for Practice

Pronounce the following words:

chair	chimes	stature	natural	drenched
champion	cheese	structure	match	French
choose	future	richly	stitch	batch

Read the following sentences:

1. Chapter Three ended with a number of suggestions and a choice of the questions to be answered.
2. Research on the nature of literature appealed to the students.
3. The feature picture dealt with problems of the future.
4. Church architecture was symbolic of the culture of the times.
5. The child watched for a chance to snatch the cherries.

Read the following quotations:

1. Agriculture is the foundation of manufactures, since the productions of nature are the materials of art.
   —EDWARD GIBBON
2. The best books of all kinds are taken to the heart, and cherished as his most precious possessions. Others to be chatted with for a time, to spend a few pleasant hours with, and laid aside, but not forgotten.
   —JOHN ALFRED LANGFORD
3. Unrighteous fortune seldom spares the noblest virtue; no one with safety can expose himself to frequent danger.
   —SENECA
4. The most wretched fortune is safe, for it lacks fear of anything worse.—OVID
5. Health and cheerfulness mutually beget each other.
   —ADDISON

Consonant Sound in *Joy*. (Other spellings: *ge*m, gran*d*eur, ver*d*ure, sol*d*ier.) This consonant is a combination of two voiced consonants. To produce it, press the tip of your tongue lightly against your upper gum ridge, as for the consonant *d;* then draw it back slightly as for the final consonant in *garage*.

Material for Practice

Pronounce the following words:

jury	germane	ingenious	engine	diverge
generous	genuine	religious	wedge	George
genius	submerge	imagine	knowledge	judgment

Read the following sentences:

1. The surgeon managed to read several pages on the origin of the legends about the regiment's exploits.
2. Engineers worked logically through the emergency.

3. Both imagery and poetic language projected the mood of the tragedy.
4. For strategic reasons the budget was rejected.
5. The cottage was surrounded by the pungent odor of ginger plants.

Read the following quotations:

1. Forgiveness is better than revenge; for forgiveness is the sign of a gentle nature, but revenge the sign of a savage nature.—EPICTETUS
2. Books are the legacies that a great genius leaves to mankind, which are delivered down from generation to generation, as presents to the posterity of those who are yet unborn.—ADDISON
3. The desire of power in excess caused the angels to fall; the desire of knowledge in excess caused man to fall; but in charity there is no excess, neither can angel or man come in danger by it.—FRANCIS BACON
4. Natural gifts without education have more often attained to glory and virtue than education without natural gifts.
—CICERO
5. This glorious Union shall not perish! Precious legacy of our fathers, it shall go down honored and cherished to our children. Generations unborn shall enjoy its privileges as we have done; and if we leave them poor in all besides, we will transmit to them the boundless wealth of its blessings!—EDWARD EVERETT

Exercises

1. Make a list of voiceless and voiced consonants.
2. Explain the difference in pronunciation between *singer* and *finger*.
3. From the examples on pages 217 to 219, try to formulate a rule about the kind of word that begins with a voiceless *th* and the kind that begins with a voiced *th*.
4. Make a list of twenty-five words that contain silent consonants. Trace the history of these words to see if you can find out whether these silent consonants were ever pronounced.
5. List ten words in which you ordinarily use assimilation.

18

Speech Pathology

A detailed study of such a highly specialized field as speech pathology is not within the scope of this book. Since an intelligent and sympathetic attitude toward speech defectives is important, the most common types of speech defects are classified in the following pages.

The bibliography for this chapter is divided into two parts: one containing titles of books dealing with speech defects, and the other containing titles of manuals to be used in correcting various types of speech disorders. Since incorrect practice may prove to be extremely harmful, however, *speech therapy should not be conducted without the aid of a professional speech instructor.*

Speech defects may be grouped under three general headings: (1) functional; (2) organic; and (3) emotional or psychological.

FUNCTIONAL SPEECH DISORDERS

Functional speech disorders affect the largest group of speech defectives, namely, the group having articulatory faults. These errors include sound substitutions, such as *v* for *th* (in *bruvver* for *brother*); sound omissions, such as *axe* for *acts,* or *probly* for *probably;* and sound distortions, such as *she* for *see.*

If these mistakes continue despite intensive study and practice of the correct production of sounds, they may suggest faulty hearing or an immature approach to life. In the latter case, the desire not to grow up is indicated by a speech pattern which is inconsistent with the age of the speaker. This type of speech involves behavior maladjustment as well as a speech problem.

"Baby Talk." In cases where there is no organic cause of articulatory faults, the defects are generally due to inadequate training, duplication of poor models, or poor imitation of good models.

Frequently, the defects are remnants of *baby talk*. Sound substitutions occurring predominantly in baby talk include *w* for *l* (*wake* for *lake*); *l* for *r* (*led* for *red*); *th* for *s* (*thend* for *send*); and *t* for *k* (*take* for *cake*).

Many children are unaware that they are making speech sounds incorrectly. Sometimes their parents or other adults either do not notice the errors or else think the mistakes amusing and make no effort to correct them. Again, many parents, eager to keep their children young and dependent, actually encourage them to continue an immature type of speech. Unfortunately, these parents fail to realize that speech which is regarded as merely amusing at the nursery age is definitely not attractive at fifteen, and at twenty may constitute a vocational as well as a social handicap.

Lisping. To many, lisping is merely the substitution of *th* for *s*, as in *think* for *sink*. More broadly, however, lisping may be defined as the imperfect production of any of the sibilant sounds, *s, z, sh,* or *zh*. Since *s* is the most intense of these sounds, it is the most troublesome to produce and requires more training and precision. For the correct production of *s*, see page 223.

There are three common types of lisps: *lingual, lateral,* and *nasal emission*. Although a hearing loss may account for failure to reproduce sibilant sounds correctly, as a rule incorrect tongue positions are to blame.

LINGUAL LISP. One of the most common forms of lisping is known as *lingual protrusion*. This lisp, as its name implies, is caused by the projection of the tongue between the teeth on the sibilant sounds. When a child loses his first teeth, he sometimes pushes his tongue into the spaces left by the missing teeth. If he continues this practice, he may have difficulty in producing sibilant sounds even after his second teeth have appeared. He will continue to say *thight* for *sight* and *thay* for *say*.

LATERAL LISP. The lateral lisp occurs when air passes through the sides of the teeth, causing *s* to sound like *sh*, as in *shay* for *say* and *thish* for *this*. If this defect is present without an organic cause, it may be the result of imitation.

NASAL EMISSION. In this type of lisp, the tongue is curled back so far that the sounds are emitted through the nose. Such a lisp is usually caused by poor control of the soft palate. The resulting sound may be described as a snort.

Lalling. *Lalling* is characterized by defective *r* and *l* sounds generally, although there may be other sounds involved. Its main characteristic is the substitution of *r* for *l*, as in *right* for *light*, or *rate* for *late*.

Slovenly Speech. Slovenly or vulgar speech, such as *dese* and *dose* for *these* and *those*; *probly* for *probably*; *filum* for *film*; *athe-letic* for *athletic*; and *ice' cream* for *ice' cream'*, abounds in sound substitutions, omissions, poor stress, and extreme assimilation, as in the substitution *Wherejueat?* for *Where did you eat?* Extreme assimilation may be the result of carelessness, laziness, or ignorance of correct speech, or a combination of all three. The middle way lies somewhere between speech that is word-wise and too formal and that which is overassimilated and careless.

Foreign Accent. Many foreign-born persons think that once they stop speaking their native languages and concentrate on English, they will no longer have foreign accents. No belief could be more fallacious. The influence of a foreign language may persist long after the language itself has been forgotten. Sometimes, although a speaker has not heard or used a foreign language since childhood, the basic and subtle characteristics of the native language may be apparent to the trained ear. The major faults which persist are: errors in vowel, consonant, and diphthong length; sound substitutions, such as *ch* for *j*, *s* for *z*, *d* for *th*, *v* for *w*; pronunciation of silent letters; and a faulty intonation pattern; and incorrect pronunciation of consonants. Two common errors in the production of consonants are dentalization and palatalization. In *dentalization* the tip of the tongue hits the upper front teeth in producing the tongue-gum sounds; in *palatalization* the tip of the tongue hits the lower front teeth in producing these sounds.

The most effective way of overcoming the influence of a foreign language is to make a thorough study of the sounds of English and their use in connected speech. In addition, a study of the use of Klinghardt markings (page 182) for intonation is invaluable.

Regional Dialects. In cases where regional dialects are so marked that they interfere with intelligibility, they may be as difficult to improve as foreign accent. A great deal depends upon the vocational goals of the speaker. If he wishes to preach, to teach, or to act, especially in a community wider than his local one, he may have sufficiently strong motivation to work at modifying his speech. If he lacks a strong vocational goal, or clings to his regional dialect in spite of good reasons for changing it, the fault may lie in his hearing or in his mental attitude toward the dialect. Although intellectually he may see the advantages of changing it, emotionally he may be unable to change because of immaturity, or inability to free himself from the habits of his childhood, or the influence of members of his family.

ORGANIC SPEECH DISORDERS

Organic speech disorders are those caused by some physical disability affecting the speech or voice organs. These disorders include: defects due to impaired hearing; malformation of the jaw (malocclusion); tongue-tie; cleft palate and cleft lip; and defects due to brain injuries.

Defects Due to Impaired Hearing. Speech problems caused by impaired hearing are numerous and sometimes of a very serious nature. The three types of hearing loss are: *conductive, perceptive (inner-ear impairment)*, and *mixed.*

CONDUCTIVE HEARING LOSS. In the conductive type, there is an interruption of the passage of sound-wave energy from the outer to the inner ear. Such interference may be caused by any hard substance, such as wax, obstructing the outer canal or impacted against the eardrum, restraining its movement. The result is an equal reduction of the loudness of all tones or sounds.

PERCEPTIVE HEARING LOSS. Perceptive or inner-ear impairment is caused by damage to the nerve of hearing and affects high pitch sounds more than low ones. Frequently this impairment is present at birth, but it may be caused by disease or injury.

MIXED TYPE OF HEARING LOSS. The mixed type is a combination of the other two types. Here, the conductive mechanism of the middle ear may have become defective through a chronic condition which has affected the nerve of hearing as well. A person suffering from this impairment will have more difficulty in hearing high-pitched sounds than low-pitched ones.

REMEDIAL MEASURES FOR IMPAIRED HEARING. The problems of the hard of hearing depend to a large extent upon the age of the patient when his hearing was impaired. If he had learned to speak normally before that time, he may suffer a deterioration in some sounds, but he may be helped greatly through a study of lip reading and the use of a hearing aid. If, however, his hearing were defective at birth or shortly thereafter, he has been deprived of the usual opportunity a child has of imitating the sounds around him. Though his position in a hearing world is a difficult one, the help of specialists will aid him in his adjustment.

Malocclusion. Malformation of the jaw, generally called *malocclusion,* is a common physical disability which may affect speech. It may be divided into four classifications: the overshot jaw, the undershot jaw, the open-mouth bite, and endentition.

When the upper jaw protrudes above the lower one, the jaw is *overshot.* When the lower jaw protrudes past the upper one, the jaw is *undershot.* If, when the teeth are closed, the jaws meet on the sides but not in front, the condition is called an *open-mouth bite.* When there is a marked irregularity in the plane of the teeth, *endentition* is present.

Although the causes of malocclusion are not all known, thumb sucking, tongue mannerisms, or neglected adenoids are almost certain to affect the formation of the jaw. Whatever the cause of malocclusion, the result is usually a poor production of the sibilant sounds. For the correct production of these sounds, see Chapter 17.

Tongue-Tie. Underneath the tongue is a cord called the *frenum.* If this cord is too short, the tongue will not have enough freedom to make some of the sounds of English correctly. If, for example, the tongue does not reach the gum ridge, sounds such as *t, d, n,* and *l,* as well as the sibilants, cannot be produced properly.

Surgical clipping of the frenum is the only way to ensure freedom of the tip of the tongue. Ordinarily, this minor operation is performed on infants, but, occasionally, the condition is overlooked and the impairment is found in adults. If the cord cannot be stretched sufficiently through exercise, it should be treated surgically in adults as well as in children.

Cleft Palate and Cleft Lip. The formation of the palate, or roof of the mouth, and of the upper lip may be defective at birth. In some cases, the cleft or opening is in the hard palate; in others, the soft palate is improperly formed; in still others, soft and hard palates as well as the jaw are involved. Sometimes the cleft extends through the upper lip and the upper gum ridge.

Beyond the fact that disturbances in prenatal life apparently cause these defects, little is known about them. Whenever possible, surgery should be used to close the cleft.

In addition to the question of surgical or medical help in the early life of the person with a cleft palate, there is the problem of speech. Explosive consonants, such as *p, b, t, d, k, g, ch,* and *j,* are almost impossible to produce. Sibilant sounds are usually difficult; vowel sounds may be nasalized; and the whole speech pattern is likely to be distorted. Because the cleft prevents any closure between the nose and the mouth, the cleft-palate patient usually has a nasal voice with little resonance or carrying power. The size of the cleft naturally affects voice quality.

If surgery is unsuccessful or for some reason cannot be used, the patient may be helped by a device known as an *obturator.* This appliance serves as a substitute for the missing part of the palate.

Whether he has surgery or wears an obturator, the cleft-palate patient needs to have speech and voice therapy. Patients and their families too often expect surgery or the use of an appliance to bring about normal speech automatically. Unfortunately, no matter how skilled the surgeon or how adequate the appliance, there is no substitute for the normal formation of the palate and lip. Surgery or appliances prepare the way for speech therapy.

Defects Due to Brain Injuries. A person who has a brain lesion may have difficulty in speech as a result. The problem involved in this kind of case is not articulation so much as a search for words. The person who has a brain injury may not be able to recall the words he needs to carry on in normal speech situations. This disability, in an extreme degree, is called *aphasia.*

The brain-injured patient needs the diagnosis and prescription of a neurologist before he begins speech therapy. The task of retraining may be a long and arduous one during which he needs to be reassured of his successes and encouraged in spite of his failures. Perhaps in no area of speech therapy is more imagination, resourcefulness, patience, and ingenuity needed than in the training of aphasics.

PSYCHOGENIC DISORDERS

It may be apparent that some disorders of speech and voice seem to have no physiological, neurological, biochemical, or anatomical cause. Sometimes a speaker shows no sign of a defect, and at other times the disorder is acute. Such disorders are called *emotional,* or *psychological,* or *psychogenic.*

Stuttering. The term *stuttering,* used interchangeably with *stammering,* characterizes speech marked by interruptions in fluency and rhythm which make it impossible for the stutterer to say anything for several seconds. He may be able to start to speak only by repeating sounds, words, or phrases. Such hesitancy and repetition are called *primary symptoms.*

Stuttering may also be accompanied or preceded by muscular and respiratory spasms; by general muscular tension and contortions; and by any number of mannerisms. Such devices, which the stutterer always thinks aid him, are called *secondary symptoms.*

While there is a lack of agreement on the exact cause or causes of stuttering, it is safe to say that a deep-seated anxiety seems to be a predominant factor. Stuttering may be but one manifestation of such anxiety. Consequently, the stutterer should be in the hands of a specialist rather than at the mercy of well-intentioned friends and relatives who think they can "cure" him by urging him to "speak slowly," "take a deep breath," or "repeat the sentence." Such advice may add to the stutterer's tension and anxiety and may succeed in making him stutter more violently.

The most important fact for the lay person to bear in mind is that ridicule of the stutterer is a remnant of the barbarous cruelty shown all handicapped persons hundreds of years ago. Those who would not laugh at a cripple or a blind person are occasionally incredibly thoughtless toward a speech defective. The stutterer should be given an opportunity to talk without fear of interruption and without fear that someone else will finish his sentence for him.

Cluttering. *Cluttering* is characterized by very rapid, indistinct speech, sometimes difficult to differentiate from stuttering. Like stuttering, it is a manifestation of a deep-rooted disturbance, usually of a psychogenic nature. Unlike stuttering, it is not accompanied by muscular spasms.

Neurotic Lisp. The so-called *neurotic lisp* occurs when there seems to be no organic reason for lisping. In adults, this lisp represents a behavior as well as a speech problem since it generally accompanies an immature point of view about life and may be a manifestation of a desire not to grow up.

Voice Defects. Many defects of voice quality, such as a very high or low pitch, are also of a psychological nature. Some are due to physical causes. If a nose and throat specialist can find no physiological impairment, the vocal problems may be attributable to a pattern of faulty breath control. If, however, the voice does not respond to proper exercise and training, psychiatric help may be needed to discover the psychological factors affecting the voice quality.

Hysterical Aphonia. Even when there is no organic cause of loss of voice, a speaker may lose his voice completely because of hysteria or emotion, such as anger, fright, or joy. Such a condition may be acute, the result of immediate tension or anxiety, or chronic, the result of tension built up over a long period. As with all psychogenic disorders, a psychiatrist as well as a speech therapist may be needed to help cases of chronic hysterical aphonia.

Neurotic Hoarse Voice. Neurotic hoarse voice is frequently associated with extreme nervousness or hysteria or a deep-rooted feeling of inferiority. If a throat specialist can find no organic cause for hoarseness, a speech therapist and a psychiatrist may be able to help the patient establish new methods of breath control and a more wholesome and affirmative attitude toward life. Such therapy, plus a strong desire to improve, will eventually result in better quality.

Exercises

1. Investigate the facilities for speech correction in your community.

2. Compare the results of (1) above with some other community of comparable size that you can investigate.

3. Assume that you have been asked to speak to a lay audience on one of the areas in speech pathology mentioned in this chapter. Select the area; plan an outline for a half-hour speech.

4. List the programs you hear on radio or television that ridicule the speech defective. What is your attitude toward such programs?

5. To what extent has a marked speech defect impeded the vocational progress of some speech defective of your acquaintance? To what extent has he tried to overcome his speech handicap?

Selected References

1—Introduction

Ayer, A. J. *Language, Truth and Logic.* New York: Oxford University Press, 1936.

Backus, Ollie. *Speech in Education.* New York: Longmans, Green & Co., 1943.

Black, Max. *Language and Philosophy: Studies in Method.* Ithaca, New York: Cornell University Press, 1949.

Blackmur, R. P. *Language as Gesture.* New York: Harcourt, Brace & Co., 1952.

Lee, Irving J. *The Language of Wisdom and Folly.* New York: Harper & Bros., 1949.

Murray, Elwood. *The Speech Personality.* Philadelphia: J. B. Lippincott Co., 1944.

Rasmussen, Carrie. *Speech Methods in the Elementary School.* New York: The Ronald Press Co., 1949.

Reid, Loren D. *Teaching Speech in the High School.* Columbia, Mo.: Artcraft Press, 1952.

Robinson, Karl F. *Teaching Speech in the Secondary School.* New York: Longmans, Green & Co., 1951.

Thonssen, Lester, and Fatherson, Elizabeth. *Bibliography of Speech Education.* New York: The H. W. Wilson Co., 1939.

Thonssen, Lester, and Robb, Mary Margaret. *Bibliography of Speech Education Supplement; 1939–1948.* New York: The H. W. Wilson Co., 1950.

Weaver, Andrew T., Borches, Gladys L., and Smith, Donald K. *The Teaching of Speech.* New York: Prentice-Hall, Inc., 1952.

2—Semantics: The Understanding of Word Meanings

Ayer, A. J. *Language, Truth and Logic.* New York: Oxford University Press, 1936.

Britten, K. *Communication: A Philosophical Study of Language.* New York: Harcourt, Brace & Co., 1939.

Chase, Stuart. *The Tyranny of Words*. New York: Harcourt, Brace & Co., 1938.

Dodge, Martin. *Know Your Isms*. New York: Farrar, Straus and Young, 1950.

Greenough, James B., and Kittredge, George L. *Words and Their Ways in English Speech*. New York: Macmillan Co., 1930.

Hayakawa, S. I. *Language in Action*. New York: Harcourt, Brace & Co., 1941.

———. *Language in Thought and Action*. New York: Harcourt, Brace & Co., 1949.

Johnson, Wendell. *Language and Speech Hygiene: An Application of General Semantics*. Lakewood, Conn.: Institute of General Semantics, 1939.

Korzybski, Alfred. *Science and Sanity: An Introduction to Non-Aristotelian Systems and General Semantics*. 2nd ed. Lancaster, Pa.: Science Press Printing Co., 1941.

Lee, Irving. *How to Talk with People*. New York: Harper & Bros., 1952.

———. *Language in Human Affairs*. New York: Harper & Bros., 1942.

———. *The Language of Wisdom and Folly*. New York: Harper & Bros., 1949.

Mencken, H. L. *The American Language*, Supplement I. New York: Alfred A. Knopf, 1945.

Murray, Edwood. *The Speech Personality*. Rev. ed. Philadelphia: J. B. Lippincott & Co., 1944.

Ogden, C. K., and Richards, I. A. *The Meaning of Meaning*. 3rd ed. rev. New York: Harcourt, Brace & Co., 1939.

Pyles, Thomas. *Words and Ways of American English*. New York: Random House, Inc., 1952.

Sapir, Edward. *Language*. New York: Harcourt, Brace & Co., 1921.

Schlauch, Margaret. *The Gift of Tongues*. New York: Viking Press, Inc., 1942.

Walpole, Hugh. *Semantics*. New York: W. W. Norton & Co., 1941.

3—*Public Speaking*

Baird, A. Craig, and Knower, Franklin H. *General Speech: An Introduction*. New York: McGraw-Hill Book Co., Inc., 1949.

Brembeck, Winston L., and Howell, William S. *Persuasion*. New York: Prentice-Hall, Inc., 1952.

Brigance, William N. *Speech Composition.* New York: F. S. Crofts & Co., 1937.

———. *Speech: Its Techniques and Disciplines in a Free Society.* New York: Appleton-Century-Crofts, 1952.

Bryant, Donald C., and Wallace, Karl R. *Fundamentals of Public Speaking.* New York: D. Appleton-Century-Crofts, 1953.

Cooper, Lane. *The Rhetoric of Aristotle.* New York: D. Appleton Co., 1932.

Crocker, Lionel. *Public Speaking for College Students.* New York: American Book Co., 1941.

Gray, Giles Wilkeson, and Braden, Waldo W. *Public Speaking: Principles and Practice.* New York: Harper & Bros., 1951.

Mouat, Lawrence H. *A Guide to Effective Public Speaking.* Boston: D. C. Heath & Co., 1953.

Oliver, Robert T., Dickey, Dallas C., and Zelko, Harold P. *Essentials of Communicative Speech.* New York: Dryden Press, 1949.

O'Neill, J. M. *Extemporaneous Speaking.* New York: Harper & Bros., 1946.

Parrish, Wayland Maxfield. *Speaking in Public.* New York: Charles Scribner's Sons, 1947.

Sanford, William Phillips, and Yeager, Willard Hayes. *Principles of Effective Speaking.* 5th ed. New York: The Ronald Press Co., 1950.

Soper, Paul L. *Basic Public Speaking.* New York: Oxford University Press, 1949.

Thonssen, Lester, and Scanlan, Ross. *Speech Preparation and Delivery.* Philadelphia: J. B. Lippincott Co., 1942.

Williamson, Arleigh B., Fritz, Charles A., and Ross, Harold Raymond. *Speaking in Public.* 2nd ed. New York: Prentice-Hall, Inc., 1948.

Winans, James A. *Speech-Making.* New York: D. Appleton-Century Co., 1938.

4—Group Discussion

Auer, J. J., and Ewbank, Henry L. *Handbook for Discussion Leaders.* New York: Harper & Bros., 1947.

Baird, A. Craig. *Argumentation, Discussion, and Debate.* New York: McGraw-Hill Book Co., Inc., 1950.

Bowman, LeRoy C. *How to Lead Discussion.* New York: Woman's Press, 1934.

Cahn, Joseph, and others. *The Story of a Discussion Program.* New York: New York Adult Education Council, 1946.

Clapp, John M. *Effective Talking in Conference.* New York: The Ronald Press Co., 1948.

Dunn, Frederick S. *The Practice and Procedure of International Conferences.* Baltimore: Johns Hopkins Press, 1929.

Elliot, Harrison S. *The Process of Group Thinking.* New York: Association Press, 1932.

Ewbank, Henry Lee, and Auer, J. Jeffery. *Discussion and Debate.* New York: Appleton-Century-Crofts, 1951.

Fansler, Thomas. *Creative Group Thinking.* New York: Harper & Bros., 1950.

———. *Discussion Methods for Adult Groups.* Washington: American Association for Adult Education, 1934.

Garland, J. V., and Phillips, C. F. *Discussion Methods, Explained and Illustrated.* Rev. ed. New York: H. W. Wilson Co., 1940.

Haiman, Franklyn S. *Group Leadership and Democratic Action.* Boston: Houghton Mifflin Co., 1951.

Heyel, Carl. *Standard Business Conference Technique.* New York: Funk & Wagnalls Co. in association with *Modern Industry Magazine,* 1948.

Leigh, Robert D. *Group Leadership.* New York: W. W. Norton & Co., Inc., 1936.

McBurney, James H., and Hance, Kenneth G. *Discussion in Human Affairs.* New York: Harper & Bros., 1950.

Myer, Walter E., and others. *Talking It Through, A Manual for Discussion Groups.* Washington: National Education Association, Department of Secondary School Principals, 1938.

Nichols, Alan. *Discussion and Debate.* New York: Harcourt, Brace & Co., 1941.

Sheffield, Alfred D. *Creative Discussion.* 3rd ed., rev. and enl. New York: Association Press, 1939.

Studebaker, John W. *The American Way.* New York: McGraw-Hill Book Co., Inc., 1935.

Utterback, William E. *Group Thinking and Conference Leadership.* New York: Rinehart & Co., Inc., 1950.

Wagner, Russell H., and Arnold, Carroll C. *Handbook of Group Discussion.* Boston: Houghton Mifflin Co., 1950.

Walser, Frank. *The Art of Conference.* Rev. ed. New York: Harper & Bros., 1948.

Wiese, Mildred, Bryson, Lyman, and Hallenbeck, W. C. *Let's Talk It Over.* Chicago: University of Chicago Press, 1936.

Wileden, A. F., and Ewbank, H. L., *How to Conduct Group Discussion*. Madison: Extension Service of the College of Agriculture, University of Wisconsin, Circular 276, 1935.

5—Argumentation

Baird, A. Craig. *Argumentation, Discussion, and Debate*. New York: McGraw-Hill Book Co., Inc., 1950.

Baker, George Pierce, and Huntington, Henry Barrett. *The Principles of Argumentation*. Boston: Ginn & Co., 1925.

Crocker, Lionel. *Argumentation and Debate*. New York: American Book Co., 1944.

Foster, William Trufant. *Argumentation and Debating*. Boston: Houghton Mifflin Co., 1932.

Fritz, Charles A. *The Method of Argument*. New York: Prentice-Hall, Inc., 1931.

Graves, Harold F. *Argument*. New York: Cordon Co., 1938.

McBurney, James H., O'Neill, James M., and Mills, Glen E. *Argumentation and Debate*. New York: Macmillan Co., 1951.

McCall, Raymond J. *Basic Logic*. New York: Barnes and Noble, Inc., 1952.

O'Neill, James M., Laycock, Craven, and Scales, Robert Leighton. *Argumentation and Debate*. New York: Macmillan Co., 1925.

Pellegrini, Angelo M., and Stirling, Brents. *Argumentation and Public Discussion*. Boston: D. C. Heath & Co., 1936.

Reeves, J. Walter, and Hudson, Hoyt H. *Principles of Argument and Debate*. Boston: D. C. Heath & Co., 1941.

Wagner, Russell H. *Handbook of Argumentation*. New York: Thomas Nelson & Sons, 1936.

Winans, James A., and Utterback, William E. *Argumentation*. New York: Appleton-Century-Crofts, 1930.

6—Debate

Baird, A. Craig. *Argumentation, Discussion, and Debate*. New York: McGraw-Hill Book Co., Inc., 1950.

Behl, William A. *Discussion and Debate*. New York: The Ronald Press Co., 1952.

Courtney, Luther W., and Capp, Glenn R. *Practical Debating*. Chicago: J. B. Lippincott Co., 1949.

Crocker, Lionel. *Argumentation and Debate.* New York: American Book Co., 1944.

Ewbank, Henry Lee, and Auer, J. Jeffery. *Discussion and Debate.* New York: Appleton-Century-Crofts, 1951.

Foster, William T. *Argumentation and Debating.* Boston: Houghton Mifflin Co., 1932.

Howes, Raymond F., ed. *Debating.* Boston: D. C. Heath & Co., 1931.

McBurney, James H., O'Neill, James M., and Mills, Glen E. *Argumentation and Debate: Techniques of a Free Society.* New York: Macmillan Co., 1951.

Nichols, Alan. *Discussion and Debate.* New York: Harcourt, Brace & Co., Inc., 1941.

Nichols, Egbert Ray, and Baccus, Joseph H. *Modern Debating.* New York: W. W. Norton & Co., Inc., 1936.

7—*Parliamentary Procedure*

Auer, J. J. *The Essentials of Parliamentary Procedure.* 2nd ed. New York: Appleton-Century-Crofts, 1942.

Bolles, Albert S. *Cushing's Manual of Parliamentary Procedure.* Philadelphia: The John C. Winston Co., 1928.

Cruzan, Rose Marie. *Practical Parliamentary Procedure.* Bloomington, Illinois: McKnight & McKnight, 1947.

Hegarty, Edward J. *How to Run a Meeting.* New York: Whittlesey House, 1947.

Leigh, Robert D. *Group Leadership.* New York: W. W. Norton & Co., 1936.

O'Brien, Joseph F. *Parliamentary Law for the Layman.* New York: Harper & Bros., 1952.

Reeves, J. Walter. *Parliamentary Procedure.* Boston: D. C. Heath & Co., 1931.

Robert, Henry M. *Parliamentary Law.* New York: Appleton-Century-Crofts, 1923.

———. *Parliamentary Practice.* New York: Appleton-Century-Crofts, 1921.

———. *Rules of Order Revised.* Chicago: Scott, Foresman & Co., 1951.

Sturgis, Alice F. *Standard Code of Parliamentary Procedure.* New York: McGraw-Hill Book Co., Inc., 1950.

Tilson, John Q. *A Manual of Parliamentary Procedure.* New Haven: Pub. by the author, 1948.

8—*Oral Interpretation of Literature*

Anthologies of Prose and Poetry

Adshead, Gladys L., and Duff, Annis, eds. *An Inheritance of Poetry*. Boston: Houghton Mifflin Co., 1948.

Auden, W. H., and Pearson, Norman Holmes, eds. *Poets of the English Language*. 5 vols. New York: The Viking Press, 1950.

Bates, Gladys deSilva, and Kay, Helena. *Literature for Interpretation*. Boston: Expression Co., 1939.

Buck, P. M., and Alberson, H. S. *Anthology of World Literature*. 3rd ed. New York: Macmillan Co., 1952.

Eastman, M. *Anthology for Enjoyment of Poetry*. New York: Charles Scribner's Sons, 1951.

Matthiessen, F. O., ed. *The Oxford Book of English Verse*. New York: Oxford University Press, 1950.

Neider, Charles, ed. *Great Short Stories from the World's Literature*. New York: Rinehart & Co., 1950.

Quiller-Couch, Sir Arthur. *The Oxford Book of English Prose*. Oxford: The Clarendon Press, 1930.

Schorer, Mark, ed. *The Story: A Critical Anthology*. New York: Prentice-Hall, Inc., 1950.

Untermeyer, Louis, ed. *Modern American Poetry and Modern British Poetry*. Combined edition. New York: Harcourt, Brace & Co., 1942.

Van Doren, Mark, ed. *The Oxford Book of American Prose*. New York: Oxford University Press, 1932.

Williams, Oscar, ed. *A Little Treasury of Great Poetry: English and American, from Chaucer to the Present Day*. New York: Charles Scribner's Sons, 1947.

Reference Books

Bassett, Lee Emerson. *A Handbook of Oral Reading*. Boston: Houghton Mifflin Co., 1917.

Boas, Ralph Philip. *The Study and Appreciation of Literature*. New York: Harcourt, Brace & Co., 1931.

Brooks, Cleanth. *The Well Wrought Urn: Studies in the Structure of Poetry*. New York: Reynal and Hitchcock, 1947.

Clark, S. H., and Babcock, Maud May. *Interpretation of the Printed Page*. New York: Prentice-Hall, Inc., 1940.

Crocker, Lionel. *Interpretative Speech*. New York: Prentice-Hall, Inc., 1952.

Crocker, Lionel, and Eich, Louis M. *Oral Reading.* New York: Prentice-Hall, Inc., 1947.

Cunningham, Cornelius C. *Literature as a Fine Art.* New York: The Ronald Press Co., 1941.

————. *Making Words Come Alive.* Dubuque: Wm. C. Brown Co., 1951.

Frankenberg, Lloyd. *Pleasure Dome: Reading Modern Poetry.* Boston: Houghton Mifflin Co., 1949.

Hubbell, Jay B., and Beaty, John O. *An Introduction to Poetry.* Rev. ed. New York: Macmillan Co., 1938.

Johnson, Gertrude E. *Studies in the Art of Interpretation.* New York: Appleton-Century-Crofts, 1940.

Lee, Charlotte I. *Oral Interpretation.* Boston: Houghton Mifflin Co., 1952.

McLean, Margaret P. *Oral Interpretation of Forms of Literature.* New York: E. P. Dutton & Co., Inc., 1936.

Parrish, Wayland Maxfield. *Reading Aloud.* New York: The Ronald Press Co., 1953.

Tassin, Algernon. *The Oral Study of Literature.* New York: Alfred A. Knopf, 1933.

Woolbert, C. H., and Nelson, Severina E. *The Art of Interpretative Speech.* Rev. ed. New York: Appleton-Century-Crofts, 1934.

9—Dramatics

Albright, H. D. *Working Up a Part.* Boston: Houghton Mifflin Co., 1947.

Boleslavsky, Richard. *Acting: The First Six Lessons.* New York: Theatre Arts Books, 1941.

Bosworth, Halliam. *Technique in Dramatic Art.* New York: Macmillan Co., 1929.

Brown, Ben W. *Upstage-Downstage; Directing the Play.* Boston: Walter H. Baker, 1946.

Brown, G., and Garwood, Alice. *General Principles of Play Production.* New York: Samuel French, 1936.

Campbell, Wayne. *Amateur Acting and Play Production.* Macmillan Co., 1931.

Carroll, Sydney W. *Acting for the Stage.* New York: Pitman, 1938.

Cheney, Sheldon. *The Theatre.* New York: Tudor Publishing Co., 1929.

Cornberg, Sol, and Gebauer, Emanuel L. *Stagecrew Handbook*. New York: Harper & Bros., 1941.

Crocker, C., Fields, V. A., and Broomall, W. *Taking the Stage*. New York: Pitman, 1939.

Davis, Eugene C. *Amateur Theatre Handbook*. New York: Greenberg, 1945.

Dean, Alexander. *Fundamentals of Play Directing*. New York: Farrar & Rinehart, 1941.

———. *Little Theatre Organization and Management*. New York: D. Appleton & Co., 1926.

Dillon, Josephine. *Modern Acting*. New York: Prentice-Hall, Inc., 1940.

Dolman, John, Jr. *The Art of Play Production*. Rev. ed. New York: Harper & Bros., 1947.

Franklin, Miriam A. *Rehearsal: Principles and Practices of Acting for the Stage*. Rev. ed. New York: Prentice-Hall, Inc., 1942.

Gassner, John, and Barker, Philip. *Producing the Play*. New York: Dryden Press, 1941.

Halstead, William Perdue. *Stage Management for the Amateur Theatre*. New York: Appleton-Century-Crofts, 1937.

Heffner, Hubert, Selden, Samuel, and Sellman, Hunton D. *Modern Theatre Practice*. Rev. ed. New York: Appleton-Century-Crofts, 1946.

Hewitt, Barnard. *Art and Craft of Play Production*. Philadelphia: J. B. Lippincott Co., 1940.

Lees, C. Lowell. *A Primer of Acting*. New York: Prentice-Hall, Inc., 1940.

———. *Play Production and Direction*. New York: Prentice-Hall, Inc., 1948.

McCleary, Albert, and Glick, Carl. *Curtain's Going Up*. New York: Pitman, 1939.

Morosco, Selma, and Lounsbury, A. *Stage Technique Made Easy*. McLeod, 1942.

Nelms, Henning. *Play Production*. New York: Barnes & Noble, Inc., 1950.

———. *Primer of Stagecraft*. New York: Dramatists' Play Service, 1941.

Pardoe, T. Earl. *Pantomimes for Stage and Study*. New York: Appleton-Century-Crofts, Inc., 1931.

Selden, Samuel. *First Principles of Play Direction*. Univ. of North Carolina Extension Div., Bull. Vol. XVII, No. 4, Nov., 1947.

Selden, Samuel. *First Steps in Acting*. New York: Appleton, 1947.

————. *The Stage in Action*. New York: Appleton-Century-Crofts, 1941.

Smith, Betty. *Twenty Prize-Winning Non-Royalty One-Act Plays* (compiled by Betty Smith). New York: Greenberg, 1943.

Smith, Milton. *Play Production*. Rev. ed. New York: Appleton-Century-Crofts, 1947.

Somerscales, Marjorie. *The Improvised Stage*. New York: Pitman, 1932.

Stanislavski, Constantin. *An Actor Prepares*. New York: Theatre Arts Books, 1936.

10—Speaking over the Air

Abbot, Waldo. *Handbook of Broadcasting*. New York: McGraw-Hill Book Co., Inc., 1937.

Bryson, Lyman. *Time for Reason about Radio*. New York: George W. Stewart, 1948.

Cantrel, Hadley, and Allport, Gordon W. *The Psychology of Radio*. New York: Harper & Bros., 1935.

Chester, Giraud, and Garrison, Garnet R. *Radio and Television*. New York: Appleton-Century-Crofts, Inc., 1950.

Crews, Albert R. *Radio Production Direction*. Boston: Houghton Mifflin Co., 1944.

Dimond, Sidney A., and Andersson, Donald M. *Radio and Television Workshop Manual*. New York: Prentice-Hall, Inc., 1952.

Duerr, Edwin. *Radio and Television Acting*. New York: Rinehart & Co., Inc., 1950.

Hubbell, Richard. *Television Programming and Production*. New York: Rinehart & Co., Inc., 1945.

Kirby, Edward M., and Harris, Jack. *Star-Spangled Radio*. Indianapolis: Bobbs-Merrill Co., 1946.

McGill, Earle. *Radio Directing*. New York: McGraw-Hill Book Co., Inc., 1940.

Siepmann, Charles A. *Radio's Second Chance*. Boston: Atlantic Monthly Press, 1946.

Sposa, Louis. *Television Primer of Production and Direction*. New York: McGraw-Hill Book Co., Inc., 1947.

Wylie, Max. *Radio and Television Writing*. New York: Rinehart & Co., Inc., 1950.

11—*The Mechanisms of Speech and Hearing*

Anderson, Virgil A. *Training the Speaking Voice*. New York: Oxford University Press, 1942.

Barrows, S. T., and Pierce, A. E. *The Voice: How to Use It*. Boston: Expression Co., 1938.

Brigance, W. N., and Henderson, F. L. *A Drill Manual for Improving Speech*. 2nd ed. Philadelphia: J. B. Lippincott & Co., 1945.

Fairbanks, Grant. *Voice and Articulation Drillbook*. New York: Harper & Bros., 1940.

Fillebrown, Thomas. *Resonance in Singing and Speaking*. Boston: Oliver Ditson Co., 1911.

Fink, David H. *Release from Nervous Tension*. New York: Simon & Schuster, 1943.

Hedde, Wilhelmina G., and Brigance, William N. *Speech*. Philadelphia: J. B. Lippincott & Co., 1946.

Manser, Ruth B. *Speech Correction on the Contract Plan*. 3rd rev. ed. New York: Prentice-Hall, Inc., 1951.

———, and Finlan, Leonard. *The Speaking Voice*. New York: Longmans, Green & Co., 1950.

Orr, Frederick W. *Voice for Speech*. New York: McGraw-Hill Book Co., Inc., 1938.

Todd, Mabel E. *The Thinking Body*. New York: Paul B. Hoeber, Medical Department of Harper & Bros., 1937.

12—*Basic Drills for Speech and Voice*

Anderson, Virgil A. *Training the Speaking Voice*. New York: Oxford University Press, 1942.

Brigance, W. N., and Henderson, F. L. *A Drill Manual for Improving Speech*. 2nd ed. Philadelphia: J. B. Lippincott & Co., 1945.

Fairbanks, Grant. *Practical Voice Practice*. New York: Harper & Bros., 1944.

———. *Voice and Articulation Drillbook*. New York: Harper & Bros., 1940.

Fink, David H. *Release from Nervous Tension*. New York: Simon and Schuster, 1943.

Grim, Harriett E. *Practical Voice Training*. New York: Appleton-Century-Crofts, 1948.

Hahn, E., Lomas, C. W., Hargis, D. E., and Vandraegen, D. *Basic Voice Training for Speech*. New York: McGraw-Hill Book Co., Inc., 1952.

Jacobson, Edmund, *Progressive Relaxation*. Chicago: University of Chicago Press, 1929.

———. *You Must Relax*. New York: Whittlesey House, 1934.

Karr, Harrison M. *Developing Your Speaking Voice*. New York: Harper & Bros., 1953.

Manser, Ruth B. *Speech Correction on the Contract Plan*. 3rd rev. ed. New York: Prentice-Hall, Inc., 1951.

———, and Finlan, Leonard. *The Speaking Voice*. New York: Longmans, Green & Co., 1950.

Van Dusen, C. Raymond. *Training the Speaking Voice*. New York: McGraw-Hill Book Co., Inc., 1945.

13—The Sounds of English

Barrows, Sarah T. *Introduction to the Phonetic Alphabet*. Boston: Expression Co., 1930.

Bloomfield, Leonard. *Language*. New York: Henry Holt & Co., 1933.

Bodmer, Frederick. *The Loom of Language*. New York: W. W. Norton & Co., Inc., 1944.

Brown, Hazel P. *Speechphone Method. Books and Records: Elementary, Intermediate, Advanced*. (Phonetic Transcription by Dorothy Mulgrave.) New York: Linguaphone Institute, 1953.

Carhart, Paul W., and Kenyon, John S. "A Guide to Pronunciation." In Neilson, Knott, and Carhart (eds.), *Webster's New International Dictionary of the English Language*. 2nd ed., unabr. Springfield, Mass.: G. & C. Merriam Co., 1934.

Gough, Harvey B., Rousseau, Lousene, Cramer, Mary E., and Reeves, J. Walter. *Effective Speech*. New York: Harper & Brothers, 1930.

Heffner, R. M. S. *General Phonetics.* Madison: University of Wisconsin Press, 1949.

Jones, Daniel. *English Pronouncing Dictionary*. New York: E. P. Dutton & Co., Inc., 1952.

Kenyon, John S. *American Pronunciation*. 8th rev. ed. Ann Arbor: George Wahr, 1940.

Kenyon, John S., and Knott, Thomas A. *A Pronouncing Dictionary of American English*. Springfield, Mass.: G. & C. Merriam Co., 1944.

Krapp, George P. *English Language in America.* 2 vols. New York: Appleton-Century-Crofts, 1925.

McLean, Margaret P. *Good American Speech.* Rev. ed. New York: E. P. Dutton & Co., Inc., 1952.

Needleman, M. H. *A Manual of Pronunciation.* New York: Barnes & Noble, Inc., 1949.

Raubicheck, Letitia E. *Your Voice and Speech.* New York: Prentice-Hall, Inc., 1953.

Ripman, Walter. *Sounds of English.* New York: E. P. Dutton & Co., Inc., 1946.

Sapir, Edward. *Language.* New York: Harcourt, Brace & Co., Inc., 1921.

Sweet, Henry. *A Handbook of Phonetics.* Oxford: Clarendon Press, 1877.

Thomas, Charles K. *An Introduction to the Phonetics of American English.* New York: The Ronald Press Co., 1947.

Ward, Ida. *The Phonetics of English.* New York: Appleton-Century-Crofts, 1928.

14—Sounds in Connected Speech
(See references listed under Chapter 13.)

15—English Vowels
(See references listed under Chapter 13.)

16—English Diphthongs
(See references listed under Chapter 13.)

17—English Consonants
(See references listed under Chapter 13.)

18—Speech Pathology

Reference Books

Ainsworth, Stanley H. *Speech Correction Methods.* New York: Prentice-Hall, Inc., 1948.

Backus, Ollie. *Speech in Education.* New York: Longmans, Green & Co., 1943.

Benda, Clemens E. *Developmental Disorders of Mentation and Cerebral Palsies.* New York: Grune & Stratton, 1952.

Berry, Mildred F., and Eisenson, Jon. *The Defective in Speech.* New York: Appleton-Century-Crofts, 1942.

Carlson, Earl R. *Born That Way.* New York: John Day Co., 1941.

Cass, Marion T. *Speech Habilitation in Cerebral Palsy.* New York: Columbia University Press, 1951.

Gifford, Mabel Farrington. *Correcting Nervous Speech Disorders.* New York: Prentice-Hall, Inc., 1939.

Goldstein, Kurt. *Language and Language Disturbances.* New York: Grune & Stratton, 1948.

Gottlober, A. B. *Understanding Stuttering.* New York: Grune & Stratton, 1953.

Johnson, Wendell. *Because I Stutter.* New York: Appleton-Century-Crofts, 1930.

———, et al. *Speech Handicapped School Children.* New York: Harper & Bros., 1948.

Ogilvie, Mardel. *Terminology and Definition of Speech Defects.* New York: Teachers College, Columbia University, 1942.

Van Riper, C. *Speech Correction Principles and Methods.* Rev. ed. New York: Prentice-Hall, Inc., 1947.

Wepman, Joseph. *Recovery from Aphasia.* New York: The Ronald Press Co., 1951.

West, R., Kennedy, L., and Carr, A. *The Rehabilitation of Speech.* Rev. ed. New York: Harper & Bros., 1947.

Manuals of Speech Correction

Brigance, W. N., and Henderson, F. L. *A Drill Manual for Improving Speech.* 2nd ed. Philadelphia: J. B. Lippincott & Co., 1945.

Fairbanks, Grant. *Voice and Articulation Drillbook.* New York: Harper & Bros., 1940.

Manser, Ruth B. *Speech Correction on the Contract Plan.* 3rd rev. ed. New York: Prentice-Hall, Inc., 1951.

Mulgrave, Dorothy. Pocket Guide to Speech Practice 2: *Correcting a Lisp.* New York: Dorothy Mulgrave, 250 Fourth Ave., New York 3, 1951.

———. Pocket Guide to Speech Practice 3: *Correcting Common Errors.* New York: Dorothy Mulgrave, 1951.

Raubicheck, Letitia. *Speech Improvement.* New York: Prentice-Hall, Inc., 1952.

Index